Keswick

The Story of a Lake District Town

GEORGE BOTT

Cumbria County Library

CUMBRIA SUPPLIES

CHAPLINS OF KESWICK-BOOKSELLERS

First published in Great Britain by Cumbria County Library, Cumbria Supplies and Chaplins of Keswick Booksellers.

PUBLISHED BY
CUMBRIA COUNTY LIBRARY
CUMBRIA SUPPLIES AND
CHAPLINS OF KESWICK-BOOKSELLERS

ISBN 0 905404 50 5
ISBN 0 9512404 1 2

PRINTED BY TITUS WILSON & SON   DESIGNED BY CUMBRIA SUPPLIES GRAPHIC DESIGN

About the Author

For 45 years a passion for all things Cumbrian has been at the centre of George Bott's life.

His first real introduction to the Lake District was a battle camp in Martindale during the war. In 1949 he seized the chance to move to Cockermouth where he was Head of English and Librarian at the Grammar School for the next 30 years.

He has edited a selection of George Orwell's essays, a biography of Shakespeare and a trio of text books for students in Sweden and Norway, Holland and Germany. In the1960's he helped to found Scholastic Publications and as Book Editor held a key role in a scheme for supplying paperbacks to schools.

For many years he has reviewed books for a wide variety of publications, from the *Times Educational Supplement* to the *Cumberland Evening News* and the *Keswick Reminder*, and also for Radio Cumbria. He contributes regularly to local newspapers and periodicals.

As a popular lecturer, his audiences range from a National Parks Annual Conference to university groups, from Lake District visitors to W I's galore. As president of the Cumbrian Literary Group since 1957, Keswick Lecture Society since 1964 and Keswick Historical Society since 1982, he is actively involved in local organisations.

Author's Introduction

For most people, the word 'Keswick' conjures up a picture of a superbly situated Lake District town, a tourist centre in the heart of the northern fells, a place for holidays, a convenient base for walking and climbing.

It has, however, more claims to fame than those of a popular resort for visitors from all over the world. It boasts one of the finest neolithic stone circles in Britain; it was a thriving industrial complex in the reign of Queen Elizabeth I; the riches of its literary associations vie with those of any other town in the country outside London; it is the home of the pencil industry and the venue of a unique religious convention; one of its leading citizens was largely responsible for the founding of the National Trust.

KESWICK: THE STORY OF A LAKE DISTRICT TOWN is designed for the general reader, for visitors who are the modern equivalent of the 'curious travellers' of earlier centuries, for (I hope) local people interested in finding out what happened on home ground in the past. My most daunting task has been the reduction of a manuscript of nearly 200,000 words to a manageable 80,000 or so.

I have aimed to tell the story rather than the history of Keswick. So there are no long extracts from enclosure awards, parish registers, inquisitions or probate inventories; no barrage of footnotes; no academic minutiae – though such vital sources have been consulted.

Inevitably, I owe a great debt to earlier recorders of Keswick's past but I was unable to research much of the original work of historians such as Jonathan Otley, John Fisher Crosthwaite, Joseph Broatch and Tom Wilson. Their published material is available but their other papers regrettably appear to have vanished or been destroyed.

The county and especially the Lake District have inspired many thousands of books and other printed material, much of it repetitious but at least providing a select nucleus of information. The history of Cumbria is extensively documented in a long run from 1866 of the *Transactions* of the Cumberland and Westmorland Antiquarian and Archaeological Society though it must be admitted that Keswick is minimally represented in comparison with, say, the Roman Wall. So, for readers who wish to know more, I have provided a bibliography with an ample selection of relevant titles.

Evidence of Keswick's past is unevenly distributed. The sparsely documented period of medieval Keswick, for example, is matched by the large number of accounts written by visitors in the eighteenth and nineteenth centuries, though many of these tend to comment on obvious features and give little insight into the more mundane aspects of daily life in the town. The Newlands and Borrowdale mining ventures of Queen Elizabeth I's reign, the Convention, or the Cockermouth, Keswick and Penrith Railway have been well researched: the life of Sir John Bankes, Hutton's Museum, or the origins of Crosthwaite Old School and its eighteen sworn men, on the other hand, remain tantalisingly vague.

My story, then, has gaps but I hope inaccuracies and misinformation are rare. Gremlins are always at work in the study of local history as they are elsewhere. I take comfort and inspiration from the wisdom of that eminent historian, Sir Charles Oman:

> 'What is required is zeal, insatiable curiosity, a dogged determination to work at all times and in all places, and then a stern resolve to print the results – even though they seem incomplete, and though there may be a danger of their being superseded on account of later discoveries.'

Although the story of Keswick begins with Castlerigg Stone Circle, it may be justly claimed that its true origins lie in geological time; that the great dynamic forces of earth movements, erosion and ice have shaped the landscape and provided the fundamental location for the first settlement.

Geologically, the Keswick area is significant and has long been a happy and profitable hunting ground for those enthusiasts and experts for whom a million years are but a moment. Certain obvious features may, however, be recognised by the layman.

To the north and west of the town, the landscape is composed of Skiddaw Slate, the oldest rocks in the Lake District, formed mainly as muds in the depths of a great sea. The dominant visual pattern is that of smooth slopes with the debris of shattered shale dotted here and there, caused, as Jonathan Otley put it, by 'the shivery and crumbling nature of this rock'.

By contrast, south of Keswick is Borrowdale Volcanic country, a rock formed according to J E Marr, a nineteenth century authority, from 'ejectments shot or poured out from volcanoes'. The characteristic landscape of Borrowdale Volcanic is rough and rugged, craggy and precipitous, the typical mountain heart of Lakeland.

A visit to Castlehead on the outskirts of the town, apart from providing a grandstand view of some of Lakeland's prime scenery, will crystallise the geological pattern – and, according to some experts, you are standing on the plug of an ancient volcano. The smooth slopes of Skiddaw, Grisedale Pike, Catbells and Causey Pike contrast with the near vertical faces of Walla Crag and Falcon Crag and the broken, bristly masses of Great End and the Scafells in the distance.

Of course, the detailed picture is infinitely more complex, a topic for the professionals: the layman has to be content with generalisations and a simplified explanation of how local scenery acquired its most significant characteristics and variety.

Choosing Castlerigg Stone Circle as my starting point and the ill-fated Timeshare venture of the late 1980s and early 1990s as the final curtain means that the whole period of human settlement is included. The presence of man becomes increasingly evident as the dominant thread through the centuries and the basic plan of KESWICK: THE STORY OF A LAKE DISTRICT TOWN is one of successive invasions, each establishing or modifying a culture, exploiting and destroying, shaping and altering the landscape, imposing a range of social and occupational structures.

My story is of the past, but what of the future, of Keswick in the third millennium? The possibilities are disturbing. The number of cars in Britain, it has been forecast, will increase dramatically and no doubt roads will be 'improved' to accommodate them. Unless action is taken, the visitor invasion of Keswick – for many people already at saturation point in 1994 – will swell to overwhelming proportions: tourism, long regarded as the life-blood of the town and its economy, could suffocate the facilities that have to cope with the visitors and adversely affect the very attractions that have brought them here. Professor C E M Joad predicted many years ago that one day the roads of Britain will be a stationary mass of immovable metal; motorists will crawl from the traffic jams of the towns and cities to the traffic jams of the countryside.

What was once a busy, pleasant small market town, with its distinctive characteristics, will be in danger of becoming indistinguishable from many another holiday centre.

Keswick's position at the heart of a unique and vulnerable countryside calls for care and constraint rather than rampant development and unfettered commercialism. Without strict controls, the extremes of the entrepreneur threaten: chair lifts and a funicular to the summit of Skiddaw; artificial snow-making machines cluttering the mountain slopes to create a winter sports centre; fell paths eroded, widened, smoothed and re-routed to accommodate anything from bicycles to mini-cars capable of climbing to a fell top without effort; a road over Styhead to Wasdale, with a roundabout by the tarn to link with a road to Langdale; the lower fells peppered with chalets and cottages, the second homes of the affluent; helicopters and light aircraft buzzing round the hills, noisy intruders hopping from landing pads and airstrips dotted liberally over the district.

The depressing catalogue could go on and on and, in any case, it is nothing more than imaginative speculation. Other factors – the decline of fossil fuel, for example – could weigh against so alarming a future for places like Keswick. But so long as there is a presumption towards more and more commercial exploitation for its own sake, the dangers are there.

It would be a sad day if the principles of the founders of the National Park were forgotten or ignored – and top of the list is the responsibility of the Park Planning Authority to conserve and enhance the landscape. Ironically, a survey of 6,000 visitors to the Lake District in 1975 revealed that centres like Windermere, Bowness and Keswick were no longer enjoyed by a significant proportion of holiday-makers because they were too commercialised, too crowded and too choked with traffic. The commitment is clear: we have a duty to posterity. The organisations devoted to safeguarding the district – the Special Planning Board, the National Trust, the conservation bodies – are fully aware of their vital role and will no doubt continue to exercise their functions of caring for a vulnerable landscape and its special features with an unshakeable conviction that they are the guardians of a unique and precious heritage.

I hope that KESWICK: THE STORY OF A LAKE DISTRICT TOWN will be both a reminder of Keswick's past and a stimulus to keeping a sharp eye on its future. It can no longer claim, as Ruskin did, to be a place 'almost too beautiful to live in'; but for many of us, in spite of all the pressures, frustrations and devastation, it is still the centre of our world. We have no wish to live anywhere else.

Acknowledgements

I should like to acknowledge my debt to a number of people and record my grateful thanks to all those who have helped in so many ways.

First I must thank the three partners – Cumbria County Library, Cumbria Supplies and Chaplins of Keswick – for their role as publishers and the Publications Committee of the County Library (especially John Smith and David Marsden) for support, advice and encouragement.

I appreciate the kind commendation of the book by Lord Rochdale and by the Chairman of the County Council.

David Bowcock and the staff of the Cumbria Record Office have been unfailingly helpful and courteous. The librarians and staff of Keswick Library have dealt with queries and requests with cheerful and friendly efficiency. The editors and staffs of the *Keswick Reminder*, the *Cumberland and Westmorland Herald* and the Cockermouth office of the *Times and Star* have been more than generous in allowing me to consult their files at length. The trustees and curators of Fitz Park Museum have made much essential material freely available.

I am indebted to many individuals for information and assistance but I should like to thank particularly Gordon Larkins and Jim Scott for their sustained interest; Stephen White, Janice Warren, Christine Strickland and Guy Pawle for help with photographs; Anne Dick for her professional co-operation with assembling the bibliography and checking the text; Mary Norris for compiling the index; Sheila Gilder for transferring my typescript on to disc; Andy Warlow for design; Susan Johnson, Frederick Benjamin and Alan Hankinson for both documentary material and pertinent comment; Keith Graham for photocopying facilities.

Four friends deserve a very special thank you. Gordon and Peggy Barnes drew on their historical perspectives and intimate knowledge of Keswick and district to make valuable suggestions and improvements. Professor Thomas Kelly, whose eye for a misprint was disturbingly uncanny, read and discussed the original manuscript. Above all, I enjoyed and profited enormously from the expert guidance of Alan Hill, known internationally as a leading bookman and editor and described by a colleague as 'probably the greatest British educational publisher of the twentieth century'. He gave unstinting, page-by-page advice and his invaluable collaboration played a considerable part in shaping the final version of the book.

Most authors willingly acknowledge the help of their wives and I am no exception. Throughout, Elizabeth has been counsellor and critic, supporter and patient consultant – and the most reliable of alarm clocks. Without the early morning sessions with pen and typewriter, it is doubtful whether the book would ever have been written.

Contents

Foreword

by Lord Rochdale

Keswick, as it is perceived today, is a town whose very existence is based on tourism, and, without it, the place would die. This is probably true and is not unique to Keswick. After all, tourism is one of the fastest growing industries in the world. What can so easily be overlooked by both inhabitant and visitor is the history, going back many thousands of years, which has determined what we see today. We come across spoil heaps when walking on the surrounding fells and perhaps vaguely wonder why and when they came into being. What are the origins of the National Trust, a large land owner in this area? Wordsworth and his friends; why are so many eminent writers associated with this neighbourhood? Suddenly Keswick is no longer just another tourist town, albeit in a beautiful setting, but a place full of unique historical interest. If you do have a feeling that this may be the case and want to know more, it is not always easy to find sources of information to satisfy your curiosity, certainly without a lot of research. In this book George Bott has done that for us, and it is exactly what I would have been looking for because it is so wide-ranging and entertaining in its account. I would commend it to anyone who enjoys learning how the past has shaped the present.

ST JOHN ROCHDALE
LINGHOLM

Foreword

by Bill Cameron

It is a great pleasure for me to welcome this history of Keswick and the surrounding area. The wealth of well-researched local history will, I'm sure, make a significant contribution to our knowledge of the locality, especially how a long history has contributed to the scene, traditions and life we find today. The book is a tribute to the knowledge and dedication of its author; it is particularly valuable in that it provides a very readable and interesting illustrated account which will appeal to both Keswickians and visitors alike, and also provides a gateway to further in-depth research for the more serious student. I am pleased that two departments of the County Council, the County Library and Cumbria Supplies, are strongly associated with the book's publication. I thank them and the third partner, Chaplins of Keswick, Booksellers, for joining together to produce this important work.

CHAIRMAN OF
CUMBRIA COUNTY COUNCIL

1

Stones, Soldiers and Saints

In June, 1818, the young John Keats was staying in Keswick. He clambered among the rocks of Lodore Falls and climbed Skiddaw – with the help of two glasses of rum.

He also visited Castlerigg Stone Circle, 'the Druid Temple' as he called it. At the time, he was writing his poem 'Hyperion' and it is surely possible that this ancient monument inspired the lines:

'...like a dismal cirque
Of Druid stones upon a forlorn moor,
When the chill rain begins at shut of eve...'

Most of the early tourists were attracted to this ring of stones. William Stukeley, the antiquarian, was here in 1725, recording the local name of 'The Carles' and the existence of a second circle in an adjoining field, no trace of which has ever been found.

Thomas Gray, immortalised as the author of the 'Elegy in a Country Churchyard', left a prosaic description of the circle after his visit on 5 October 1769 – 'a druid circle of large stones, 108 feet in diameter, the biggest not eight feet high, but most of them still erect: they are fifty in number'.

It is possible, as Jonathan Otley, a local geologist and guidebook writer, suggested in 1849 that the circle may have been a continuous ring of stones, many of which had been removed over the centuries 'for secular purposes'. It is not unknown for canny farmers (and others) to appropriate suitable and easily accessible building material, irrespective of its historical or archaeological importance.

Castlerigg, a neolithic stone circle some four thousand years old, has collected its share of legends and wild surmise, much of it linked with the Druids. The stones, it has been claimed, are men petrified for their sins; it is impossible, says another flight of the imagination, to count the number of stones accurately. Gruesome tales of sacrifice and unexpected miracles are told along with the grim details of strange rites and primitive ceremonies.

The sense of awe remains. Aubrey Burl, a leading twentieth century authority on stone circles, is lavish in his appreciation. 'Of all the superb rings in the Lake District,' he wrote in 1979, 'the Castlerigg Stone Circle is the most exciting and the most mysterious.'

'A dismal cirque of Druid stones upon a forlorn moor'

Technically, Castlerigg is classed by one modern expert, Professor A Thom, as a Type A flattened circle. Its date is about 3000-2500 BC, a neolithic structure that predates the great sarsens of Stonehenge by a thousand years. A recess on the eastern side gives it a unique place among the stone circles of Britain. Excavations in 1882 revealed only stones and bits of charcoal: the purpose of this singular feature remains a mystery.

Three stone axes were unearthed inside the circle during the last century, sparse evidence but enough to prove the existence of prehistoric man in the Keswick area. Further support came from the discovery in 1901 of four stone axes at Mossgarth in Portinscale and several in the Blencathra – Helvellyn Street area during building operations. Bristowe Hill yielded pieces of a crude quern and an axe in 1903: a stone adze was found at the Forge and a hammer at Brigham.

What, then, was the purpose of Castlerigg Stone Circle? It could have been a trading post, a central market for stone implements made at the axe factory on the slopes of Pike of Stickle in Langdale, one of a complex of 'workshops' in the central fells and within easy reach of Castlerigg along ancient paths and trackways.

It could have been a meeting place, either for social gatherings or for religious ceremonies and rituals. It is not unreasonable to suppose that at this tribal or inter-tribal rallying point, people would assemble to worship their gods (possibly even the stones themselves) and would also use the occasion for secular purposes – settling disputes, deciding boundaries, exchanging goods. Some of Cumbria's fifty or so stone circles were used for funerary purposes but Castlerigg has yielded no evidence of burials.

Professor Thom gave a measure of academic respectability to the theory – complex and strictly for the experts – that Castlerigg was a kind of astronomical observatory, with the stones aligned to the sun, the moon and the stars. It would then be possible to keep a sophisticated check on the progress of the changing seasons and determine the appropriate time for such vital activities as sowing and reaping.

Whatever the purpose of Castlerigg – market place, assembly point, temple or primitive Jodrell Bank – there is no doubt that our ancestors chose a superb site, surrounded by panoramas of supreme natural beauty and ringed by the high fells. It is equally certain that the popular name of 'The Druids' Circle' is a misnomer; the stones existed long before the time of the Druids.

Artist's impression of neolithic man at Castlerigg

It is not surprising that it has always attracted tourists. Lavish appraisals are legion but on occasion there are reports of vandalism. When Wordsworth and Coleridge visited the site in November 1799, they found 'the Keswickians have been playing Tricks with the stones'. A century later, it was reported that 'huge char-a-bancs daily discharge large numbers of tourists and trippers at the circle, who proceed to cut their initials on the stones'.

Protection was needed and in 1888 Castlerigg was one of the first sites to enjoy official custody under the provisions of the Ancient Monuments Protection Act. In 1913, the field in which the Carles stand was up for sale and the indomitable Canon Rawnsley made sure it was bought for the National Trust.

A monument as old as Castlerigg has inevitably attracted mystical associations and even in modern times strange stories crop up now and again. Some years ago, there were rumours of a witches' coven meeting in the magic circle – an eerie, isolated setting, the sort of location linked in popular imagination with witchcraft. The rumours died quickly: perhaps a typical Cumbrian winter's night sent peaked hats flying and broomsticks were whisked away in a force eight gale...

It is difficult to decide whether Castlerigg was a permanent settlement or a special site for special occasions. Evidence from elsewhere in Cumbria suggests fringe occupation by early man, where the lowlands and the coastal strip offered a reasonably hospitable landscape, well away from the forest-choked valleys and the forbidding fell tops.

In the period that followed the Neolithic – the Bronze Age – stone circles, cairns and tumuli, however, are often found on higher ground – say, up to about 1,000 feet – as the earlier Castlerigg was. This would seem to indicate an expansion of occupation from the skirts of Lakeland towards the central fells, involving the clearance of valley woodland and scrub.

Analysis has revealed a sharp drop in elm pollen in about 3000 BC Does this indicate greater activity by early man, felling trees for fuel and implements and feeding leaves and young shoots to their animals? Or was the decline due to a disease, like the Dutch elm disease of recent years?

Whatever our speculations about the rest of Cumbria, evidence in the Keswick area of a transition from outlying flat land to the lower fells, with deforestation of the valleys and upland slopes, is insufficient to draw any satisfactory conclusions.

One feature of the pre-Roman landscape, however, does support the claim for some form of settlement: the hill forts, dating from about 500 BC and typical of the Iron Age, at Castle Crag in Borrowdale, Castle How at Peel Wyke near the foot of Bassenthwaite, and Carrock Fell, one of the largest sites in Cumbria.

Smaller hill forts have been discovered at Reecastle near Lodore, Raven Crag above Thirlmere and at Threlkeld above the disused quarries on the lower slopes of Clough Head, a setting that has been described as 'truly a panorama fit for the gods'.

Archaeologists are certainly not agreed on the details and dates of hill forts. Excavation at Threlkeld, for example, uncovered only meagre finds and the experts were 'not disposed to think this is a prehistoric settlement'.

When the next invaders arrived – the Romans – they found an indigenous population scattered over Cumbria in small communities and isolated farmsteads, possibly units of the Brigantes, the Celtic tribe that dominated much of northern England. Ill-equipped and unprepared as they were, they offered little resistance as the triumphant legions pushed their conquest further and further north.

Evidence of Roman occupation in Cumbria is abundant: Hadrian's Wall, Hardknott Fort, Ravenglass Bath-house, for example, are typical remains of the victorious invaders, but Keswick poses a problem.

A Roman road ran westwards from Voreda (Old Penrith near Plumpton Wall) to Troutbeck on today's A66 about nine miles from Keswick. Here there was a cluster of temporary camps for marching troops. Beyond Keswick at Braithwaite, near the site of the former railway station, a metalled causeway was discovered in 1952. This may be a section of an ancient road, the 'magnum chiminum' mentioned in a thirteenth century charter of Fountains Abbey and possibly the preliminary approach of a Roman road over Whinlatter Pass to Derventio (Papcastle) and Alauna (Maryport).

Recent research has found distinct traces of an agger – the raised platform on which the Romans generally built their roads – extending westwards from Troutbeck to the edge of Keswick via Wallthwaite, Guardhouse and parts of the Golf Course at Threlkeld.

Assuming a Roman highway existed west and east of Keswick, is it reasonable to accept some form of occupation on the site of the present town? Was there a signal station high on Castlerigg? Or a camp where Greta Hall now stands? Was a military presence supported by a civilian settlement? Such notions remain pure speculation and we can only hope that one day archaeological evidence will settle the debate.

The period following the departure of the Romans is one of legend and romance. The influence of several centuries of military occupation probably continued to dominate the life-style of the Celtic inhabitants. Reliable evidence is sparse: place names help to support the simple fact of settlement but little more. Blencathra, for example, is a Celtic name, the first element corresponding with the Welsh 'blaen' meaning point or top, and the second with 'cateir', a chair, as in Cader Idris.

Local river names are often Celtic in origin. Derwent derives from 'derva' meaning oak; those two tongue-twisters, Glenderamackin and Glenderaterra, include the Welsh 'glyn', a wooded valley. Dock Tarn and Thirlmere have Old English elements: 'docca', a water lily or some other aquatic plant, and 'thyrel', a hollow.

These Celtic names obviously indicate settlement of some kind, though it is reasonable to assume that the population was scattered and sparse – but numerous enough to attract the next group of invaders, the saints. The line-up is formidable: Patrick, Ninian, Cuthbert, Herbert, Kentigern. Only the last two play any significant role in the story of Keswick.

St Herbert was a pupil and close friend of Cuthbert, Bishop of Lindisfarne. 'There was,' Bede tells us, 'a certain priest revered for his uprightness and perfect life and manners named Hereberte, who had a long time been in union with the Man of God (Cuthbert) in the bond of spiritual love and friendship.'

J M W Turner's romantic conception of St Herbert's simple cell

Herbert lived on an island in Derwentwater. He met Cuthbert regularly and on one occasion in Carlisle his friend warned him that 'we shall see one another no more in this world, for I am sure that the time of my dissolution is at hand'.

Herbert begged that he might die at the same time as his master and was told that his wish would be granted. Tradition claims that the two men died on 20 March 687.

Several centuries later, on 13 April 1374 (oddly 687 years after Herbert's death in 687), Bishop Appleby of Carlisle issued a charter of indulgence to the vicar of Crosthwaite for those parishioners who made a pilgrimage to St Herbert's Island and took part in a special mass. Canon Rawnsley, in a sermon preached on St Herbert's Day, 13 April 1885, paints a vivid picture of such a pilgrimage, though with what degree of accuracy it is impossible to determine.

He imagined it as a colourful procession of musicians and candle-bearers, banners and ecclesiastical hardware, with the vicar of Crosthwaite magnificently robed in his embroidered vestments. This impressive assembly of clergy and laity wound its way across the Howrahs to a landing at Nicol End and so to St Herbert's Island for a service at the tiny chapel marking the site of the saint's rough and primitive hermitage.

Pilgrimages there certainly have been over the centuries but whether they were ceremonies of such striking proportions as Rawnsley suggested is very doubtful.

When the stone axes were unearthed at Mossgarth in Portinscale in 1901, the workmen also found a mould of the type used to make small crosses and crucifixes to be pinned on the clothes of pilgrims. This one produced a replica of an emaciated Christ on the cross on one side and a pattern for pins and buttons on the other. It has been dated late fourteenth or early fifteenth century and Canon Rawnsley, ever ready with an explanation, suggested it was used to make 'badges' for sale to pilgrims en route from Crosthwaite to St Herbert's Island via Nicol End.

An annual mass is held on the Island by Keswick's Roman Catholic priest and in 1987, to commemorate the 1300th anniversary of St Herbert's death, the vicar of St John's organised a pilgrimage which attracted a large number of people anxious to pay their respects to the saint.

In the 1700s, St Herbert's Island was owned by the Lawson family. About 1760 Sir Wilfrid Lawson cut down the trees, planted new ones, and alongside the ruins of the saint's simple cell built 'a rustic summerhouse'. The island became a favourite location for parties and picnics: today, the summerhouse has gone but the tree-clad island is a popular destination for visitors in hired rowing boats.

Crosthwaite Church

Crosthwaite Church is dedicated to St Kentigern (Kyentyern means 'head lord') who was also known as Mungo, a pet name meaning 'dearest friend'. The story goes that on a journey from Glasgow to Wales in 553, Kentigern arrived at Carlisle to be told that the local people had lapsed into heathen ways. He turned aside from his planned route and visited a number of settlements, marked today by the eight Cumbrian churches which bear his name.

At one of them, Crosfeld (later Crosthwaite), he set up his cross in the clearing and preached to the people – possibly a small British group at nearby Bristowe Hill. Tradition claims the existence of a holy well in the immediate vicinity and the 'high' of High Hill, a peculiarly flat area near Crosthwaite Church, may be a corruption of 'holy'.

Modern scholarship questions the date of 553 and plumps for a twelfth century church founded during a revival of the cult of Kentigern, sparked off by a life of the saint written by Jocelyn, a monk of Furness Abbey, about 1180.

Therein lies the problem. Professor Kenneth Jackson, in 'Sources for the Life of St Kentigern' (in NK Chadwick's *Studies in the Early British Church*, 1958) stresses the unreliability of Jocelyn's 'Life', dated some six centuries after the saint's death. It was intended to glorify Kentigern and omits anything detrimental to him. Conflicting details and a barrage of miracles and mysterious happenings further undermines a positive ratification of 553, though Jackson does admit that 'one may reasonably accept that Kentigern was a real person, founder of the church at Glasgow and missionary in Cumbria'.

The tantalising question is unanswered: did Kentigern set up his preaching cross on the site of Crosthwaite Church over fourteen centuries ago? We may never know with absolute certainty but it must always remain a possibility. The 'thwaite' element of the place-name is Scandinavian: does it indicate a clearing the Viking invaders found, perhaps with its cross still standing, or were they themselves responsible for it?

Among the spate of miracles associated with Kentigern, four have a special link with Keswick. The emblem of Crosthwaite Church, seen in the mosaic floor of the sanctuary, and the badge of Keswick School, shows four objects, also incorporated in the city arms of Glasgow: a bell, a tree, a bird and a fish with a ring in its mouth.

The bell is said to represent a gift to Kentigern from the Pope on one of his seven visits to Rome. The tree is a reminder of the rising up of a hill to provide a natural pulpit when

Kentigern preached to the crowds at Hoddom near Dumfries. Another version links the tree with a bush that bore everlasting blackberries.

The bird recalls a decapitated robin: Kentigern replaced the head and brought the bird back to life. The fish with the ring in its mouth symbolises a story connected with Langueth, the Queen of Strathclyde. As a token of her affection she gave the king's ring to a young soldier or courtier. The king saw the ring, removed it from the young man while he was asleep and threw it into the river Clyde. When he asked Langueth where the ring was, she approached the soldier, who had to confess that he had lost it. In despair, she appealed to Kentigern for help: he told her to send someone to fish for salmon in the river. The very first catch was opened and there inside the fish was the missing ring. The king forgave his wife and the soldier and harmony reigned once more.

St Kentigern - a stained glass window in Winster Church

2

Settling Down

The secular history of these early centuries, like the ecclesiastical, is vague. The Anglian spread from the east in the seventh century, which gave Northumbria control over most of northern England, appears to have had little effect on the scattered communities of Cumbria, then part of the vast kingdom of Rheged and later of Strathclyde.

The rarity of Anglian place-names in the central fell country argues for minimal influence. The Britons of Cumbria clung to their fastnesses, adopting the name 'Cumberland' from their Celtic kinsmen in Wales – 'the land of the Cymry'. Place-name elements such as 'pen', 'blaen' and 'glyn' suggest a unified culture; the native methods of counting sheep in Cumbrian, Welsh, Cornish and Breton show marked similarities – all use 'pimp' for five and 'dick' for ten, for example. Place-names ending in the Old English 'ham' or 'tun' (both indicating a village or homestead) show that Anglian settlements tended to cling to the fringes of the Lake District.

There are rogue names, Keswick included, which cut across the accepted pattern. Stockley Bridge near Seathwaite in Borrowdale, for example, is pure Anglian: 'stoc', the trunk of a tree, and 'lah', an open place. Old English 'mere' in Thirlmere and Buttermere hints at some penetration into the central fells.

The Anglian domination was disturbed by the Scandinavian invasion which possibly began as early as the eighth century in the Orkneys and Shetlands and on the coast of Northumberland. Halfden the Dane sacked Carlisle in 875 but the thrust of Viking colonisation in Cumbria came from the west, not the east. The invasion was not by fierce, blood-thirsty pirates, who pillaged and raped, but by more peaceful men from Ireland and the Isle of Man who, over several generations, had moved south from north-west Scotland to integrate with the Irish.

In the valleys of the fell country, these Norse-Irish found a landscape not unlike the native Scandinavia, Norway in particular, of their forebears. Though the immigration of intruders no doubt generated its share of skirmishes and quarrels, it would seem that a peaceful integration rather than a forced domination characterised the Viking period in Cumbria.

The overwhelming claim for Scandinavian settlement is in place-names, many of them in the fringe areas close by Anglian communities – surely a strong argument against an invading force hell-bent on destruction?

The landscape around Keswick is thick with Scandinavian place-names. We still use, as elsewhere in Cumbria, pure Scandinavian words to identify topographical features – beck, tarn, fell, force – and existing names on the map point unerringly to Viking ancestors. It has been estimated that there are over forty Scandinavian place-names within six miles of Keswick, with a handful of elements dominating: 'thwaite' (thveit, a clearing), 'scale' (skali, a shepherd's summer hut), 'keld' (kelda, a spring) and 'seat' or 'side' (saetr, a summer pasture or farm). So Braithwaite is the broad clearing, respectable Portinscale the hut of the harlot, Threlkeld the spring of the thrall or serf, Seatoller the summer pasture with the alder tree.

Detailed place-name interpretation is an expert's domain where amateurs must tread warily. Many local names have defied explanation or at best have inspired informed speculation – Skiddaw, Latrigg, Helvellyn. The generally accepted interpretation of the name 'Keswick' is that it means 'cheese farm', a combination of two Anglian elements, 'cese' and 'wic'. The earliest extant dating is about 1240 when 'Kesewic' appears in a Fountains Abbey cartulary and ultra-violet light, it has been claimed, has revealed 'Keswike' on the Gough map of about 1360. Other theories suggest a derivation from 'kesh' (water hemlock), a contraction of 'Ketelswick' (the bay of Ketil, some ancient Scandinavian settler) and as recently as 1988 an eminent local industrial archaeologist has argued a case for 'kis', a Norwegian word for the mineral pyrites.

The Norse settlers of the eighth and ninth centuries continued the process of clearing the forest which had begun in prehistoric times, changing the face of Lakeland and leaving a legacy which is still apparent. Pollen analysis has shown that fell sides were covered in trees and shrubs until man got to work. Sheep and pigs feeding on acorns and beech-mast must have helped to block regeneration and to maintain the treeless slopes, so providing the modern tourist with open landscape views.

The years before the next invasion by the Normans were not entirely peaceful but how far the remote and insignificant hamlet that became Keswick was affected by attacks and incursions, we have no idea. One skirmish came uncomfortably close in 945, when Edmund of Northumbria defeated Dunmail, ruler of Cumbria. Traditionally, he is buried under the cairn on the col between the southern end of Thirlmere and Grasmere – Dunmail Raise on today's A591. The authenticity of the story is seriously undermined when we discover that some years later Dunmail turns up in Rome as a pilgrim...

Whatever the truth about Dunmail, the facts about the next group of invaders are reliably documented. The date when the Normans arrived in Britain – 1066 – is imprinted on our minds as firmly as our own telephone number and by the end of the century their presence and power had a profound effect on Cumbria.

The Domesday Book of 1086 has no mention of Cumbria, except for the southern fringe, but in 1092 King William Rufus marched north, took over Carlisle, and 'sent thither very many English peasants with wives and stock to dwell there to till the ground'.

The impact of the Normans on the Keswick area came with the creation of the great Baronies and in particular Allerdale below Derwent (north of the river), Allerdale above Derwent (south of the river) and Greystoke: Keswick stood at the junction between these three administrative units.

The symbol of Norman power was the castle: examples still remain at such places as Cockermouth and Egremont. Most of the sites were on the fringes of the fell country but it is just possible that Keswick may have had a castle, the seat from the thirteenth century, at least, of the de Derwentwaters, later the Radcliffes, who were the dominant family in the district for several centuries. The obvious site would be Castlerigg but no evidence has been found, in spite of confident statements by later writers. Nicolson and Burn's *History and Antiquities of the Counties of Westmorland and Cumberland* (1777), for example, categorically declares that 'the Ratcliffs built an house of pleasure in one of the islands of Derwentwater' from the remains of a ruined castle on Castlerigg.

Keswick may not have had its castle but another development of the Norman invasion certainly affected the region round 'the cheese farm'. The twelfth century was the age of abbey and monastery building in Cumbria, from Carlisle in 1123 to Shap in 1199. Like the Norman castles, these religious houses were positioned on the softer edge of the mountain dome, easy for communication but remote enough to ensure solitude.

It was Furness Abbey (founded in 1127) that influenced Keswick and Borrowdale. Its Cistercian monks were farmers and wool merchants whose products were distributed abroad as well as at home. Their flocks of sheep nibbled away at the woodlands, sustaining a process begun by neolithic man and continued by the Norsemen as they cleared their thwaites.

Furness grew wealthy on its thriving wool trade and extended its property from the immediate area round the abbey to large blocks of land between Coniston Water and Windermere and between Eskdale and Borrowdale.

In 1208, Alice de Rumelli, a descendant of the first overlord of the Barony of Allerdale, sold much of Borrowdale to Furness Abbey for a total sum of £156.13s.4d. As a local administrative centre for this vast sheep-rearing tract of fell country, the Abbey established a grange or farm at what is now Grange-in-Borrowdale.

The double-arched bridge at Grange in Borrowdale

Furness, however, was not the only abbey with a stake in Borrowdale. Alice de Rumelli also negotiated a sale of land and property in the valley with Fountains Abbey in Yorkshire, which included Derwent Island, Watendlath, and the mill of Crosthwaite on the 'land of Kesewic', the earliest mention we have of the name.

Both the Fountains Cartulary and the Furness Coucher Book – the monastic records and registers – provide many details which give positive evidence of the social and economic patterns of the twelfth and thirteenth centuries, with Keswick at the hub of smaller, scattered communities such as Braithwaite and Thornthwaite. Monk Hall, now the site of Keswick's hospital, may have been the local headquarters for Fountains Abbey: here, states James Clarke in his Survey of the Lakes (1789) 'the monks had a steward and here the tenants paid their rents'.

Holy men though the Cistercian monks of Furness and Fountains were, they were also entrepreneurs, jealously guarding their rights and their territories. Inevitably quarrels flared over boundaries, culminating in the great dispute of the late twelfth and early thirteenth century, when both institutions claimed the vaccary (dairy farm) of Stonethwaite. Eventually King Edward was consulted: he confiscated the property into his own hands and promptly sold it to Fountains for forty shillings.

The Normans not only built their castles and actively encouraged the founding of abbeys and monasteries; they also established vast areas of forest, primarily to preserve game for hunting. These forests were not necessarily wooded and were, legally speaking, merely tracts of land subject to forest laws.

Keswick was strategically positioned in the heart of the Cumbrian forests, with Skiddaw and Inglewood to the north and east, Derwent Fells, Copeland and Ennerdale to the west and south. Some parts of the forest were cleared to allow pigs and cattle to graze and gradually domestic colonisation spread, with rents from increased holdings compensating the landowners for loss of ground. The rich man's playground slowly evolved into the grazing grounds of the rural population.

There is little doubt that Keswick, on a small scale, was developing as a centre of population by the Norman period. The newly built church at Crosthwaite, the work of Alice de Rumelli in the early 1190s, was a focus for the community as well as a place of worship.

An incident in 1306 illustrates its importance and the extent of its activities. The citizens of Cockermouth raised a petition objecting to 'a great concourse of people every Sunday at Crosthwaite Church' where all manner of goods were sold. This Sunday trading, the Cockermothians claimed, was affecting their market. Their petition was successful and the buying and selling at the church stopped.

The incident suggests that there must have been a community large enough to support and patronise the market and that there was more mobility than might have been expected. This 'unseemly usage' is all the more surprising when we realise that it happened thirty years after Keswick was granted its market charter. In 1276 Thomas, Lord of the Manor of Derwentwater, was allowed to hold a Saturday market and an annual five-day fair in July. It is a matter of local pride that the Saturday market still survives after seven centuries and possibly on its original site.

Some idea of what the cluster of buildings that was thirteenth century Keswick was like comes from an inquisition of the lands and tenements of Thomas de Derwentwater on his death in 1303. There is a reference to '30 tenants who hold in burgage in a place called Kesewik, each of whom pays for each burgage per annum 6d.' Burgage was property held on a yearly rent. Excavation in Cockermouth has shown that these early burgage plots were some forty feet wide and built in a regular pattern with height and line controlled.

The Keswick burgages fronted the Market Square, timber-framed houses with an enclosure behind for a garden, an orchard or other domestic use. The pattern is still discernable today, in spite of considerable alterations. More durable stone has replaced timber; the enclosures no long serve as gardens or orchards – they, too, have been adapted for cottages, workshops and storerooms.

A map of 1787 shows the layout quite distinctly, with the rear enclosures appropriately marked by symbolic trees and with open fields beyond. The population in 1787 has been estimated at about 1,000, which means the houses and their yards must have been thickly populated.

It used to be thought that the yards, with their narrow entrances, were for defence against marauding Scots, the next invaders in our catalogue.

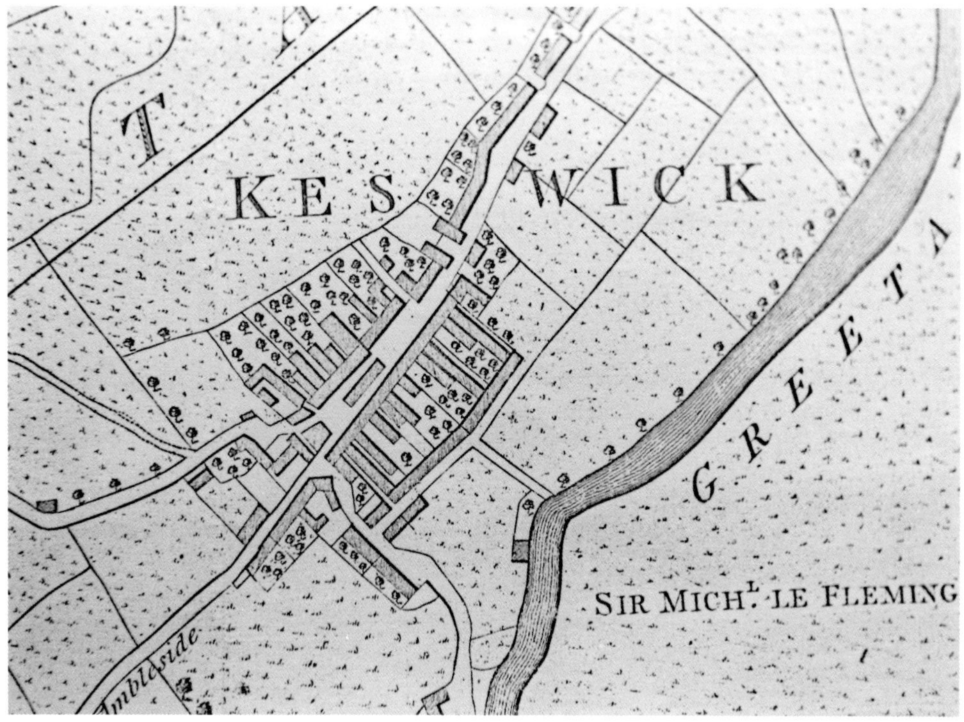

Keswick in 1787

The incursions from over the border stretched through several centuries. As early as 1138, the Scots attacked Calder Abbey, only four years after its foundation. Increased raids called for extended defence: churches were fortified, pele towers were built as refuges. The central fells appear to have escaped the full force of the Scottish raids: the nearest pele tower to Keswick was at Greystoke. The problems of approach over difficult terrain and the prospect of meagre pickings no doubt persuaded the Scots that it was easier and more profitable to pillage the fertile areas and the richer settlements, particularly around Carlisle and in the Eden valley.

Keswick appears to have escaped, though there is an enigmatic entry in a document of 1317 which reads: 'the said manor (of Castlerigg) is now worth per annum £13 and no more, because it is destroyed by the Scots: in time of peace it used to be £30'. The manor of Castlerigg reached as far as Gilcrux and Tallantire and the damage to the estate might have been to fringe properties.

A raid of 1322 came dangerously near to Keswick: it reached Embleton, about nine miles to the west, burning twelve of the twenty-four peasant holdings to the ground. By the beginning of the fifteenth century, the attacks were confined to Border country and any fears that Keswick might suffer vanished.

We can only guess at the effect on Keswick of that other scourge of these centuries: the plague. It has been estimated that the 1349 epidemic, for example, reduced the population of Cumbria by up to 40% and it seems unlikely that Keswick escaped the pestilence, though there is no firm evidence.

Natural disasters, too, must have affected the local economy. Crops failed, sheep and cattle caught diseases – the dreaded 'murrain' – and the Cumbrian climate added yet another potential enemy to undermine sound husbandry.

Even so, Keswick developed as the economic centre for the surrounding district, its hamlets and isolated farmsteads. The dissolution of the monasteries in the early 1500s meant a change of ownership of the land and an adjustment of the economy. The sheep and wool of Furness and Fountains were handled locally by new landlords and tenants. The geographical location of Keswick makes it the obvious focal point on which paths, tracks and roads have converged for centuries. This favourable position was a vital feature in the town's development as a medieval market, though Leland's description of it in the 1530s as 'a lytle poore market town' is a reminder that we must not imagine it as a community bustling with activity and thriving with prosperity.

As more land was claimed from the forests and wastes, there emerged a class of farmers popularly known as 'Statesmen' or 'Estatesmen'. It is not easy to define the term precisely. These yeomen, with the right to hand on their estates to their next of kin, have all-too-often been transformed into romantic figures – strong, sturdy, independent dalesmen, who lorded it over their own little kingdoms and cared not a fig for anyone.

The reality is more prosaic. For the most part, they were hard-working farmers on a small scale, paying their rents and fines to the lord of the manor and struggling to eke out a living in a hostile environment and unfavourable weather. Crops were limited: oats, barley, beans and a little wheat and rarely potatoes until the end of the seventeenth century. Equipment was primitive: transport was by packhorse, clumsy carts or rough sleds.

An element of stability inspired the building of typical Cumbrian farmhouses and barns; many are still in use, often modernised and modified, but as much part of the traditional landscape as the rocks themselves. Medieval tenure is something of a minefield but it is reasonable to assume that some statesmen remained little more than labourers, while others, more successful, graduated to minor gentry – a hierarchy mirrored in the rural buildings.

The mainstay of the economy was the Herdwick sheep, a hardy, resilient animal able to withstand extremes of weather and unique to the area. How they came to Cumbria is a mystery. One traditional story suggests they were washed ashore from the wreck of a Spanish Armada ship; another that they were brought by Norse invaders; yet a third traces them back to neolithic settlers. Though decreased in numbers and changed by crossbreeding, they still remain a familiar sight on the fells.

Sir John Bankes

3

Elizabethan Klondike

The picture of Keswick to the middle of the sixteenth century has necessarily been sparse but with a new wave of invaders our knowledge of the town becomes more definite.

The arrival of expert miners from Germany in the mid-1500s transformed a small rural community into a busy industrial complex which, for a time, enjoyed a measure of prosperity unknown in its more normal capacity as a medieval market centre.

It is possible that the Romans mined copper in the Keswick area and there is evidence of mining activity before the reign of Queen Elizabeth I – a grant to dig for precious metals made by King Edward IV in 1475 to his younger brother, Richard, for example.

The project of the 1560s was on a much grander scale than any previous enterprise – 'the most famous at that time in England, perhaps in Europe' as Thomas Robinson called it in his *Essay towards a Natural History of Westmorland and Cumberland* (1709). The Society of Mines Royal was set up to finance and organise the operation. Profit was certainly one motive but copper was needed for the production of arms and the strengthening of warships at a time when the country was threatened by foreign attack. Copper was also essential for making brass, which in turn was manufactured into equipment for producing woollen cloth, a major export.

Elizabeth, anxious to satisfy the demand for copper, turned to Germany for expert miners. The prime location of this know-how was Augsburg, a Bavarian city founded in Roman times and, in the sixteenth century, a financial and commercial centre.

In June 1564, Daniel Hechstetter, Hans Loner and twelve workmen arrived in Keswick and found workable deposits of copper not far away. Six months later, the Queen gave official permission for Hechstetter to 'search, dig, try, roast and melt all manner of mines and ores of gold, silver, copper and quicksilver' not only in the Keswick area but also in Coniston, Cornwall and Wales.

For the Queen herself, the glittering prizes were there: first claim on nine-tenths of all gold and silver at a favourable rate, royalties on the copper, and one tenth of any precious stones found in the mines.

The Society or Company of Mines Royal was finally incorporated in May 1568, its twenty-four shareholders including a Lord Mayor of London; Elizabeth's secretary, Lord Burghley; the Earls of Leicester and Pembroke; and the Lord Lieutenant of Dorset – a formidable and far-reaching selection of Elizabethan businessmen and establishment power. Letters patent – the grant from the monarch of privileges, holdings, appointments and monopolies – were granted to Daniel Hechstetter and Thomas Thurland, master of the Savoy hospital or poorhouse in London, who had contacts with the German mining community.

Their early efforts identified considerable deposits of copper in the Newlands and Borrowdale valleys. In July 1566, Thurland reported the discovery of copper at Scope End 'which they say is the best in England'.

Spoil heaps still remain at Goldscope

Goldscope, as the mine was called, was probably a corruption of the German 'gottesgab' – God's gift – rather than an indication of deposits of gold. This rich source of high-grade ore was supplemented by other mines in the area: Dale Head, Stoneycroft, Ellers and, further afield, at Coniston, Caldbeck, Wythburn and St John's in the Vale.

The expanding enterprise needed large quantities of fuel and timber was obtained locally, though at one stage a twelve-acre plot was bought in Workington for the construction of a wharf to handle the import of wood from Ireland.

Lady Katherine Radcliffe, wife of the Lord of the Manor and a descendant by marriage of the de Derwentwater family, owned much of the woodland. She was unco-operative and it was proposed that her holdings and those of the Earl of Northumberland should be taken over by the Crown. In a letter to Queen Elizabeth in May 1567, George Nedham, one of the twenty-four shareholders of the Company of Mines Royal, described her as 'so froward that nothing could be obtained at her hands, neither by entreaty or otherwise'; she charged exorbitant prices for her trees and was 'marvellous unreasonable and sore to deal with'. It was even suggested that she should be removed from Keswick and given another ladyship elsewhere.

A year later, in a letter of June 1568, Daniel Ulstet, assistant governor of the Company, writing to Lord William Cecil echoed Nedham's strictures: 'we cannot occupy these mines quietly so long as my Lady has possession and rule of this town. For she is the cause of all hindrance and unquietness to us.'

Apart from the mines themselves, where each day the Germans were producing up to fifteen hundredweight of 'as pure copper as any in the world', two associated projects were making their impact on Keswick, one on Derwent Island, the other at Brigham on the eastern outskirts of the town.

In February, 1569, John Williamson of Crosthwaite sold Derwent Island to the Company for £60. Earlier known as Hestholm (stallion island) or Vicar's Island – 'full of trees, like a wilderness' Leland described it in 1539 – it became a vital centre of activity for the settlers. Tradition has it that the Germans took refuge on the island to escape from the hostile attacks of the local people but there seems to be little hard evidence to support this claim.

The new owners set to work, tidying up the island, removing stones, digging up hedges and weeds. They built a brewery and a bakehouse, a pigeon cote, a pigsty and a windmill: they laid out a garden and planted an orchard of some 300 apple and pear trees, dressing the ground with manure transported by cart from Lady Radcliffe's estate over the frozen lake in the winter.

The Company's account books reveal all kinds of tiny but significant details. John Buckbank carted 3200 slates from Underskiddaw for £1.12s; a dozen rings for the pigs cost 10d; a plumber was paid 6s.8d. for 'mending the great brewing kettle'; a tailor's fee for making the sail for the windmill was 4s.4d.

For so small an island – a mere 250 yards long and 170 yards wide – the efforts of the German colony represent considerable and intensive development but, with the decline of the industry, Derwent Island also suffered and by the middle of the seventeenth century all that remained was 'a little ruinous house'.

Although each of the mines had its own cluster of essential buildings, the complex at Brigham was on an impressive scale. Here the ore was sent for smelting, some of it transported by water if the name of Copperheap Bay on Derwentwater has any significance.

At the Forge (as it is still called) the Company rented land from 'Miladi Catherina Radcliefl' at one shilling a year and built on a lavish scale. In its heyday, the concentration of workshops and assay chambers, smelting houses and smithies, accommodation and a bath-house for the work force, was said to be the biggest in England and possibly in Europe. A little way upstream, the waters of the Greta were harnessed to provide a source of power: a weir was built across the river and the water was channelled to the smelting works through a tunnel and a mill race, which can still be traced today.

Today's flyover spans the site of Brigham Forge

It is not difficult to imagine Brigham Forge at the peak of its activity, with the great hammers pounding away, the bellows sighing loudly, wheels creaking on their axle-trees. The workmen would be busy at their anvils; the furnaces would be roaring, clouds of smoke would be rising, and everywhere a scene of bustling, animated industry would be evidence of a successful commercial project.

Daniel Hechstetter's notebook provides some statistics. In 1567 only ten hundredweights of copper were smelted; the annual average for the years 1567 to 1584 was just over sixty times as much – some thirty tons – with a peak in 1570 of 1,250 hundredweights. From 1570 to 1584 over 5,000 ounces of silver were extracted.

Whatever prosperity the Company generated, success was marred by the famous legal battle of the 1560s and the decline that set in during the later years of the seventeenth century.

The law case was between the Queen and Thomas Percy, seventh Earl of Northumberland. In October 1566, Percy's men stopped the Germans removing ore from Newlands on the grounds that Northumberland owned the land, that any minerals therefore belonged to him and that the workmen were trespassing. The Queen ordered him to allow the mining to continue but Northumberland argued his case. A trial in 1567 resolved that mines of gold and silver (and he admitted that Newlands copper contained gold) were Crown property and that the royal mines did not pass to Northumberland with a grant of the land. The Queen, not surprisingly, had won her case. Northumberland did himself no good by championing Elizabeth's rival, Mary, Queen of Scots, who landed at Workington in May 1568. The following year he was one of the leaders of the unsuccessful Rising of the North, an abortive challenge to Elizabeth's power that resulted in his execution in 1572.

Rich though Goldscope was in high-grade copper, the Company's affairs were in something of a tangle by 1570. Expenses were high; debts were outstanding; there was a trade depression in England. Exports suffered from troubles abroad and even the Queen was failing to pay her dues.

The problems reached a climax in 1580 with the bankruptcy of Haug, Langnauer and Co., the Augsburg entrepreneurs who were the main financial backers of the Keswick industry. Two commissions in 1600 and 1602 examined the affairs of the Company of Mines Royal: their recommendations stirred Newlands into a period of modest prosperity in the expert hands of second generation Hechstetters.

We cannot be certain when the operation finally ended. Economic factors certainly played an important part but other reasons for the ultimate decline have been suggested. Fuel may have run out; at its peak, it has been estimated, the Brigham smelter used 5,000 horseloads of charcoal produced from about ninety acres of woodland – a sizeable amount but hardly enough to devastate the landscape and cause a shortage. Moreover, peat and coal were used more and more to fuel the fires of the Forge.

Another theory claims that the industry petered out when there were no Hechstetters at the helm to ensure perseverance and enthusiasm, technical expertise and intelligent business acumen.

Traditionally, Cromwell's troops are said to have destroyed the Brigham complex during the Civil War but confirmatory evidence is lacking. *The History and Antiquities of the Counties of Westmorland and Cumberland* by Joseph Nicolson and Richard Burn (1777) states categorically: 'the smelting houses and works were destroyed, and most of the miners slain, in the civil wars'. In 1648, a group of Roundheads was despatched from Penrith to relieve the besieged garrison at Cockermouth, the only Parliamentary stronghold in the district. Nicolson and Burn, incidentally, mistakenly describe the castle at Cockermouth as a Royalist stronghold. These soldiers would surely pass through Keswick and it is possible that they might have been responsible for the destruction, though it is difficult to understand the motive behind such an action.

Keswick does appear to have escaped any significant involvement in the conflicts of the Civil War, its isolation a protection from warring factions. Even the claim that Stair House in Newlands was the home of the Parliamentarian, General Thomas Fairfax, is doubtful. The initials 'FF' and the date '1647' inscribed over the door are more likely to be those of Francis Parratt of Stair who married Thomas Fairfax of Caldbeck in 1628.

Sir Daniel Fleming, writing in 1671, compared Brigham Forge at that date with its former glory. Keswick, he wrote was 'wel knowne many years ago by reason of ye mines of copper...and much inhabited by minerall men who had their smelting houses near Greata Syde... And tho' these smelting houses within memory were so numerous as they looked like a little Towne yet now there is not one house standing.'

The invasion of a small market town by a group of foreign workmen certainly had a profound social impact. Estimates of just how many Germans came to Keswick differ widely, reaching the ridiculous figure of 4,000; a sensible total would be around 150 or 200. Friction and suspicion were inevitable and in October 1565 it was reported that between 'the Almain strangers' and 'others of the common people of this country of the meanest sort there falleth some discord'.

There was at least one death. Leonard Stoultz was attacked by twenty locals, led by a man called Fisher. Daniel Hechstetter was anxious and angry, condemning the bragging and the threats of future attacks and 'especially that naughty man Fisher, who has been ring-leader and chief occasion of the villainous murdering of Leonard Stoultz'.

Serious antagonism seems to have mellowed into acceptance as the foreigners were integrated into the community. Before long, the miners started to marry local girls and by 1580 there had been nearly 40 such marriages. Crosthwaite parish registers record the births of 176 children to German fathers between 1565 and 1584.

The Hechstetters in particular left their mark on the town. It has been claimed that during repairs some years ago to a house near Keswick Bridge, carved oak panelling was uncovered with the initials D H and I H, possibly those of Daniel and Jane Hechstetter. Their descendants include a Lord Mayor of London, a Dean of Carlisle, a master of Carlisle Grammar School, and the Calvert family, whose name still lives on in 'The Calvert Trust', a local organisation which provides activity holidays for disabled people.

Inter-marriages apart, it did not take the canny Keswickians long to realise that the exploitation of the mines meant, as never before, employment and money. Local men found work as carriers of coal from Caldbeck and Workington, peat and slates from Skiddaw, timber from Borrowdale. At the mines, they took on the more menial tasks of digging foundations and loading sacks, transporting ore and maintaining buildings.

Important as copper was, the discovery of another source of underground wealth was to have far-reaching effects on Keswick's economy, effects which continue to the present day. Like much of Keswick's early history, the discovery of wad is enveloped in mystery and tradition. This deposit, variously known as black lead, plumbago, graphite or black cauke, was found at Seathwaite in Borrowdale, a tiny hamlet which claims to be the wettest inhabited place in England.

The story goes that about 1550 a shepherd accidentally uncovered a cache of wad under the roots of a fallen tree on the fell side.

When it was found that this unfamiliar substance could be used to make a mark, it became a popular means of branding sheep. Other uses were discovered: 'a present Remedy for the Cholock; it easeth the Pain of Gravel, Stone and Strangury; and for these and the like Uses, it's much bought up by Apothecaries and Physicians'. Local sufferers ground the wad into powder and dissolved as much 'as will lie upon a Sixpence' in white wine or ale.

Seathwaite - the home of wad and rain

In addition to its medicinal properties, wad reduced friction in machines and was suitable for glazing and hardening crucibles and other vessels of earth or clay which were subject to intense heat. Rubbed on guns and other weapons, it acted as a preservation against rust; dyers used it to ensure the permanence of their colours, though it has been suggested that for this process 'wad' has been confused with 'woad'. For armament manufacturers, it was commonly employed for casting bomb shells and cannon balls.

This multi-purpose material was obviously highly prized as well as highly priced: its scarcity and purity added even further to its value. It was mined from two holes 1,000 feet or so above Seathwaite, a network of pipes and adits, stages and levels, veins and drifts. Digging out the wad was not a continuous process. The workings were opened every five or seven years and sufficient wad to meet demand was extracted. Bishop Nicolson, who visited Seathwaite in 1710, reported that one section ('the old level') had been closed for thirty-two years but the day before he arrived a new and rich deposit had been found.

Throughout its life, the Seathwaite mine was vulnerable to thieves in search of easy and profitable pickings. The workmen themselves could easily hide the light-weight wad; organised gangs of looters operated with aggressive efficiency, stealing, it has been estimated, thousands of pounds' worth of wad in a year.

An account of a visit to Seathwaite in 1749 asserts that the poorer inhabitants of Keswick lived mainly by 'stealing or clandestinely buying of those that steal, the black lead, which they sell to Jews, or other hawkers'. Traditionally the George Hotel was the base where the Jews carried on their illegal wheeling and dealing.

At least one wily thief carried his fraud too far. He owned the land adjoining the mine and sank his own shaft. He then tunnelled into the workings, 'where, with secret joy, he continued his depredations for some time undiscovered'. He was eventually caught and tried at Carlisle.

Such incidents were instrumental in convincing the mine owners to seek legal protection for their property and its valuable deposits. In 1752 an Act of Parliament was passed, making it a crime 'to break into any mine or wad-hole of wad or black cawke, commonly called black-lead, or to steal from thence'. Buildings and guards protected the mine workings; miners were searched; an armed escort accompanied consignments of wad on their way to London.

Whatever the truth of the stories about smuggling and shady dealing, one fact is certain: Borrowdale wad provided the raw material for Keswick's major industry, the manufacture of pencils.

The town likes to boast that it is the home of the first pencils in the world. There is no hard evidence to prove the claim and its validity depends on what is meant by the word 'pencil'. It is derived from the Latin 'penicullus' (literally, a small tail) and was used to describe small, fine pointed brushes for painting. Egyptian painting brushes existed as early as 1500 BC; metal styluses were common in classical times.

The ancestor of the familiar wood-encased pencil may be traced to at least 1565 when it was used to illustrate a book on fossils published in Zurich. Various dates have been suggested for the first pencil works by the Greta in Keswick but Molly Lefebure's authoritative article in her *Cumberland Heritage* (1970) puts forward a tentative date of 1792. One local tradition credits a Keswick joiner with making the first important step of encasing wad in wood. Another insists that pencils were made in the town in Elizabethan times – the raw material was certainly available.

The description of 'pencil maker' begins to appear in the Crosthwaite parish registers in the early 1800s. How many firms were operating in the early days and on what scale, we don't know: the manufacturing process was probably some form of cottage industry. Speaking in 1877, Mr Peter Harrison, who had lived in Keswick for nearly fifty years, recalled that when he was a boy pencils were wholly made by hand and sold from 1s. to 1s.6d. each.

Scarcity of records makes it impossible to sketch a full or accurate picture of the early pencil industry in Keswick. The first significant firm date is 1832 when Banks and Co. set up in business at Forge Mill, to be followed by Hogarth and Hayes at Greta Bridge and Abraham Wren on Penrith Road.

Early pencil works in the shadow of Greta Hall

By 1886 the Wren and Hogarth firms had combined in well appointed premises at Southey Hill and over the road at Greta Bridge Ann Banks and Co. started making pencils in a disused woollen mill – today it is a youth club. Although there were two firms with the name Banks, they had no connexions: Ann Banks and Co. were commercial rivals to Banks and Co.

In 1906 Henry Birkbeck took over Banks and Co. at Forge Mill after some years as manager. His son, Simon, succeeded him and transferred the business in 1919 to Mr H J Billinge. A disastrous fire in 1940 destroyed much of the building and Mr Billinge continued to use part of what remained as an antique furniture showroom.

Ann Banks and Co. was bought by the Greenwood family in 1908. Four years later, they moved across the road into Hogarth's premises at Southey Hill, trading as the Cumberland Pencil Company. Eventually the Twinlock Group took over and in 1980 Rexel, a subsidiary of the Ofrex Group, became the new owners.

The Borrowdale deposits of wad were exhausted many years ago and today's sophisticated processes depend on raw materials from abroad: graphite from Sri Lanka, Korea and China; gums from America and Turkey; cedar-wood from America; clay from Bavaria and southern England. A staff of about 140 produces a wide range of pencils: up to seventy-two colours are available in hard to soft grades from 9H to 6B. Types vary from outsize 'Beginners' to slim diary pencils, from artists' Colour Blocks to carpenters' Blackedge.

In 1981, the Company opened its Museum and Exhibition Centre, a well-arranged and professionally presented display telling the story of pencil making. Among other intriguing exhibits is the world's largest pencil – seven feet long, three and a half inches wide, with lead one inch in diameter – hand-made by one of the staff to raise funds for the Keswick Mountain Rescue Team.

The world's biggest pencil

4

Picking a Living

The decline of the Newlands and Borrowdale mines and the return of the miners to their native Germany did not signal the end of mining activity in the Keswick area.

Over the years, attempts have been made to revitalise Goldscope. Clarke reports in his *Survey of the Lakes* (1787) that a group of Dutchmen came over with William, Prince of Orange, about 1690 to investigate the mine and 'stayed until the place was not worth the working'. In the 1850s a rich vein of lead was discovered and for several years the 'Great Bunch' kept some fifty workmen busy – and sparked off a long and expensive legal battle between the owners. Sporadic efforts, all on a small scale and much bedevilled by water, have failed to find deposits of either copper, lead or galena of sufficient quantity or quality to justify extraction on a commercial basis.

The same sad saga of repeated exploitation and failure is told of the other mines in Newlands and Borrowdale: Dale Head, Yewthwaite on the western flank of Catbells, Castlenook and Long Work near Goldscope, Barrow and Stoneycroft (traditionally the scene of a disaster when a dam burst and workmen were buried in sand and mud as the shaft in which they were digging was swamped).

On the fell side between Sail and Scar Crags in Newlands, a vein of cobalt was discovered in the 1840s. A two-mile access road and a tramway were built from Stoneycroft; machinery for crushing, smelting and dressing the raw product was installed. A very expensive venture collapsed when only a few ounces of cobalt were produced: 'to this mine,' writes John Adams in his *Mines of the Lake District Fells* (1988), 'goes the distinction of having been the worst mining investment in the whole of the district.'

The spoil heaps of Brandelhow Mine at the southern end of Derwentwater are all that remain of a once rich and ancient mine. A series of ever bigger wheels tried to cope with water but the mine finally had to close in 1891.

Force Crag Mine near Braithwaite is one of the few local sites that has been worked in modern times, producing a variety of minerals. Signs can still be seen of the tramway that carried ore to Braithwaite for grinding and of the aerial ropeway built in the early 1940s.

There are remains, too, of the mines at Threlkeld, once productive and prosperous, but, like all the other mines in the Keswick area, subject to periods of closure. During the years 1881 to 1901, a total of over 10,000 tons of galena and 13,000 tons of blende were mined by a workforce of some 100 men. A fierce dispute in 1890 with the Derwentwater Angling Association, who accused the Threlkeld Mining Company of seriously polluting the River Greta, went to a public enquiry. The Company, in spite of protests that the complaints were causing loss of money and putting jobs in jeopardy, was found guilty.

Quarrying, like mining, has provided a vital contribution to the economic life of Keswick. Small operations apart, two major quarries, both no longer operating, provided a measure of steady employment and financial stability for many years.

Honister slate quarries straddled the summit of the popular road from Seatoller to Buttermere. The workings almost certainly go back beyond the first date for which documentary evidence is available – a lease of 1728 to John Walker for extracting slate from 'Ewecrag and Fleteworth'.

A visit by George Smith of Wigton in 1750, recorded in the *Gentleman's Magazine*, paints a typically romantic and exaggerated picture. 'The scene was terrifying...the mountains heaped on mountains that were piled around us, desolate and waste, like the ruins of a world which we had survived, excited such ideas of horror as are not to be expresed.' He suggested the name of this fearful place should not be Honister but Finisterre – the end of the world.

The tunnels driven into the fellside are easily identified but they give no hint of the vast chambers hollowed out inside the mountain – up to 600 feet long, eighty feet wide and forty feet high, and big enough, the quarrymen used to boast, to hold the population of a large city.

The traditional method of transporting the hewn slate was by sledge, a back-breaking, muscle-testing slog along narrow paths and unstable scree, fraught with danger and demanding great strength and considerable dexterity. Stories are told of prodigious feats, some true, some perhaps apochryphal. Joseph Clarke of Stonethwaite is said to have brought down forty-two-and-a-half loads in seventeen journeys in one day, a staggering total of nearly five tons of slate.

In the 1880s, tramways and aerial ropeways replaced sledges. One minor quarry, Dubbs, was linked by a tramway to the workshops; it was abandoned long ago but still provides a well-worn path for walkers en route to Great Gable and Haystacks via the ruins of the Drum House.

In 1907, horses were still used to transport the slate to Keswick but in that year a traction engine was harnessed to take the daily load of twelve tons, using the old toll road from the workshops to Seatoller, a contoured track which is still the favoured route for walkers on the Pass.

Apart from the task of handling heavy hunks of slate, other factors turned Honister quarrymen into a race apart. The summit of the Pass is wet and windy: up to 100 inches of rain a year are usual and ferocious gales, shrieking through 'the Crack', have reputedly torn off roofs, ripped men and sheep off the crags and lifted a wagon loaded with thirty hundredweight of slate off its tracks.

In the early days, some of the quarrymen lived in primitive huts among the crags; others walked long distances from their homes. In 1893, eight cottages were built at Seatoller for the workmen, with six more in 1918. In 1927, a hostel for fifty men was built on site: it has, for some years, done welcome service as a Youth Hostel.

Under the control of the Buttermere Green Slate Company, the Honister quarries flourished.

Over 100 men were employed and production reached 3,000 tons a year. More recently, the quarries have suffered the fate of so many once profitable local enterprises: falling demand and rising costs brought final closure in 1986.

Honister - with its 'mountains heaped on mountains'

Threlkeld Quarry has provided a century of employment, though it has few historical highlights and none of the romance of Honister. Started in 1878 by Herman Harkewitz, a German who came to Keswick from Yorkshire, it has had a number of owners, the most recent in 1965 the Amalgamated Road Stone Corporation.

The quarry, still visible on the lower slopes of Clough Head, produced stone blocks and coloured floor tiles, setts and kerbs, flags and chippings. Major schemes such as the building of the Thirlmere reservoir and the expanding network of roads, the M6 and the A66 in particular, required the kind of material that Threlkeld could supply. Modernisation in 1939 streamlined production and drastically reduced the size of the workforce. In the busy days some 200 men were employed but by the 1970s the staff was down to fifty, half of them engaged in transporting the 150,000 tons annual output.

The quarry was finally closed in the early 1980s and abandoned but in 1989 planning permission was given to develop it into a mining museum and industrial workshops.

Within Keswick itself and its immediate environs, a number of trades and occupations provided employment. The Greta supplied a natural and cheap source of power which was harnessed by a string of some twenty mills on its banks. They stretched from the Briery bobbin works (now a holiday village) to Greta Bridge pencil mill, with a concentration at Brigham Forge and on the river side opposite what is now Fitz Park. The old mills have either disappeared or been converted into flats; sympathetic planning has meant that the structure of their original design is easily recognised.

The local labour force produced a wide variety of goods. In 1688, Thomas Denton wrote: 'The number of tanners and shoemakers which dwell about the town causeth the markets to abound with raw hides and leather'. A century later, it was reported that a market at Settle in Yorkshire had destroyed the leather trade in Keswick.

Pencils and bobbins apart, other products included course woollens and fancy waistcoats, straw hats and nails, blankets and beer, spades and scythes. A thriving woollen mill operated at Millbeck from the mid 1700s; in 1903 the premises were converted into a substantial dwelling house, later known as Millbeck Towers.

The industrial and commercial activities of the eighteenth and nineteenth centuries operated on a small scale but Keswick was no longer Leland's 'a lytle poore market town'. Its continued prosperity and the exploitation of its next wave of invaders – tourists – were dependent on an adequate road system, particularly as pack-horses were replaced by wheeled transport.

Road maintenance had never had top priority. In 1555 an act laid the duty of caring for the roads on the parish, with elected overseers to organise necessary repairs. Parliament set a minimum standard in 1691: main roads were to be level and at least eight feet wide, packhorse tracks to be three feet wide. Improvements in the eighteenth century were almost wholly due to the Turnpike Trusts which, by the 1770s, were responsible for thousands of miles of roads throughout the country. To raise revenue to finance repairs and maintenance, the Trustees were empowered to erect toll gates or bars and to charge a fee for traffic passing through. The normal practice in Cumbria was to let the toll gates to the highest bidder at a public auction.

Keswick had several of these barriers where travellers were halted to pay their dues.

The Brigham toll house is easily identified today by the side of Calvert Bridge on Penrith Road. The High Hill building, altered and modernised, is opposite the big bend in the river just before the junction with the road to Bassenthwaite and Carlisle. At some auctions, this gate was let along with the 'Chain or Side Bar at Crosthwaite'.

Over the years there appears to have been either a gate or a bar at three locations on the Ambleside road. Maps of 1787, 1832 and 1852 show a bar by the modern entrance to Castlehead Close just beyond St John's Church.

Further along the road, the toll at Brow Top was sited at the top of the bends of Manor Brow (which used to be known as Skinner's Kiln Hill) opposite Castlerigg Manor. In 1774 it was auctioned for £27 and it continued in use until 31 October 1883, just eight months before the controlling authority, the Penrith, Keswick and Cockermouth Turnpike Road Trust, was wound up in June 1884.

The third location for a bar on this road was at its junction with today's main road to Ambleside, the A591. Here, at Toll Bar Cottage, is presumably the site of 'Castlerigg Brow' which is listed in the auction notices of the nineteenth century. That for January 1878, for example, gives a rate of £267 for 'Brigham and Brow Top Gates with the Chain on Castlerigg Brow'.

The first Turnpike Trust in Cumbria was Whitehaven in 1739. The Cockermouth-Keswick-Kendal and the Keswick-Penrith roads were turnpiked in 1762. Thomas Gray, travelling from Keswick to Ambleside in 1769, found the highway 'in some few parts is not completed, yet a good country road, through sound but narrow and stony lanes, very safe in broad daylight' and by Thirlmere it earned the compliment of 'excellent'. Thomas West, writing in the late 1770s, found the Keswick to Penrith route offered '17 miles of very good road'.

The traveller from Keswick to Cockermouth had a choice of two turnpike roads: the comparatively easy route on the east side of Bassenthwaite via Mirehouse and Ouse Bridge, or by the steep Whinlatter Pass and Lorton. Hutchinson, writing in 1794, leaves no doubt about the nature of this latter road, even allowing for typical romantic exaggeration: 'The steep and alpine pass of Whinlatter forms an ascent of five miles, up stupendous heights, by a winding path, contrived in an excellent manner...to render the advance more gradual.'

The side roads were not so well treated. A traveller in Borrowdale was liable to meet falling rocks and on occasion to find the road completely blocked. It reminded Thomas Gray of an Alpine pass and he went no further than Grange. In 1783, Peter Crosthwaite's map of Derwentwater shows four routes up the valley, one on the east and three on the west. Of these three only one (today's motor road) was usable; the upper track along the flank of

Catbells, still a popular footpath, and the lowest along the lake shore were impassable.

The great John Macadam was active in Cumbria both as an adviser to several Turnpike Trusts and as a builder of roads. In 1824, following a report to the Trustees in the Keswick area, he supervised the construction of ten miles of new road between Keswick and Penrith and four miles between Keswick and Cockermouth.

The Keswick to Penrith route, he considered, 'has been laid out upon a very injudicious line and the surface has been neglected or mismanaged in such a manner as to have rendered the road very inconvenient, if not dangerous'. Whinlatter was 'so steep as to present the greatest obstacle to carriages of every kind'. Improving it would have cost a great deal and would have meant increasing the distance: much better, he suggested, to concentrate on 'the level line by the west side of Bassenthwaite Lake'.

His advice was accepted and, modified and upgraded over a century and a half, the route remains the main highway westwards as the A66.

Improved roads meant that the way was open for the tourist invasion – modest in comparison with today's millions but increasingly popular for the curious travellers as war in Europe brought 'The Grand Tour' to an end. By 1783, Thomas Kitchen's Travellers' Guide revealed that 'Keswick, though a poor village, receives great benefit from the resort of gentry to see the romantic lakes and mountains that surround it'. Even at this early date, Skiddaw was on the tourist trail.

5

Curious Travellers

Broadly speaking, we can classify the early visitors to Keswick into two categories, Romantic and Picturesque, with some travellers fitting firmly into both groups.

The pioneers were John Dalton (1709-1763) and John Brown (1715-1766). Dalton, son of the rector of Dean near Cockermouth, was brought up in Whitehaven, where his father was the minister of Holy Trinity Church. A prebendary of Worcester Cathedral, he had literary aspirations and adapted Milton's 'Comus' for the stage, donating the proceeds to the poet's daughter who was oppressed by age and poverty.

John Brown grew up at Wigton vicarage. He was appointed a canon of Carlisle Cathedral in 1737 and took an active part in the 1745 siege of the city. His literary output was considerable but he was dogged throughout his life by attacks of acute depression. In 1766, on his way to Russia to advise the Empress on an educational system, he committed suicide. He was very fond of Keswick and paid an annual visit 'not only as an innocent amusement but as a religious act'.

The Romantics were overawed by Lakeland scenery and their descriptions were appropriately exaggerated. John Dalton's *Descriptive Poem Addressed to Two Young Ladies at their Return from Viewing the Mines at Whitehaven* (1755) paints a picture of stupendous crags and impending woods, savage grandeur and menacing eagles, softened a little by the 'verdant isles' of Derwentwater – in all, 'a pleasing, though an awful sight'.

John Brown's *Letter describing the Vale and Lake of Keswick* (1767) echoes Dalton's imaginative flights of fancy. Waterfalls tumble 'in vast sheets, from rock to rock, in rude and terrible magnificence'; fell tops pierce the clouds; woods climb up the steep and shaggy sides of the mountains 'where mortal foot never yet approached'. Brown did at least venture to the top of Walla Crag, where 'azure groups of craggy and broken steeps form an immense and awful picture'. To round off his visit, he walked by Derwentwater in moonlight, 'a scene of such delicate beauty, repose and solemnity as exceeds all description'.

It was Brown who provided the key words for the Romantic traveller.

The full perfection of Keswick, he suggested, consists of three qualities: beauty, horror and immensity – the smooth and gentle, the rugged and rough, the high and majestic. The reaction of the Romantic visitor is neatly typified by Mr Avison of Newcastle, who stood at Friars' Crag, looked at the well-known view of Derwentwater and described it as 'beauty lying in the lap of horror'.

Stupendous crags and savage grandeur in Borrowdale

The earliest significant account of a visit to Keswick was Thomas Gray's journal of 1769, tinged, not surprisingly, with Romantic tones. Gray wrote his diary – a sort of 'wish-you-were-here' extended postcard – for his friend, Dr Wharton, who had been forced through illness to abandon the tour at Brough.

On 2 October 1769, Gray approached Keswick from the east and some two miles outside the town gazed on 'the vale of Elysium in all its verdure'. He was to spend more than half of his ten-day visit to the Lakes in and around Keswick. He has little to say about the people or their way of life: he is primarily concerned with the scenery and his own reactions to it, epitomised in his excursion into Borrowdale with the landlord of the Queen's Head as his companion.

Gowdar Crag by the side of Lodore Falls evoked the inevitable Romantic response. The rocks were 'hanging loose and nodding forwards, seen just starting from their base in shivers'. Gray was reminded of his visit to the Alps when the guides had urged speed as his party crossed a glacier and warned against talking 'lest the agitation of the air should loosen the snows above and bring down a mass that would overwhelm a caravan'. He looked up at the solid mass of Gowdar Crag, afraid that it was about to fall on him, and 'hastened on in silence'.

He went no further than Grange where he was entertained by a farmer who provided milk, oat cakes, butter and ale. Gray was very impressed by the farmer's account of the destruction of an eagle's nest in the valley. The predators appear to have bred regularly, a menace to lambs and game. While fellow dalesmen shouted and made enough noise to keep the parent bird away, the farmer was lowered on a rope to remove an eaglet and an egg from the nest.

Like most tourists in his day and since, Gray was drawn to the Lake. He looked at Derwentwater from Crow Park, then rough pasture, and from Cockshot, planted with oak, spruce and Scots fir, and, for Gray, preferable to Castlehead as a viewpoint. He awards the rosette, however, to the panorama from Crosthwaite vicarage, 'the sweetest scene I can yet discover in point of pastoral beauty'. Oddly enough, he makes no mention of the islands in Derwentwater, even when he visited Calf Close Bay, which he called Carf-close-reeds. Here, he tells us, 'the glass played its part divinely'.

This peculiar item of the well-equipped traveller was a Claude Glass, a plano-convex mirror about four inches in diameter, set in black foil and bound like a pocket-book.

Calf Close Bay, where Thomas Gray's Claude Glass 'played its part divinely'

To use it, the traveller selected a view, turned his back on it and saw it reflected in the Glass, neatly framed and reduced to the size of a postcard. Taking advantage of different coloured inserts, it was possible to gain a range of artificial effects: midday sun could be converted into moonlight, stooks of corn into snow drifts.

Gray's journal is a mixture of romantic absurdities and sober statements of fact. For example, it might be thought that Castlerigg Stone Circle would have inspired him to excessive comment rather than the prosaic statistics he recorded. On the other hand, when he went to Bassenthwaite, it is said that he asked for the blinds of the chaise to be drawn, so terrifying were the slopes of Skiddaw above him.

He left Keswick with regret. As he looked back from Castlerigg over the town, the two lakes, the valley and the fells, he admitted 'I had almost a mind to have gone back again' – a sentiment shared by many a visitor since Gray's day. He certainly did an effective public relations job for Keswick. His journal was read widely, a magnet that drew later tourists to sample the delights of Lakeland and to experience something of the beauty, horror and immensity that had so impressed Gray.

If Thomas Gray is seen as the epitome of the Romantic Traveller, William Gilpin, who came to the Lakes in 1772, is the Apostle of the Picturesque. A Cumbrian by birth – at Scaleby Castle near Carlisle in 1724 – he took holy orders and worked as a schoolmaster for twenty-five years before retiring in 1777. He devoted the rest of his life to his passion for art, drawing in particular, and to his wish to spread the gospel of the Picturesque.

The key volume is his *Observations relative chiefly to Picturesque Beauty, made in the Year 1772, on several Parts of England; particularly the Mountains and Lakes of Cumberland and Westmorland* (1776). In this bible for picturesque tourists, he records his travels and catalogues the necessary criteria for judging a landscape.

At its simplest, picturesque beauty is 'that kind of beauty which would look well in a picture'. Nature needed to be 'improved' by the hand of man and for Gilpin this meant a detailed formal analysis of the various aspects of scenery – mountains, lakes, woods and so on – to provide the would-be artist with a framework of assessment. Islands, for example, cannot be objects of beauty if they are round or regular in shape; they must be scattered and certainly never dead centre of a lake; they must not be heavily wooded – close to they appear 'a heavy lump' and at a distance 'a murky spot'.

With such artificial restrictions, it is not surprising that Gilpin warns the Picturesque Traveller assessing Derwentwater: 'Great care therefore should be taken in selecting views of this lake'. Keswick itself he dismissed as a place of no consequence but at least it was superior to Ambleside.

The nearby valleys fared rather better. Borrowdale was wild and desolate enough even for Gilpin; Lodore Falls inspired the standard descriptions: nobility, grandeur, dignity, simplicity, repose (an odd word for a waterfall).

The inhabitants of the valley, according to Gilpin, lived at subsistence level, with crops that matured late, violent rain storms and just enough produce from sheep, cattle and the land to keep them alive. Peat was dug from high on the fells and brought down to the valley by sledge. At Rosthwaite, writes Gilpin, 'the sons and daughters of simplicity enjoy health, peace and contentment.'

The nearest he came to climbing a fell was a visit to Watendlath by the track from Rosthwaite. Today it is a popular walk offering little difficulty: for Gilpin it was 'steeper than the tiling of a house...a painful perpendicular march of nearly two miles'. He was amply rewarded by the picturesque setting of Watendlath, with its ring of fractured rocks and beetling cliffs, a scene of wild and majestic irregularity.

St John's in the Vale he found disappointing: the meadows, farm-houses and clumps of trees cohered into a confusion that was rich rather than picturesque. He did, however, find space to recount the details of the devastating storm of 22 August 1749, even though he casts doubt on the credibility of the local inhabitant who told him the story.

The effusive descriptions of Gray and Gilpin set the tone and subsequent travellers followed the established trend, though some added their individual stamp and widened their perceptions.

Among them, William Hutchinson, a Barnard Castle solicitor, deserves special mention if only for his monumental history of Cumberland (1793-1797), a prime though not always reliable source. He came to the Lakes in 1773 and 1774; his journals are packed with the exaggerated responses of his day. The fells round Derwentwater, for example, rise in rude and ruinous confusion, a stupendous 'circus' of convulsive chaos and grotesque crags.

Keswick itself earned no bouquets. Hutchinson dismissed it as 'a mean village, without any apparent trade; the houses are homely and dirty'. Even the distinctive Moot Hall was condemned as 'of the most uncouth architecture' and tourist accommodation was quite inadequate. The weekly market flourished, selling salmon, eels, perch and trout and 'the finest mutton in the island of Great Britain'. Hutchinson could find few signs of industry or manufactory but rather contradicts himself by listing Keswick's products: coarse woollen goods, blankets, kerseys, happings, linen. A new cotton mill was operating on the banks of the Greta, helping to swell the number of looms in the town to eighty; the leather trade, once considerable, had declined.

James Clarke, a Penrith land surveyor, published his *Survey of the Lakes* in 1787. He, too, was rooted in the romantic tradition but his local knowledge tempered excessive reactions and provided more detailed and reliable information about Keswick than some of his contemporaries who based their accounts on a brief visit. He cast a slightly contemptuous eye on Gray, surprised that he had failed to mention Blencathra and concluded that he 'was not a mountaineer'.

Clarke approached Keswick from the east. At Brigham Forge he found the remains of the old smelt mills with walls still standing some four or five feet high. Keswick itself he described as a small town without any remarkable buildings, except for the 'poor's House'.

William Green's etching of 'the poor house'

The Saturday market was thriving and three fairs were held each year. Clarke mentions only the one held on St Mary Magdalene's Day and called the Morlan Fair. It was held on 22 July when rainfall could be heavy. A local rhyme, 'Morlan fluid Ne'er did guid' was, said Clarke, 'most wonderfully poetic lines': his tongue must surely have been firmly in his cheek.

The former prosperous leather trade may have declined but by 1787 Keswick was beginning to wake up to the economic advantages of the tourist invasion. The town's romantic situation, Clarke claims, 'draws every summer, vast numbers from all parts of the kingdom to visit the many natural curiosities in its neighbourhood'.

The standard itinerary included Crow Park, the rounded field at the head of Derwentwater which still remains a favourite picnic site for today's visitors. In the 1740s, it was covered in a dense thicket of oak trees, with a comprehensive crown of foliage 'as close and smooth as a bowling green' and so tightly clustered together that it was said local boys went from tree to tree like squirrels.

When Clarke was in Keswick, Crow Park was bare of trees. Greenwich Hospital, owners of the timber, sold it in 1749. Mr Scott, a local farmer, dug out the remaining roots and ploughed the land, starting at the bottom of the rise and cutting a single ridge and furrow in a spiral.

Borrowdale, like Keswick, was starting to realise its potential as a tourist attraction. Clarke dined at the 'neat and commodious little inn at Lodore', where even the cat and the dog seem to have welcomed him. If we are to believe Clarke, drastic changes had transformed Borrowdale in the twenty years since Gray had been there. The road round the lake, he claimed, was very good, even for carriages; it was 'made purposely by the inhabitants for the accommodation of travellers; so that at present a journey into Borrowdale may be performed with both ease and pleasure'.

Thirty years previously, Clarke maintained, the valley was hardly in a state of civilisation: agriculture was primitive and the ground was sparsely cultivated. Carts or any other wheeled vehicle were unknown and Clarke reckoned hay was still being carried by horse in the streets of Keswick when he was there. In summer, Borrowdalians fed on fish and mutton; in winter, on bacon and hung meat. Clarke saw seven sheep hanging in one cottage chimney and was told of much greater numbers of carcases in other farmhouses.

Grange Bridge, built in 1678, was in poor condition but the hamlet itself earned Clarke's commendation as 'a pretty well kept village'. When the water of the river was high enough, boats were used to carry slate, wood and other commodities to Crow Park and adjacent landing places at the northern end of Derwentwater.

Clarke acknowledged the attractions of Millbeck and Applethwaite, though they remained anonymous among 'many pleasant villages' (!) on the road near Lyzzick Hall. This was a favourite spot where 'several gentlemen take up lodgings in the Summer time, and pitch Marquees to enjoy the beauty of the place'. The road to Applethwaite and Millbeck passed Crosthwaite Vicarage, giving 'the grandest view for the artist of any in the country'. The nearby church, Clarke said, was dedicated to St Cuthbert! Such howlers cast doubts on Clarke's reliability.

How true was his account of the Penny Fair at the church of St John's in the Vale? On the Sunday before Easter, he tells us, all the inhabitants of the parish, young and old, men and women, adjourned to the nearby ale house after evening service. Everyone paid a penny – hence the name of Penny Fair – and the money was spent on liquor. On one occasion, £3 was collected, which must have meant that 720 people attended evensong – a figure quite incompatible with the capacity of the small church or the population of the parish.

As a surveyor, Clarke was interested in the topography of the landscape and his maps of the lakes and their immediate surroundings are perhaps the most valuable part of his *Survey:* presumably they are more accurate than some of his stories.

By the early 1800s a small library of journals and accounts of tours was available for the curious traveller in the Lake District. Most were repetitious, quoting freely from previous writers, Gilpin and Hutchinson in particular, and adding little to our picture of Keswick and district in the late eighteenth century.

One of the more lively and reliable accounts comes from Joseph Budworth, later Joseph Palmer, who hides his identity as the author of *A Fortnight's Ramble to the Lakes* (1792) under the pseudonym of 'A Rambler'. A soldier by profession – he lost an arm in the siege of Gibraltar in 1779 – he was honest enough to admit in the second edition of his Ramble that the first was 'very incorrect', a warning perhaps that we should read all these early journals with a measure of scepticism.

If Gray saw the Lakes as a Romantic, Gilpin as an apostle of the Picturesque and Hutchinson as an historian, Budworth's perspective was that of a fell-walker. In his fortnight – the last week in July and the first in August – he travelled over 240 miles and climbed a number of fells in consistently fine weather. One of the merits of his 'Journeying Companion' is that it does not rely on earlier descriptions or reactions: Budworth was his own man.

Unlike Gilpin and Hutchinson, he found Keswick a neat town. The local people were unassuming and obliging, friendly and hospitable; many of them lived to a great age. Their food was simple and homely: oat cake, buttermilk and whey, ale, fish and whatever they could produce from the land. Budworth did not call at any cottage that had fewer than three children. Visitors were welcomed with respect and kindness, unlike southerners whose 'rapaciousness to strangers is a disgrace to the country'.

Borrowdale pleased him but it did not send him into wild raptures: indeed, the vast amphitheatre of the upper valley was 'neither so magnificent or pleasing as the one around our chaste favourite, Grasmere lake'. A footnote records a little-known scrap of information. In 1745, during the rebellion, the local farmers drove their cattle into Borrowdale for safety. It is generally believed that the 1715 and 1745 Jacobite uprisings had little direct effect on the Lake District but Budworth's note raises a doubt. 'The days of incursions', he wrote, 'are imprinted on the minds of the people about the Lakes; and the rebel army entered into a part of England where they had the most rooted enemies.'

In both 1715 and 1745, the main Jacobite thrust was in the east of Cumbria –

Carlisle, Penrith, Kendal – and traditionally the last skirmish on English soil was at Clifton near Penrith in 1745. James Radcliffe, third Earl of Derwentwater, was executed in 1716 for his part in the first rebellion but it seems reasonable to assume that Keswick, isolated and well away from any action, was minimally affected by the uprisings. Perhaps news of the siege of Carlisle and Bonnie Prince Charlie's march through Penrith were threats enough to stir the men of Borrowdale to take precautions.

Above all, Budworth is remembered for his account of Mary, the Beauty of Buttermere, an encounter that began in arcadian innocence and generated a romantic story of seduction and fraud that has held its interest until our own day. Few readers of Melvyn Bragg's *The Maid of Buttermere* (1987) realise that it was Budworth who first introduced Mary to the world outside her remote valley.

Complementing the written journals and diaries of the early tourists were the efforts of the artists who were attracted by the landscape. Some, like Gilpin, slot into the categories of both writer and artist but others earn their place in the story of Keswick by the pictures they drew and painted – and that usually meant Derwentwater.

One of the earliest was inspired by the felling of trees on Crow Park. The artist is unknown, though a case has been argued for Salathiel Court, who was born at Papcastle near Cockermouth. The timber was bought by the Speddings of Whitehaven, who commissioned the artist to record the sale in the mid 1700s.

The sale of oaks at Crow Park

While workmen chop and saw, two gentlemen chat and supervise in the shade of rather spindly trees which have little resemblance to the sturdy oaks of Crow Park. The group of men and trees forms the foreground to a full-length view of Derwentwater, the surrounding fells sharp and peaked, typical of the exaggerated contours of the Romantic style.

Among the earliest identifiable artists were William Bellers, who used Castlehead as a viewpoint in the 1750s, and Thomas Smith of Derby whose 'View of Derwentwater from Crow Park' (1761), like that of the earlier unknown artist, is characterised by the familiar excesses of slope and height. The impact of Smith's engraving arises from the turbulence of swirling cloud over Borrowdale, contrasting sharply with two human figures and a blasted tree in the foreground.

At least two artists drew a circular panorama, an ingeniously conceived and continuous strip embracing the whole landscape round Derwentwater. One is by an unknown artist; the other, now lost, is by Thomas Hearne who, according to Southey, made a sketch of the circle of fells from Crow Park in the 1770s.

In the footsteps of the pioneers came a whole tribe of artists of varying degrees of competence, anxious to record the prospects offered by 'the Vale of Elysium', drawing and sketching, etching and engraving the landscape of Keswick and district with a wide span of accuracy, imagination and artistic response.

Joseph Farington (1747-1821), born at Leigh in Lancashire, produced a plethora of prints, including many of the Lake District and a lengthy diary covering nearly thirty years of his life. Henry William Bunbury (1750-1811) the caricaturist, moved to Keswick about 1800. He won the approval of Sir Joshua Reynolds and exhibited his landscapes at the Royal Academy. The *Cumberland Pacquet* of 14 May 1811 described him, perhaps too generously, as 'the celebrated caricaturist, doubtless the greatest genius in that line of his day'.

Sir George Beaumont (1753-1827) was both a committed artist and a generous patron of the arts. He visited the Lakes on a number of occasions, at times with fellow artists such as Hearne and Farington. His first picture to be accepted by the Royal Academy was 'A View of Keswick 1779'. A close friend and correspondent of the Wordsworths, it was he who bought a cottage and ground for the poet at Applethwaite Ghyll. He is also remembered as one of the founders of the National Gallery.

The Rev. Joseph Wilkinson (1764-1831) was born in Carlisle and for a time lived at Ormathwaite near Keswick with Dr and Mrs William Brownrigg, relations of his wife, before taking over a parish in Norfolk. He deserves a mention if only because Wordsworth wrote the text to his *Select Views in Cumberland, Westmoreland and Lancashire* (1810).

Although the poet's contribution was eventually to be revised and expanded into his own guidebook to the Lakes, Wordsworth regretted his association with Wilkinson's artistic efforts and was pleased to remain anonymous. On 10 May 1810, he wrote to Lady Beaumont: 'The drawings, etchings or whatever they may be called, are, I know, such as to you and Sir George must be intolerable. You will receive from them that sort of disgust which I do from bad poetry.'

J M W Turner (1775-1851) visited the district in 1797. His most famous picture associated with the Lakes is 'Morning on the Coniston Fells', with Adam and Eve as central figures in a rural paradise of the kind that Thomas Gray and others found in Borrowdale. Among his pictures of Keswick and Derwentwater is one of St Herbert's Island which leans heavily on romantic exaggeration and transforms the crude cell of the saint into a gothic edifice of cathedral-like proportions.

John Constable (1776-1837) included Keswick on his tour of the Lakes in 1806 and painted more than seventy watercolours of the district. William Westall (1781-1850) was a friend of Wordsworth and the members of his circle. From 1811 to 1820 he spent the winters in Keswick: Southey provided the letterpress for his 'Views of the Lake and of the Vale of Keswick' (1820) and Westall supplied the sketches for Southey's *Colloquies*.

Joseph Flintoft (fl.1827-1843), best known for his relief model of the Lake District in the Fitz Park Museum, was also a landscape painter. Thomas Knox, yet another painter of local scenes, was living in Keswick in the 1840s and exhibited at the Royal Academy and elsewhere.

Frederick Clive Suker (1847-1894), who changed his name to Newcome to avoid confusion with other members of his artistic family, was born near Warrington and exhibited at Liverpool Academy before he was twenty. He lived in various parts of the country, including Coniston, Carlisle, Frizington and Keswick, and was honoured by an exhibition in Carlisle in the year of his death.

Among native Keswickians who have followed a career in art was Francis Derwent Wood (1871-1926). A member of the Royal Academy and an exhibitor at a number of prestigious galleries, he was appointed Professor of Sculpture at the Royal College of Art in 1918. Among his best-known pieces of sculpture are those of Henry James and T E Lawrence of Arabia.

In more recent times, Keswick has been home to a steady stream of artists, amateur and professional, native and incomer, and today a small but active group keeps the earlier tradition alive, helped by the members of a flourishing Art Society.

Thomas Gray

6

Romantic Reactions

By the latter part of the eighteenth century, Keswick had woken up to the realisation that there was money to be made from the tourists. 'Lakers' the locals called them, and it is difficult not to agree with Norman Nicholson that the word has its ironical undertones. 'Laking' or 'laiking' is a Cumbrian dialect word for 'playing' – and what were the excesses of the Romantic and Picturesque travellers but a kind of playing with the truth?

Gradually the flow of visitors increased. Judged by the flood of tourists that swamps the Lake District today, it was little more than a trickle. Only those who could afford both time and money were able to visit: for the more affluent, a Lakes tour was a substitute for the European Grand Tour, then impossible as the Napoleonic Wars developed.

With the growth of the Industrial Revolution, the Lake District was seen as a pastoral oasis, a refuge from the grime and noise and urban squalor of the crowded conurbations of Lancashire and Yorkshire – for the select few who could join the academics and clergymen and leisured gentlemen drawn by other motives.

If the Lakers were coming, they had to be provided for. It has been claimed that the first 'hotel' specifically built to accommodate tourists in the Lake District was at Ouse Bridge at the foot of Bassenthwaite Lake. Its origins correspond more or less with the setting up of the local Turnpike Trusts in the 1760s. It appears to have functioned for about fifty years; by 1810 it had been converted, possibly reverted, to a farmhouse.

The Keswick inns offered some accommodation, not always as salubrious and comfortable as it might have been. A list of 'Names and Residences of Persons who have been Licensed to keep Common Inns and Ale Houses' printed in the *Cumberland Pacquet* of 5 December 1787 includes fourteen for Keswick; unfortunately, the premises are not identified by either name or location. A century later, in September 1889, the Brewster Sessions Records list thirty-six inns and five beer houses.

The George, once the George and Dragon, is said to be the oldest hostelry in the town. According to Joseph Broatch, a prominent Keswick solicitor in the 1920s and 1930s, a bill for a visitor to the George dated 1733 was once found but there is no evidence of the date the hotel was built. The Queen's, earlier known as the Queen's Head, was a popular base – Gray stayed there in 1769 – and the names of the Packhorse and the Woolpack indicate an ancestry that goes back to the days before wheeled vehicles were in use.

The Royal Oak has a long history, its name possibly linked with the restoration of

Charles II in 1660. Joseph Broatch records that when alterations were being made in the early part of this century, a beam was uncovered with the date 1593 – an indication of antiquity but not of function. In the nineteenth century, the Oak emerged as the principal hotel and coaching house: until recent times it remained a popular centre of social and business life in the town.

Names have changed over the years. The Oddfellows Arms used to be the Rose and Crown; a line drawn down its yard marked the boundary of the parishes of Crosthwaite and St John's. The Central Hotel, now incorporated in Ye Olde Friars Sweet Shop, was once the Shoulder of Mutton; the Derwentwater at Portinscale changed from the Black Dog to the Marshal Blucher about 1815. One result of the changing commercial pattern of the town has been the disappearance of several long established inns: the Woolpack, the Central, the Waverley, the Crown, the King's Head, the Black Lion among them.

As many visitors arrived with little or no knowledge of the district, they needed to be shown or told what was on offer, to be made aware of local amenities and curiosities. Although an increasing number of books about the district became available, they were mainly journals, accounts of travel in the Lake District rather than specific manuals designed to help tourists. Some provided pointers of where to go and what to see but Thomas West's *Guide to the Lakes* (1778) is generally regarded as the first tailor-made guidebook for visitors. It was certainly well received: by 1821, it had reached its eleventh edition.

West, a 'mercantile traveller' turned Jesuit priest, was a committed antiquarian and on occasion accompanied parties visiting the Lakes. Although his book is based on extensive travel in the district, it is by no means free of the trappings of the Romantics: a telescope and a landscape mirror were regarded as essentials for a successful tour; Glaramara was 'a mountain of perpendicular rock'; the route from Stonethwaite to Langdale over Stake Pass was 'the wildest that can be imagined...an Alpine journey of a very extraordinary nature'.

View from Crow Park, West's second station

Stupendous crags and horrendous journeys apart, West does direct the tourist to the best viewpoints – what he calls 'stations'. Keswick and Derwentwater had eight stations dotted round the lake from Cockshott and Crow Park to Latrigg and the garden of Crosthwaite Vicarage via Stable Hills, Castle Crag, Swinside and Fawe Park. West describes the view from each of the eight locations, quoting from Gray, indicating the features of the landscape and identifying fells and rivers, islands and scenic gems.

His approach is essentially visual and antiquarian: we learn little about life in Keswick, the people, the social conditions, the daily activities.

With all its imperfections and omissions, West's Guide was the pioneer in a flood of handbooks for tourists during the next 200 years. For today's readers, it is valuable not only for its historical interest but also for its clutch of appendices which includes Dr Dalton's poem (1755), Dr Brown's letter (1767), Thomas Gray's journal (1769), Richard Cumberland's *Ode to the Sun* (1776) and specimens of Cumberland dialect.

No serious visitor today would be without a map but the early tourists were inadequately served by contemporary cartographers. A map by Bowe and Kitchin of 1769, for example, shows a road from Hawkshead to Whitehaven over Crinkle Crags and Bowfell, and a lake in Eskdale. Housman's *Guide* (1800) uses the same delineation to mark the track from Seathwaite to Wasdale over Styhead as it does for the principal roads from Keswick to Penrith and Ambleside.

Thomas Martin's map of 'The Beautiful Vale of Keswick in Cumberland' deserves a special mention.

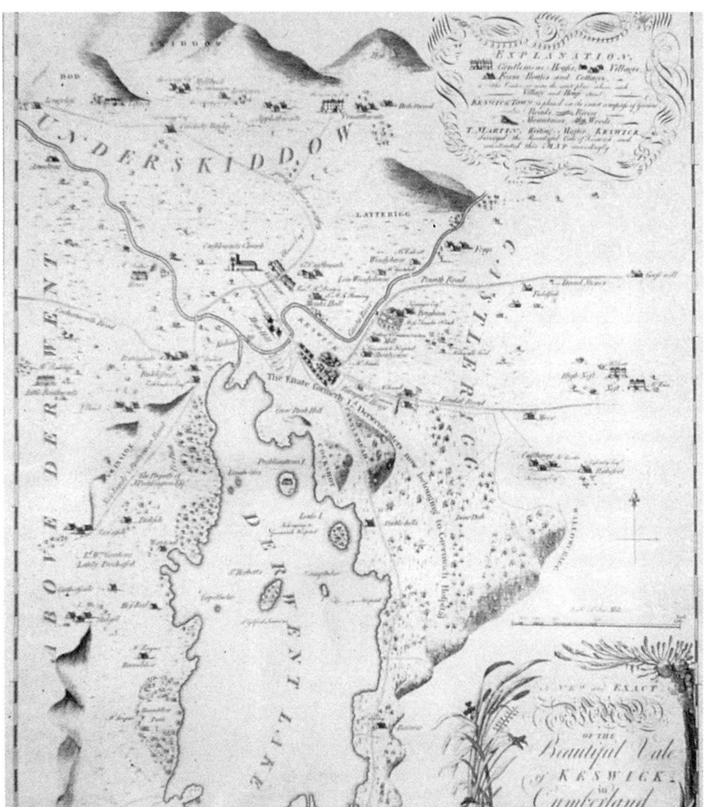

'The Beautiful Vale of Keswick in Cumberland' 1784

Published in 1784, it is the work of the writing master at Crosthwaite School. It shows the estates of the principal landowners and uses stylised drawings to indicate gentlemen's houses, farms, cottages and villages. So far as is known, only one copy of the original exists, appropriately in the Fitz Park Museum.

At least two writers of the period made some attempt to produce maps that were accurate (though falling short of modern standards) and furnished with some detail. These were James Clarke, the Penrith surveyor, and Peter Crosthwaite, a Keswick museum proprietor.

Crosthwaite's maps focused on the lakes themselves, showing West's stations, depths at various points, roads and the houses of the gentry. Drawn on a scale of three inches to the mile (except Windermere), these maps are surprisingly accurate. As each new edition appeared, it was altered and updated. Changes of ownership of property may be traced; Crosthwaite, aping West, added a trio of his own stations. The maps are decorated with drawings of local features, including an observatory at Greta Hall, and buttressed by samples of doggerel which could have been culled from Brown or Dalton. On the Derwentwater map, spread over the area at the foot of Skiddaw, he writes:

> Here lies the Splendid Spoils of Mountain Floods;
> Those Fertile Plains, brought Captive from their Sides.
> And yon Stupendous Chasms (Cloud high) have left
> Bereft of Soil.

The maps appear to have been very popular: Crosthwaite himself claimed to have sold 'many Thousand Maps of the Lakes', mainly to the tourists who visited his museum.

This astonishing collection of curiosities must surely be the first purpose-built tourist attraction in Keswick, the practical vision of a lively entrepreneur.

Crosthwaite was a local man, born at Dale Head, Thirlmere, in 1735. He spent seven years in the service of the East India Company and twelve as a Customs Officer at Blyth in Northumberland before settling in Keswick in 1780. Four years later, Museum House was built on the site of today's Herries Thwaite Shopping Centre and flourished until 1870. A plaque set into the pavement near the entrance to the shopping centre commemorates this bold attempt to provide for the growing tourist trade.

Crosthwaite's 'Cabinet of Curiosities' displayed a bizarre and motley collection of oddities, 'more of gimcracks than antiquities' commented one visitor in 1797. The exhibits ranged from a chicken with two heads and the hand of an Egyptian mummy to the rib-bone of a twenty-one-foot giant and a petrified horse-muscle found in a coal mine at Greysouthen. Room Three was known as 'Captain Wordsworth's Room'. John Wordsworth, sailor and brother of William and Dorothy, brought back items for the museum from his travels abroad, including an albatross, Chinese idols and the jaw of a shark.

One of Crosthwaite's prime exhibits was a set of musical stones, variously termed the stone dulcimer, the rock harmonicon or the geological piano. It took him six months to collect, shape and tune enough stones to make two octaves, often involving chipping away for twelve hours a day. Crude and simple though it was, it was the first of several sets of musical stones to be made by later craftsmen, including the fine example still on show in the Fitz Park Museum.

Two other items deserve special mention. One was a barrel organ, very loud, very sweet in tone, that was capable of playing seventy-seven different tunes. The other was a sixteen-pound Chinese gong with the sound of a cathedral bell and audible at a distance of four miles in the open air on a fine day.

Crosthwaite was always on the lookout for potential trade. He sat in a chair and, using a set of carefully angled mirrors, he was able to spot carriages and possible customers. To attract their attention, a drum was thumped, the gong was beaten, and the organ played. Such direct and brash publicity appears to have been successful: in 1793 some 1540 'persons of rank and fashion' visited the Museum.

Crosthwaite, ever ill-tempered and outspoken (he was once described as a 'little, purple-faced pig of a man') resented any competition and never missed an opportunity to attack his rival, Thomas Hutton, whose modest museum with its more orthodox collection of fossils and mosses, minerals and birds, was located in Lake Road near the Market Square.

Hutton, a hard-working, obliging guide and part-time weaver, had been with West on his tour and appears to have helped him in his choice of stations. A guidebook of 1810 describes him as 'a practical botanist and mineralogist and professional cicerone to the lakes and mountains around'.

Whatever the attractions for tourists of the two museums, Keswickians must have been amused or roused to partisanship by the intense rivalry between the two owners. Unfortunately, we have only Crosthwaite's side of the quarrel: his notebooks leave no doubt about his paranoic dislike of Hutton, entry after entry maintaining a flow of bitter condemnation of his rival's methods and credibility, his false claims and his dishonesty.

He accused Hutton of telling visitors that the people of Borrowdale were all red-haired and of being 'the foremost and most impudent wad Thief in the Parish'. Claims of finding rare plants were 'all vile Falsehood': 'the greatest Liar in England', as Crosthwaite called him, would do anything for gain. What Hutton's response to these outrageous accusations was we can only speculate.

Hutton was not the only target of Crosthwaite's venom. He attacked Sarah Mayson, a shopkeeper, denouncing her for consistently overcharging her customers; Mrs Southward, a widow who ran the Royal Oak, was vilified for refusing to display Crosthwaite's advertising handbills. 'I left her shewing as many impudent airs as ever I saw by any woman of Billingsgate and she hinted to me I was mad.'

Apart from keeping his museum and heaping abuse on his fellow Keswickians, Crosthwaite was active in other spheres. He kept meteorological records, including 5,381 observations in five years of the height of clouds. He surveyed a route for a canal from Skinburness on the Solway Coast to Keswick. He cooked up a plan for lowering the level of Derwentwater by twelve inches to bring nearly 200 acres of land into cultivation – a scheme, his diary tells us, that had the approval of Wordsworth and Coleridge. He made a zig-zag path up Latrigg; he wrote a 200-page treatise on healthy living, suggesting that the use of pure water, internally and externally, was the panacea for all ills; he sank a well and installed a pump at High Hill – a source of soft, clean water which remained popular with the townsfolk for many years.

This self-styled 'Guide, Pilot, Geographer and Hydrographer to the Nobility and Gentry who make the Tour of the Lakes' died on 9 June 1808 at the age of seventy-three, a controversial figure to the end. At least his obituary notice was kind, declaring that he lived 'respected by his neighbours and few men in this or any other country had so numerous an acquaintance'.

It is easy to imagine the early tourists arriving in Keswick, finding accommodation at the principal inns and arming themselves with Crosthwaite's maps. A visit to one or both museums was essential before exploring the beauties of Derwentwater with the help of West's *Guide* and his eight stations. There was no immediate rush to climb the fells and local men saw little merit in such expenditure of energy unless it was in the course of duty – gathering sheep or cutting peat, for example.

There were exceptions, like Budworth, but most visitors were content to keep to the valleys. One fell top, however, offered the thrill of ascent with the minimum of real (though not always imagined) danger. This was Skiddaw, and many of the diaries and journals of the late 1700s and early 1800s record a journey to the summit.

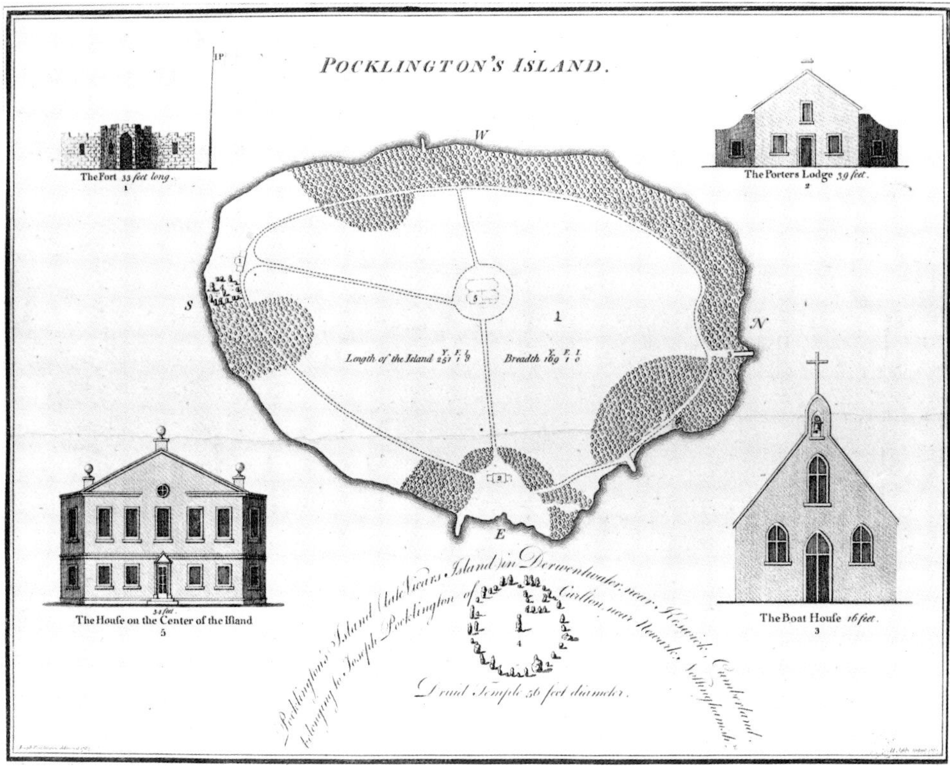

Peter Crosthwaite's map of King Pocky's island

Neither Thomas Gray nor William Gilpin ventured up the mountain. Gilpin, assessing Skiddaw as a picturesque feature, was disappointed: devoid of 'shaggy majesty', it was 'a tame, inanimate object'.

William Hutchinson in 1773 found the 'laborious ascent of five miles' well worth the effort. The view, even though the sharp, thin air caused respiration 'to be performed with a kind of asthmatic oppression', was magnificent. A sudden change to thick cloud, thunder and rain compelled the guide to lie on the ground in terror; Hutchinson's party appear to have enjoyed this manifestation of adverse weather conditions as characteristic of Skiddaw.

He also records two facts worth a special mention. In 1689, apparently, a building was erected on top of Skiddaw by John Adams, the geographer, to house his telescope and optical instruments used in surveying. Sadly, comments Hutchinson, 'being arrested by his engraver and his death soon following, his labours were lost.'

It was the custom, Hutchinson reveals, for visitors to put a stone on the summit cairn with their name and place of residence duly inscribed: 'we read the names of a multitude of friends on the slates thrown up, inhabitants of many parts of the kingdom'. Even allowing for exaggeration, this comment indicates the popularity of Skiddaw as the destination of tourist excursions by the 1770s...but what has happened to all those slate visiting cards?

James Clarke rose at four o'clock to climb through valley mist to a clear summit above. Sounds travelled with crisp clarity: cocks crowing, birds warbling, bulls and cows bellowing, shepherds whistling. He is more restrained than many of his contemporaries, agreeing that 'from the top of Skiddaw is a most noble prospect but not so great as some of our Tourists tell us'. He reminds us of a local proverb, first recorded by Camden in 1607:

Skiddaw, Lauvelin, and Casticand,
Are the highest hills in all England.
Kidstowpike, Catstycam, Helveyllin and Skiddaw-man,
Are the highest hill ever clumb by Englishman.

Most accounts of this period overestimate the height of Skiddaw. One well-known engraving by de Loutherbourg (1787) of a coach rattling along at the foot of Skiddaw carries a gloss that here was the Etna of the North, 1,500 yards high.

An exhilarating journey along the foot of the Etna of the North

John Housman recommends climbing Skiddaw with a guide and on foot rather than on horseback. Ignoring his own advice, he and his companions set off in October 1798 without a guide, their ascent sparking off the standard romantic reactions. Even before the party reached the summit, they were astonished to see 'a boiling sea of mountains, with pointed, conical and broken tops, appear rioting over each other in a most turbulent manner, like a legion of raging monsters, preparing to spread destruction on every side'.

They lost their way at one point and busied themselves 'in forming schemes for self-preservation in case we should be overwhelmed with atmospheric obscurity'. Even so, they reached the top in just over two hours, duly impressed by the 'horror' of the final ridge and its attendant 'profound precipice...chasms of enormous depth...steeps of slaty shiver'.

Perhaps the most graphic account of climbing Skiddaw in the days when it was regarded as a major challenge was that of Mrs Radcliffe in 1794. A writer of Gothic novels, stories packed with supernatural incidents, far-fetched plots, contrived situations and exciting terrors, she was ideally prepared for perspectives wrapped in superlatives and hyperbole.

Almost from the first moment of the climb, the horses were edging their way along narrow precipices. Derwentwater dwindled to the size of a pond and the panorama of mountains evoked 'ideas of the breaking up of the world'. True to type, she recoiled in horror from the yawning chasms as she rode along a path that was 'dreadfully sublime'.

The air on the summit was 'boisterous, intensely cold and difficult to inspire', the kind of raw wind which regularly blows on Skiddaw top and sends hardened fell walkers scuttling for shelter. Here, Mrs Radcliffe found an old man resting behind a cairn: he turned out to be a local farmer who had spent his life near the foot of the mountain but had never, until that day, climbed it, 'so laborious is the enterprise reckoned'.

For many early visitors, Keswick offered unusual excursions which did not endanger life and limb. Lodore Falls was an obvious attraction, particularly in spate; Castlerigg Stone Circle inspired awesome admiration of its monoliths and wild speculation about its origin and purpose. Watendlath, tucked away in its own hanging valley above Derwentwater, was something of a Mecca and the Bowder Stone near Grange in Borrowdale was a must – much the largest stone in England, declared one visitor in 1749.

Not so popular but still on the tourist trail was the salt spring at Manesty. The monks of Furness Abbey may have extracted salt here: it was certainly known in 1555 and an analysis in 1740 calls its contents 'a rough, severe purge to strong constitutions, heats the blood, much excites a thirst'. Its curative properties were said to be effective for a frightening catalogue of illnesses: 'dropsical, cacochymic, cathetic disorders; foulness of the Stomach, slipperyness of the Bowels from Relaxations, or much Mucus, some icteritious disorders'.

Clarke deplored the lack of conveniences for those taking the Manesty waters in 1787 but by 1816, perhaps earlier, the spring was syphoned off into a walled bath. Some time later, Sir John Woodford, then living at Derwent Bay not far away, sank a well at Manesty and built a house over it; bathers were admitted free of charge but the facility was not used and the building decayed. Today, no trace of either spring or building remains.

The prime magnet for tourists was Derwentwater itself. Scenic beauties apart, there were other attractions on offer. The Duke of Portland's ten-seater barge was available for hire. It was armed with a cannon to provide the simple pleasure of banging off a pinch of powder and listening to the echoes of sound reverberating round the neighbouring hills. Thomas Hutton, having no cannon, discharged a gun and produced echoes lasting up to thirty seconds; opposite Walla Crag, his shout produced five distinct echoes.

The Lodore Hotel, then an undistinguished small inn, owned two cannons. The fees for firing, quoted by various visitors, differed widely, ranging from 6d to 4s. Why, asked one traveller, put up with second-best 'instead of ordering at once the super-extra-double-superfine' with nine echoes promised?

Visitors were always intrigued to hear about the two natural phenomena associated with Derwentwater: the Floating Island and the Bottom Wind.

The Floating Island still occasionally rises at the southern end of the lake near the Lodore Hotel landing-stage and stirs up the old arguments and explanations. Its size varies and it can remain above water for periods ranging from days to weeks. The most acceptable theory is that the mixture of peat and decaying vegetable matter produces methane gas in certain conditions, particularly in hot weather. The resulting buoyancy causes the island to rise to the surface. Budworth records that 'there are very few people in the neighbourhood who have not been upon it' and it is said that at some time in the 1930s Keswick Girl Guides planted the Union Jack on it and claimed it for England!

The other curiosity, the Bottom Wind, has never been satisfactorily explained. On a perfectly calm day, suddenly the surface of the water is agitated. A swell moves from west to east and the movement can last for anything from an hour or less to a whole day. Often, though by no means always, this strange movement is the forerunner to a storm.

It was, however, not cannons, Floating Island or Bottom Wind that was the prime attraction in the 1780s: by then, two local entrepreneurs had seen the potential of the lake for activities specifically designed to pull in the crowds.

William Gilpin

7

King Pocky's Antics

Without doubt, the principal event in the 1780s was the series of specially organised regattas on Derwentwater, the brainchild of Peter Crosthwaite and Joseph Pocklington, who first visited the town in 1768 and ten years later returned to live here.

'King Pocky' has earned a special place in the story of Keswick, mainly for his eccentricities but also for his generosity. The son of a wealthy banking family in Newark, he had aspirations of grandeur. He built a mansion at Carlton near Nottingham; he acquired his own coat of arms; he was appointed High Sheriff of his native county before he was forty.

He bought Derwent Island, then known as Vicar's Island, for £300, transforming it into his own little kingdom, complete with its bizarre collection of oddities. He built a house on rising ground in the centre of the island at a cost of £1,393.4.3½. – Pocklington, as befitted a banker, kept meticulous accounts. He planted trees round most of the perimeter of his domain and made paths to give access to his eccentric creations.

King Pocky's little paradise on Derwentwater

His boathouse looked every inch a Nonconformist chapel, crowned with bell-tower and cross. Nearby was his own 'church', St Mary's, a wooden facade decorated to give the appearance of ecclesiastical doors and windows: 'a venerable white-washed gothic building rears its august head in all the pride of pasteboard antiquity' wrote William Gell who visited the island in 1797. The more substantial tower attached to the wooden shell, crenellated and adorned with flagpole and weather vane, housed a room, 'not furnished with bells,' wrote Clarke, 'but with good roast beef and claret.'

Fort Joseph, named after its creator, looked the length of the lake; it was complemented by a battery equipped with a cannon for producing echoes. A Druid Temple, modelled on Castlerigg Stone Circle, and a standing stone six feet eight inches high, added yet further touches of pseudo-antiquity. An even more outrageous manifestation of Pocklington's eccentricities was his 'ghost tree'. He cut off the branches of an oak, removed the bark and painted the pathetic remains white. Coleridge's notebook entry for 14 November 1799 reads: 'Pocklington shaved off the Branches of an Oak, Whitewashed and shaped it into an Obelisk – Art beats Nature'.

Some visitors to King Pocky's 'Paradise Island', as he renamed it, were favourably impressed by the 'very judicious improvements'. Others were appalled at 'the gingerbread erections'. One commented: 'Mr Pocklington's slime may be traced in every part of Keswick Vale. It is a pity he has no friend to advise him to blow to atoms everything he has constructed.' In Southey's opinion, Pocklington had hideously disfigured the island and Wordsworth commended the actions of his successor who 'ridded the spot of its puerilities'.

Pocklington's enthusiasm for building extended well beyond his island kingdom. At the Bowder Stone near Grange, he built a chapel and a small cottage for an old woman who was installed to make sure passing visitors did not miss the huge rock. He chipped a hole through the 'keel' of the Stone so that two people could lie, one on each side, and shake hands. No doubt many romantic tourists experience a frisson as they lay quaking under the 2,000-ton rock and grasped the hand of a companion or of Pocklington's old crone. For the faint-hearted, he provided a ladder to the top of the Stone: here they could enjoy a splendid view of upper Borrowdale stretching beyond yet another of Pocklington's erections – a 'Druid' monolith a few yards from the Stone.

In 1785, he built Finkle Street House in Portinscale at a cost of £648.15.11¼, a three-storey villa with lean-to wings, which still stands as Derwent Bank, a popular centre of the Holiday Fellowship. Two years later, he built a mansion in an idyllic situation on the eastern shore of Derwentwater. Barrow Cascade House cost him £1,652.3.6⅓: it, too, has survived and today is a Youth Hostel of considerable elegance.

Not content with adding yet another substantial property to his kingdom, Pocklington set to work on the waterfall behind Barrow House. He had it enlarged, doubling its height and diverting the stream to create what is still a fine cascade. Nearby, he set up a small hermitage and tried to find a resident anchorite who would live in it for a wage of 2s.6d. a day...under certain conditions. He must never leave his cell or speak to anyone for seven years; he must never wash or cut his hair and nails. Not surprisingly, there were no takers for the job.

Although Coleridge condemned him as 'so strange and so intensely selfish a character', Pocklington's accounts show another side to the personality of a man who today would be a successful executive in the world of high finance. Regularly he gave gifts of money to the poor of Keswick and Borrowdale and on occasion to specific individuals – '3 June 1814 Robinson from Keswick, a poor man, 2s.6d'. In January 1791, it was reported that he distributed large quantities of fine wheat bread to upwards of 150 poor families in or near Keswick.

In 1796 he moved to Barrow Cascade House and sold his island to Major General William Peachey for £2,500. He died in May 1817, leaving most of his property to a great-nephew who married into a distinguished Cumbrian family, the Senhouses of Maryport.

Pocklington is chiefly remembered as the prime mover and co-organiser of the Derwentwater regattas of the 1780s. The first of these aquatic carnivals was held on Bassenthwaite on 14 August 1780 and set the prototype for subsequent years and other venues. Pocklington was not going to be upstaged by cavortings on Bassenthwaite and on 28 August 1781 he launched the Derwentwater Regattas. His partner, Peter Crosthwaite, no doubt saw the celebrations as a magnet to draw more visitors to Keswick and to his museum.

The pattern was quickly established. Crowds assembled from eight o'clock in the morning and marquees extending for several hundred yards along the edge of the lake were erected to accommodate them. Some spectators joined the pleasure barges on the lake itself; others had to be content with a place on the shore or on Crow Park, the natural grandstand for the regatta.

Boat races and foot races, entertainments and sideshows helped to provide a red-letter day, rounded off by fireworks, a dance and a feast for the gentry.

The centre piece of the day's events was the mock battle, a noisy, boisterous skirmish which, it was claimed, could be heard at Appleby, thirty miles away. Three officials were in charge: a Steward, a Governor who was Commander-in-Chief of the defence of the Island, and an Admiral who led the attack. The post of Steward changed annually but Pocklington and Crosthwaite retained their positions as Governor and Admiral throughout the series of regattas.

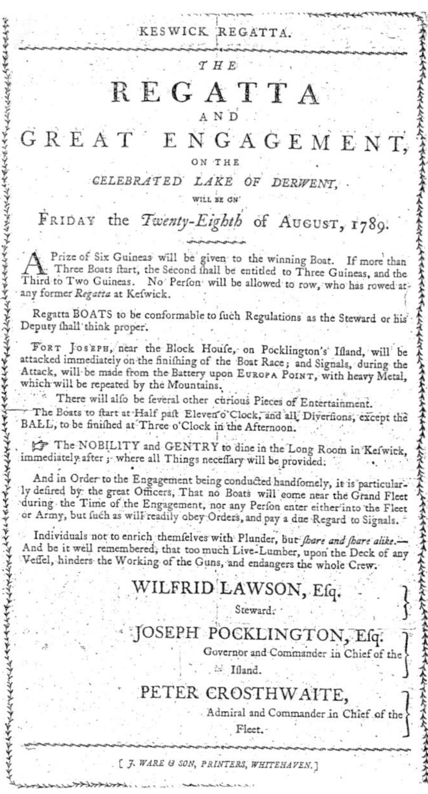

KESWICK REGATTA.

THE

REGATTA

AND

GREAT ENGAGEMENT,

ON THE

CELEBRATED LAKE OF DERWENT,

WILL BE ON

FRIDAY the *Twenty-Eighth* of AUGUST, 1789.

A Prize of Six Guineas will be given to the winning Boat. If more than Three Boats ſtart, the Second ſhall be entitled to Three Guineas, and the Third to Two Guineas. No Perſon will be allowed to row, who has rowed at any former *Regatta* at Keſwick.

Regatta BOATS to be conformable to ſuch Regulations as the Steward or his Deputy ſhall think proper.

FORT JOSEPH, near the Block Houſe, on Pocklington's Iſland, will be attacked immediately on the finiſhing of the Boat Race; and Signals, during the Attack, will be made from the Battery upon EUROPA POINT, with heavy Metal, which will be repeated by the Mountains.

There will alſo be ſeveral other curious Pieces of Entertainment.

The Boats to ſtart at Half paſt Eleven o'Clock, and all Diverſions, except the BALL, to be finiſhed at Three o'Clock in the Afternoon.

☞ The NOBILITY and GENTRY to dine in the Long Room in Keſwick, immediately after; where all Things neceſſary will be provided.

And in Order to the Engagement being conducted handſomely, it is particularly deſired by the great Officers, That no Boats will come near the Grand Fleet during the Time of the Engagement, nor any Perſon enter either into the Fleet or Army, but ſuch as will readily obey Orders, and pay a due Regard to Signals.

Individuals not to enrich themſelves with Plunder, but *ſhare and ſhare alike.*— And be it well remembered, that too much Live-Lumber, upon the Deck of any Veſſel, hinders the Working of the Guns, and endangers the whole Crew.

WILFRID LAWSON, Eſq.
Steward.

JOSEPH POCKLINGTON, Eſq.
Governor and Commander in Chief of the Iſland.

PETER CROSTHWAITE,
Admiral and Commander in Chief of the Fleet.

[*J. WARE & SON, PRINTERS, WHITEHAVEN.*]

The attacking fleet assembled behind the cover of Friars' Crag. A flag of truce was sent to Governor Pocklington but, naturally, he refused to surrender and the battle began. Cannons banged; guns were fired; everybody made as much noise as possible.

Success sparked off greater sophistication. In 1784, French horns were introduced, their music mingling with the booming of the cannons and adding its own peculiar echo. 'Balloon vessels' made their appearance in 1785: the name suggests large, air-filled replicas of boats, perhaps, or it might have been a fanciful name for simple balloons.

The 1787 regatta inspired a famous picture of the mock battle, drawn in situ by Robert Smirke, the Wigton artist.

Crosthwaite's invaders land on Pocklington's Island, armed with muskets and swords; cannons roar, smoke clouds the action, bodies are strewn in the foreground, the beef and beer are plundered. On the immediate fringes of the skirmish, well-dressed ladies and gentlemen (and a child) look on; in the background, the fells stand sentinel to a graphically depicted scene of glorious make-believe.

Plans sometimes went awry. The first regatta in 1781 was plagued by heavy and incessant rain. In 1783, the two men who were appointed to negotiate the capitulation of the Island had 'unfortunately sacrificed so liberally to Bacchus' that they were unable to speak. In 1787 the fireworks failed to arrive on time and in 1789 Pocklington was ill.

1789 was also the year that Peter Crosthwaite's anger exploded. He was convinced that a gang of his Keswick enemies, headed by Hutton, was hell-bent on destroying him and his enterprises. He accused the 'Junto of unprincipled guides...the dark sons of Envy' of fleeing their colours during the mock battles and persuading the gentry that he, Admiral Crosthwaite, would not fight. They then filled their boats with Pocklington's disappointed guests on the Island and, at a shilling a head, 'brought them speedily over to England that they might return quickly for another cargo of deluded people'.

The accusations, the hints of cut-throat rivalry, the anger and the frenetic, headlong prose of Crosthwaite's notebooks suggest that Keswick in the regatta years witnessed not only the mock battles on Derwentwater but also bitter conflicts between the warring factions in the town itself, with physical violence breaking out now and then to compound the war of words.

1790, a thinly attended event, was the last of Pocklington's regattas. From time to time, they were revived in a modified and less spectacular fashion. For example, Samuel Lewis's *Topographical Dictionary* of 1831 records 'an annual regatta takes place on the last Thursday and Friday in August, the sports chiefly consisting of rowing, horse-racing and wrestling'. Henry Irwin Jenkinson, a local philanthropist, reintroduced sports and a regatta in 1878 and the annual August Bank Holiday Sports in Fitz Park during this century were perhaps a natural development of the land-based contests of the 1780s.

From its inauguration on 3 August 1891 until 1966, it drew large crowds of local supporters and visitors. Its demise was widely regretted but it was not until 1992 that a small group of enthusiasts, with the backing of the Lions Club and the Cricket Club, revived the Sports. Its initial success, in spite of adverse weather conditions, promised well for the renaissance of a traditional event which, for so long, had been exceptionally popular.

The early tourists not only enjoyed the scenery of the Lake District and special events like the regattas: they also liked to hear stories about local people and local incidents...and the natives were not slow in providing them, some true, some embellished, some patently fabricated. 'The watermen and guides,' wrote Clarke, 'think they must tell the Tourist some extraordinary tale or other, and therefore endeavour to invent something that bears the face of probability.'

One of the most popular tales, though one bearing little of the face of probability, was that of Lady Derwentwater. She is said to have escaped from Lord's Island in 1715 and

Lady Derwentwater contemplates her line of escape up Walla Crag

climbed a prominent fissure, Lady's Rake, on the perpendicular front of Walla Crag, taking with her jewels and precious plate. En route, she dropped her handkerchief, which could be seen clearly over two centuries later: all that was needed was a regular touch of white paint on a prominent rock and the 'handkerchief' could easily be identified from a distance.

A made-up story? How, then, do we explain the discovery by Henry Lightfoot in the mid 1800s of thirty-four silver pennies scattered among loose gravel near Lady's Rake? They were coins from the reigns of Edward I and II – 1272 to 1327 – and probably had nothing to do with Lady Derwentwater and her supposed scramble up a formidable rock climb.

Neighbouring valleys and villages added their own tall stories: the Borrowdale folk who built a wall to keep in the cuckoo and ensure eternal spring; the ghost of Armboth House at Thirlmere, a bride murdered and thrown into the lake as the wedding feast was being prepared; ghostly horsemen on Souther Fell near Threlkeld; Henry Clifford, the 'Shepherd Lord' of the fifteenth century, whose story is told in Wordsworth's 'Song at the Feast of Brougham Castle'; King Arthur's daughter, Gyneth, sleeping under Castle Rock at the foot of St John's in the Vale, a romantic yarn elaborated in Sir Walter Scott's 'The Bridal of Triermain'.

Even our own day has its fantasies. In 1981, the Cumbrian Bogart Preservation Society was formed at the Twa Dogs Inn in Keswick. Its object was to protect this rare creature – a cross between a badger and a fox – though the Natural History Museum was unwilling to acknowledge that such a creature existed. The best sighting time is after midnight (and after closing-time) on Saturdays. It is perhaps no coincidence that mine host of the Twa Dogs won the World's Biggest Liar contest at Santon Bridge in West Cumbria in 1981 for his account of the Bogart, in spite of producing a stuffed specimen, five feet long with the requisite badger's head and fox's body. The Society flourishes, its subscriptions and fund-raising efforts benefiting local charities.

One story, romantic, certainly, but no invented legend, is that of Mary, the Beauty of Buttermere. It has been put into rhyme and sold as a broadsheet; presented on the London stage as a melodrama; written up in the nineteenth century as a three-decker novel; broadcast as a radio play; and as recently as 1987 turned into Melvyn Bragg's best-selling novel, *The Maid of Buttermere.*

It was Budworth who discovered Mary Robinson at the Fish Inn at Buttermere in 1792 and was charmed by her innocence, simplicity and natural grace. Once his discovery was made public, a visit to see this 'reigning lily of the valley' was firmly slotted into the tourist itinerary. Budworth realised his mistake and by the third edition of his *Fortnight's Ramble* in 1810 apologised for having mentioned Mary, but it was too late.

John Hadfield - fraudster, imposter, seducer of Mary Robinson

In 1802, John Hatfield or Hadfield, arrived in Keswick and stayed at the Queen's Head. Masquerading as Colonel the Honourable Alexander Augustus Hope, MP for Linlithgow, and brother of the respected Earl of Hopetown, this convincing imposter was accepted with deference and goodwill. His alias was in keeping with the past activities of a rogue who had twice married, had deserted his wife and children, and had spent some years in jail for fraud and forgery.

He impressed the Keswick locals, who never doubted that here was a genuine gentleman of quality, rich and aristocratic. Coleridge, then living at Greta Hall, had his reservations, not least because Hadfield's conversation was ungrammatical, and de Quincey later recorded that 'the man's breeding and deportment, though showy, had a tang of vulgarity about it'.

Mary Robinson fell a willing victim to his charms: Hadfield was handsome, a smooth talker and a plausible persuader, who had no problems seducing a simple, unsophisticated village maiden, even though he was already married and 'betrothed' to another woman, the wealthy young ward of a Colonel Moore. Hadfield married Mary at Lorton church on 2 October 1802, adding bigamy to his catalogue of crimes. Back in Keswick after a brief honeymoon, he had his bluff called by a barrister, George Hardinge, who knew the real Colonel Hope and could vouch that he was abroad at the time.

Hadfield was arrested but with typical brash assurance asked to be allowed a final fishing trip on Derwentwater. He slipped away over the fells to Ravenglass and eventually to Chester and Swansea. He was captured in South Wales and taken to Carlisle where he was charged with forgery and defrauding the Post Office by illegally using the privilege of an MP to frank his letters for free delivery...but there was no mention of bigamy and poor Mary.

He was found guilty. While he was in the condemned cell, he was visited by Wordsworth and Coleridge, who happened to be passing through Carlisle. Coleridge comments in his Notebook: '...visited Hatfield, impelled by Miss Wordsworth – vain, a hypocrite'. He was hanged on 3 September 1803 before a large crowd. Mary's child was still-born and she eventually married Richard Harrison, a Caldbeck farmer. She had seven children, five of whom survived. Her beauty mellowed into the homely features of a plump Cumbrian housewife and she died in 1837 at the age of fifty-eight. Her obscure grave in Caldbeck churchyard is seen by only a handful of the hundreds who flock to see the nearby tombstone of the famous huntsman, John Peel.

8

Gentlemen and Guides

As Keswick became better known, it attracted not only visitors who stayed for a few days but also 'off-comers' who decided to settle down. The town and its environs have suffered less than Windermere from the invasion of mansion-type houses but a scattering still remains.

Pocklington probably set the fashion. He sold his island in 1797 to Major General William Peachey, MP from Yarmouth. The new owner wisely removed Pocklington's more outrageous follies and planted trees, laid out lawns and shrubberies and renamed his home Derwent Island.

He died in 1838 and the property passed to his widow and son-in-law, Captain James Henry. A disastrous fire on 15 October 1840 caused considerable damage and may well have been the reason why Henry and his mother-in-law left the island. In 1844, it was bought by Henry Cooper Marshall, Mayor of Leeds and a member of a wealthy flax spinning family. He added wings to the repaired house, improved the gardens and planted more trees. With funds in plenty available, the inconveniences of living in the middle of a lake were quickly and efficiently dealt with: water pipes were laid under the lake; a small fleet of boats plied between island and mainland, carrying people and supplies.

Elsewhere in Lakeland, the Marshalls owned property on a vast scale – Hallsteads on Ullswater, Patterdale Hall, Monk Coniston. A 2,000 acre estate at the northern end of Derwentwater came on the market in 1832. This belonged to Greenwich Hospital, which had taken possession from the ill-fated Earl of Derwentwater after the 1715 rebellion. John Marshall, Henry Cooper's brother, bought the property, valued at £61,600, for £49,800, strongly supported in his purchase by Wordsworth, who suggested Friars' Crag as a suitable site for building a house.

Other members of the Marshall family gravitated to Keswick. Reginald Dykes Marshall bought Castlerigg Manor; Francis, a master at Harrow for over thirty years, built Hawse End.

Derwent Island remained Marshall property until 1951, when it was handed over to the National Trust.

On the western side of the lake, Lord William Gordon built a small but elegant mansion at Derwent Bay or Waterend, a few years after Lady Irvine, his mother-in-law, bought the estate for him and his wife in 1782.

Waterend, William Gordon's 'most charming little retreat'

Its centre-piece was a round dining-room, flanked by two rooms, one square and the other rectangular, all three with separate roofs – 'a most charming little retreat', imaginatively planned in its setting and avoiding the unsympathetic brashness of Pocklington on Derwent Island.

Lord William bought much of the land on the western shore of Derwentwater and planted thousands of trees on his property, which stretched from Fawe Park to Manesty. He built a new road from the northern end of Catbells to Manesty, clearly marked on Peter Crosthwaite's maps and described as 'impassable' on the 1809 edition.

On the death of Lady Gordon in 1834, the estate was inherited by her nephew, Major General Sir John George Woodford, who had had a distinguished military career before retiring to Derwent Bay. Aide-de-camp to Sir John Moore, he was wounded at the battle of Corunna, traditionally by the last shot fired, and also took part in the Battle of Waterloo.

He lived in seclusion at Derwent Bay, protected by a hoarding to prevent uninvited and inquisitive intruders staring through his windows. He venerated all living things: rats and mice were caught and carried well away from his house and released; moles burrowed freely in his lawns; jackdaws roosted unmolested in his chimneys.

Although visitors were not welcome at Derwent Bay, Sir John was quite affable to anyone he met on his walks. He liked children and, on the occasion of the Prince of Wales' wedding in 1863, organised a gang of Keswick lads to build a bonfire on Swinside. He was keenly interested in the Keswick Boys' Drum and Fife Band and every year entertained the scholars of Crosthwaite Sunday School in Silver Hill Field for their annual tea-party.

He disliked being opposed and in the 1840s had a tussle with his friend, the Rev. James Lynn, vicar of Crosthwaite, over the payment of tithes. Borrowdale, Sir John insisted, was exempt and he refused to pay the sum assessed on his estate. Eventually a compromise was reached: each year the sexton would seize one of Sir John's cows and immediately resell it to him. The custom continued until the poor old 'Vicar's Cow' died.

Reminders of both Gordon and Woodford still exist, not least in the extensive woodlands on the west side of Derwentwater. Derwent Bay House, shyly tucked away and unseen by the hordes of walkers on their way to climb Catbells, serves as a pleasant holiday home for visitors. Lord Gordon's Chair, a semi-circular shelter of stone, stands on private ground, an idyllic though somewhat uncomfortable refuge with uninterrupted views of Walla Crag across Derwentwater.

The two stately homes whose estates now occupy most of the western side of the lake are of more recent date. Lingholm was built in the 1870s for Colonel J F Greenall. During the 1890s it was often unoccupied or let furnished in the summer. Among those who rented the house were Beatrix Potter and her family: the house, grounds and immediate vicinity provided a perfect setting for the young artist to draw and write.

In the early 1900s, the house was bought by Colonel George Kemp, later Lord Rochdale.

Lingholm, the family home of Lord Rochdale

He developed the gardens and built the terraces on the lake side of Lingholm, which has remained in the hands of the Rochdale family ever since. During the First World War, it served as a convalescent military hospital and in the Second World War played host to evacuee children from the north-east.

The gardens have continued to expand, though some of the formal garden has been reduced and a water garden built in 1927 has disappeared altogether. Lingholm's glory is its collection of rhododendrons and azaleas, many of them planted in the late 1920s and 1930s and now matured into displays of rich and profuse colour.

Lingholm's near neighbour, Fawe Park, was built in 1857 as a shooting box for Mr Spencer Bell. It is not open to the public but it earns its place in the story of Keswick on two counts: like Lingholm, it was a holiday home for the Potters and was immortalised as the scene of Mr McGregor's garden in *The Tale of Benjamin Bunny* and second, it achieved some notoriety as the battleground for a footpath dispute in the 1880s.

As the gentry settled in their mansions, discerning visitors arrived on holiday in ever-growing numbers. They reacted against the excesses of the Romantic and Picturesque tourists and demanded a more faithful and reliable type of guidebook.

The satirists spear-headed the attack on the fanciful and the far-fetched. James Plumptre's comic opera, *The Lakers* (1798) unmercifully poked fun at the pretences of Miss Beccabunga Veronica, 'a great botanist and picturesque traveller'. Its satire is about as subtle as red paint on a pillar-box and the play, as far as I know, has been performed only once – at the Wordsworth Summer School at Grasmere in 1987, without music.

William Combe's *Dr Syntax's Tour in Search of the Picturesque* (1812) carried on the satirical tradition but much more important was a curious document published in 1807. Part description, part social comment, and called by its author 'an omnium-gatherum of the odd things I have seen in England', *Letters from England* by Don Manuel Alvarez Espriella is a world away from the blatant ridicule of Dr Syntax and the glaring farce of Beccabunga Veronica. Its controlled irony is balanced by its mass of detail, providing a picture of early nineteenth century England unrivalled in its variety and acute observation.

Supposed to be a translation from the Spanish, it was in fact written by Keswick's literary giant, Robert Southey: Don Manuel was no Spanish nobleman on tour.

He found Lodore Falls less of a Niagara than he had been led to expect – a common enough experience; he commended General Peachey for sweeping away the disfigurements of Pocklington on Derwent Island; he climbed Skiddaw with an effort but without any hint of danger. Warned of the terrors of Borrowdale, its horrifying precipices and stone avalanches, he 'found no difficulty in walking along a good road, which coaches of the light English make travel every summers day'.

Unlike Don Manuel, William Green was no fictionalised character. Born in Manchester in 1760, he settled in Ambleside: his work both as artist and guidebook writer clearly marks the transition from romantic exaggeration

Monk Hall, the old farm that occupied the site of Keswick hospital

to sober fact, from horror and immensity to topographical accuracy and reliable information, with, it must be admitted, an occasional lapse into the fanciful notions of his predecessors.

His annual display in a room at the back of the Queen's Head in Keswick was a popular attraction. His prolific output of aquatints, etchings and watercolours was matched by his enthusiasm for tramping the fells, an enthusiasm which underpins his guidebook of 1819 with authority and dependability. It tells visitors where to go and what to see, plotting easy walks in the valleys and longer treks on the high fells, including a twenty-three mile marathon from Keswick, taking in Borrowdale, Buttermere and Newlands.

Just how far ahead of his time Green was is illustrated by his vision of a 'Garden City' on the outskirts of Keswick, a proposal that fortunately remained an imaginative plan rather than a practical project. The suggested location of this 'ideal residential paradise' was at the foot of Castlehead, extending to the outskirts of Keswick and the shore of Derwentwater. The scheme was to cost £100,000 – probably the main reason why it remained a dream: in any case, Greenwich Hospital, the owners of the land, were unimpressed and refused to negotiate.

The plan provided for 300 houses, a church and tavern, concert hall and assembly rooms. Trees were an essential feature of the village, alongside parks and cascades; wardens would patrol the area to protect the amenities.

Had Green's scheme been realised, we should have a very different Keswick today. He certainly must not be dismissed as an entrepreneur out to make a fortune: his motives were impeccable. He had the welfare of the local people at heart and wanted to encourage the right kind of visitor.

Green set the fashion for guidebooks which regarded fact and informed comment as more important than fanciful description and over-zealous appreciation. Prominent among them was Jonathan Otley's *Concise Description of the English Lakes and adjacent mountains: with general directions to tourists.* Published in 1823, this pioneering companion, trustworthy and comprehensive, owed its success to the care and assiduous investigations of its author, a resident of Keswick. Norman Nicholson, internationally known poet and distinguished writer of our own day, assessed it as 'the basis of all sound factual writing on the district' and Otley himself claimed that 'when I first published there was no other work that had any pretension to compete with it'. Green's guidebook was conveniently ignored...

Jonathan Otley - guidebook writer, mineralogist, geologist, meteorologist

It included sections on botany and mineralogy, geology and meteorology; its details and statistics were the fruit of personal experience, local knowledge and scientific observation. It was the first of a long line of guidebooks that has continued remorselessly, though the tone and presentation of Martineau, Linton, Jenkinson, Baddeley, Wainwright and others have changed to accommodate individual attitudes and priorities and the demands of successive generations of tourists.

If there was a contemporary rival to Otley's guide, it was Wordsworth's, still in print and still well worth consulting. The first version, the anonymous introduction to Joseph

Wilkinson's *Select Views in Cumberland, Westmoreland and Lancashire* (1810), was published separately as his own *Description of the Scenery of the Lakes in the North of England* in 1822 and as the definitive *Guide through the District of the Lakes in the North of England* in 1835.

Rooted firmly and deeply in many years' residence in the Lake District, it is not only factual and practical: it also interprets and assesses. Only a short section is specifically devoted to directions and information for tourists; the bulk of the narrative analyses the characteristics of the landscape, both natural and man-made. Wordsworth offers unequivocal advice on the situation, style and colour of buildings; the most suitable trees to plant; the best time to visit the Lakes; even the order in which scenes should be viewed.

It is to Wordsworth that we owe the next invasion of Keswick: the literary establishment. Born and bred in Cockermouth in a house now owned by the National Trust, he must have passed through Keswick many times on his way to school at Hawkshead or to relations in Penrith – and he did admit in 'The Prelude' that 'distant Skiddaw's lofty height' helped to arouse his early awareness of the fell country.

In 1794, he and his sister, Dorothy, spent six weeks in the shadow of Skiddaw at Windy Brow, a house owned by the Calvert family: William Calvert had been a school friend of Wordsworth at Hawkshead.

Those few weeks were a vital period in the lives of both William and Dorothy. He was emerging from a series of personal crises and Windy Brow offered a freedom and a refuge that helped to resolve his problems. It was the first time brother and sister had been together since they were children in Cockermouth: apart from inevitable separations in the years ahead, they remained together for the rest of their lives.

The old farmhouse of Windy Brow, now overshadowed by the much more imposing mansion with the same name nearby, delighted Dorothy with its situation and views. She was equally impressed by the couple who lived at the farm, presumably tenants of the Calverts – simple, plain-living folk, poor but contented, industrious and fond of reading.

The Wordsworths, too, lived frugally, drinking no tea and spending their days walking and talking and visiting friends such as the Speddings of Armathwaite. There appears to have been only one cloud over the idyllic six weeks at Windy Brow. Aunt Christopher Crackenthorpe of Penrith condemned Dorothy for her needless extravagance and for rambling about the countryside in 'an unprotected situation'. Dorothy's spirited reply dismissed her aunt's strictures, silencing the unjustified criticisms of a disagreeable woman who was 'despised by everybody around Penrith for her excessive pride'.

Wordsworth's connexion with the Calverts had a much more significant effect on his life than providing a holiday home for six weeks. In September 1794, Wordsworth accompanied Raisley, William Calvert's younger brother, on a proposed trip to Lisbon. Raisley suffered from consumption and was so ill that the journey reached no further than Penrith.

Back in Keswick, Wordsworth nursed Raisley for three months but he died at the Robin Hood Inn in Penrith in early January 1795. In his will, he left Wordsworth a legacy of £900 – a generous gesture which helped the poet to devote himself to writing, 'enough to secure me from want if not to render me independent'.

Six years later, William Calvert invited Wordsworth to live at Windy Brow, which he was rebuilding. Wordsworth declined but a second opportunity for him to settle near Keswick arose in 1803.

Sir George Beaumont, artist and admirer of the poet, presented him with a small estate at Applethwaite, though at this date he had neither seen nor met Wordsworth. The motive behind this liberal gift was to allow Wordsworth to be near his friend, Coleridge, who was then living at Greta Hall. Wordsworth turned down the offer, pleading vaguely the 'state of my own affairs' but more likely because he realised that Coleridge was unlikely to stay long at Greta Hall.

Beaumont insisted that Wordsworth should keep the land and use the rent from the few cottages on it to plant trees or make improvements in case he ever decided to build. Wordsworth never lost his affection for Applethwaite, describing it in his *Guide* as 'a rare and almost singular combination of minute and sequestered beauty, with splendid and extensive prospects'.

The Ghyll, as the property came to be known, remained in the Wordsworth family for many years. In more recent times, it was the holiday home and later retirement home of Bishop Eric Treacy, who was known as 'the Railway Bishop' for his passionate interest in trains and his ability as a superb photographer of 'the iron horse' in action.

John Ruskin

9

Gurus of Greta Hall

Six weeks at Windy Brow, regular visits to friends in Keswick and ownership of a small estate a couple of miles away hardly qualify Wordsworth as a Keswickian. But without him, the town would not have emerged as one of the prime literary shrines of the country. The arrival of Coleridge at Greta Hall was directly due to Wordsworth; Coleridge's presence in Keswick drew Southey, who in turn acted as a magnet and host to numerous distinguished literary personalities. Greta Hall and its residents played a vital, though by no means the only role in putting Keswick firmly on the tourist map.

Wordsworth and Coleridge first met in Bristol in September 1795. Their friendship burgeoned, nurtured by a common enthusiasm for poetry and shared political sympathies. In May 1796, Coleridge, writing to John Thelwall, described Wordsworth as 'a very dear friend of mine, who is in my opinion the best poet of the age'.

The bond between the two men was firmly cemented when Coleridge moved to a cottage at Nether Stowey in Somerset on the last day of 1796 and the Wordsworths to Alfoxden House, a large mansion four miles away from Coleridge's 'old hovel', in July 1797.

Walking over the Quantock Hills and talking on every imaginable topic (they were suspected of being French spies), William, Dorothy and Samuel Taylor forged a friendship so strong that the trio became 'three persons, one soul'. The most fruitful outcome of this idyllic period was *Lyrical Ballads*, a joint production which included 'The Rime of the Ancient Mariner', 'Michael', and 'Lines written a few miles above Tintern Abbey'. A key volume in its day, it changed the course of English poetry by its directness of language, its simplicity of vocabulary and its choice of subject.

A trip to Germany in September 1798 and 'a picteresk Tour' of the Lakes in October 1799 strengthened the relationship still further. When the Wordsworths moved into Dove Cottage at Grasmere in the closing days of 1799, it seemed inevitable that Coleridge should follow them. Six months later, on 23 July 1800, he moved into Greta Hall with his family.

The house, standing proud on a hill that in 1800 was on the outskirts of the town, commanded a superb panorama of lake and fells. It was the property of William Jackson, a retired carrier, immortalised by Wordsworth as the master of Benjamin the Waggoner and brother-in-law of John Benson, the landlord of Dove Cottage. His interest in literature, coupled with the impact of Coleridge's charm, led him to offer part of the unfinished mansion rent free but Coleridge insisted on paying and Jackson accepted £45 a year.

Greta Hall, home of Coleridge and Southey

The house had twelve rooms, including the kitchen and back kitchen: two were very large, two rather less spacious and six smaller still. Coleridge hoped to convert an outhouse into a study but Jackson was unwilling to bear the cost of altering a building that would be of no use to him if Coleridge went away. In front of the house was a field and a large garden. Behind, an orchard and shrubberies fused into a small wood on a steep slope down to the Greta. Here, among the trees, was a shaded walk a quarter of a mile long by the side of the river. Much has changed but the house can still be seen.

Coleridge, his wife Sara and their son, Hartley, two months short of four years old, quickly settled in. Coleridge was mightily impressed. 'Right before me is a great Camp of simple mountains – each in shape resembles a Giant's Tent', he wrote to his friend, Samuel Purkis, just five days after his arrival at Greta Hall. To William Godwin he declared: 'I question if there be a room in England which commands a view of Mountains and Lakes and Woods and Vales superior to that in which I am now sitting.'

The early days at Greta Hall were happy and full – writing, visiting the Wordsworths, exploring the fells. On 31 August 1800, for example, Coleridge walked over Helvellyn by moonlight, arriving at Dove Cottage at eleven o'clock armed with part of his poem 'Christabel'.

Blencathra was one of his first climbs, to be followed by Helvellyn Dodds, the Coledale Horseshoe, Skiddaw and the great marathon of 1802. On 1 August 1802 at half past twelve, Coleridge set off on his nine-day trek, the Greta Hall besom stick in his hand and his knapsack filled with a few necessities – a shirt and cravat, two pairs of stockings, paper and pens, some tea and sugar, his nightcap and a book of German poems.

He headed for Portinscale through the hop field (presumably today's Howrahs) and tramped over Newlands to Buttermere and Ennerdale. St Bees was a disappointment: he stayed at a miserable pothouse, the bed a poor apology for comfort. His accommodation, a glass of gin and water, and breakfast cost under five pence. A bad night was followed by a wet morning and an unrewarding visit to the library at St Bees School, where he found only a handful of worthless Bible commentaries suitable only for fire-lighting, he suggested.

Thomas Tyson's farm, Burnthwaite in Wasdale, was much more comfortable; it is still a working farm, still accommodates visitors. From here, Coleridge climbed Scafell where he wrote to Sara Hutchinson 'surely the first letter ever to be written from the top of Sca Fell'. Pundits still argue about his route of descent off Scafell: was it by Broad Stand or Scafell Chimney? Whichever it was, it certainly alarmed Coleridge: it put 'my whole limbs in a tremble...every drop increased the palsy of my limbs'. His violent exertions brought on a rash of red heat-lumps which stayed with him for several days.

In Eskdale, he stayed at Taw House – Toes, he called it. He lost himself on the Duddon fells but eventually landed at Ulpha. Coniston he liked, 'a worthy compeer of the stateliest, an equal co-heir of nature with Keswick, Windermere and Ullswater'.

The great 'circumcursion' brought Coleridge back home by Windermere and Ambleside, a long and demanding ramble that puts him firmly among the pioneer fell walkers and rock scramblers. It was patently a happy excursion, a chance for Coleridge to soak himself in the grandeur and beauty of the fell country. A modern Keswick writer, Alan Hankinson, followed Coleridge's route in 1989: his prize-winning *Coleridge Walks the Fells* (1991) is a most enjoyable and perceptive account and comparison of both expeditions.

Back at Greta Hall, life was far from peaceful and harmonious. Wordsworth's rejection of 'Christabel' for the second edition of *Lyrical Ballads* and his critical disparagement of 'The Ancient Mariner' must have hurt Coleridge deeply. Illness, worry over financial problems, the difficulty he had in settling down to regular work, his deteriorating relationship with his wife: all helped to drive him to the panacea that was part of his life for so many years – opium.

Depression and dejection, coupled with severe pain, sent him to bed. The weather and the dampness of Greta Hall did little to help him and the leeches of John Edmundson, the local doctor, gave only temporary relief. Only opium (laudanum) eased pain, physical and mental. Coleridge claimed that reading some old medical journals loaned to him by Dr Edmundson had seduced him into taking laudanum but Molly Lefebure proves in her *Samuel Taylor Coleridge: a bondage of opium* (1974) that he had been using drugs for many years.

About this time, he may well have been introduced to the notorious Kendal Black Drop, a concoction stronger than standard laudanum and popular locally as a cure-all, a sort of nineteenth century aspirin that claimed to cope with everything from rheumatism and coughs to depression and gout.

Coleridge's *Notebooks* reveal the intensity of his afflictions. On Friday, 28 October 1803, he records: 'A sad night – went to bed after Tea – and in about two hours absolutely summoned the whole Household to me by my Screams, from all the chambers – and I continued screaming even after Mrs Coleridge was sitting and speaking to me.'

The picture of the dutiful and caring wife disguises the domestic strife that compounded Coleridge's physical illness and mental frustration. Poor Sara Coleridge, friendless, weighed down by family responsibilities in an unfinished, cold, damp house, and continually clashing with her irritable and indolent husband, flew into angry tempers. Coleridge responded; verbal battles raged; recourse to opium only intensified the quarrels. 'Scarce a day passed without a scene of discord between me and Mrs Coleridge,' he confessed.

He found some comfort at Dove Cottage, pouring out his woes and complaints to the sympathetic ears of William and Dorothy. They believed all he told them about his wife and identified her as the prime cause of strife. 'Her radical fault,' wrote Dorothy, 'is want of sensibility... She is to be sure a sad fiddle faddler.' The argument that Sara was to blame for the discord and friction and for driving Coleridge to drugs has been thoroughly scotched by Molly Lefebure's *The Bondage of Love* (1986), an in-depth study of Mrs Coleridge and a convincing analysis of conflicting personalities and relationships.

The growing dissension between husband and wife was seriously intensified by the arrival on the scene of Sara Hutchinson, sister of Mary, Wordsworth's wife.

Coleridge first met Asra, as he called her, at the Hutchinson home at Sockburn near Darlington in November 1799. A mild flirtation developed into infatuation. Asra's visits to her sister at Dove Cottage provided yet another excuse for Coleridge to quit Greta Hall and find consolation with the woman who took first place in his affections. Asra felt sorry for him and was, no doubt, flattered by his attentions but from its beginning it was an affair doomed to failure and unhappiness. Asra's innocent pity was no match for Coleridge's intense and passionate declarations, typically crystallised in the outpourings of 'Dejection: an Ode', published in the *Morning Post* of 4 October 1802, Wordsworth's wedding day.

The printed version was a toned-down rewrite of a letter to Asra, an anguished, self-indulgent wallowing in grief and despair in which he almost delighted in her misery as well as his own. It is not surprising that over the years she, too, suffered depression and nervous tension which eventually resolved themselves in a repugnance for Coleridge.

Samuel Taylor Coleridge, 'an archangel a little damaged'

In October 1801, Coleridge escaped from the marital minefield at Greta Hall to work for the *Morning Post* in London. Separation seemed the only solution to his problems but he still clung to the hope of reunion and peace. He wrote to his wife some 300 miles away: 'it is my frequent prayer and my almost perpetual aspiration, that we may meet to part no more – and live together as affectionate Husband and Wife ought to do.'

In March 1802, he was back in Keswick: any superficial reconciliation crumbled into the old routine of bickering and discord, even though Sara was pregnant. The suggestion of separation sparked off a furious quarrel, recriminations on both sides and the resolve to try again to save the marriage from the wreck it had become. The uneasy truce continued as Coleridge grew more and more dependent on opium. He suffered a range of illnesses and, looking for an explanation, decided that it was Lakeland weather that was at least partly responsible. He decided to seek warmer climes and on 9 April 1804 set sail for Malta.

Two years later he was back in Keswick. Dorothy Wordsworth was disturbed by his condition: 'never did I feel such a shock as at first sight of him...he is utterly changed'. She was convinced that leaving Sara was the only solution and in September 1808 Coleridge and his two sons moved in with the Wordsworths at Allan Bank, Grasmere. Sara's attempts to keep the marriage at least superficially harmonious failed. In the social and moral atmosphere of the early 1800s, the world would see her as the cause of the break-up; she would be condemned as the guilty partner; her reputation would be in ruins, her conduct highly suspect. As a woman, she had no property rights, no claim on the children.

The inevitable compromise left them 'good friends' and Sara continued to live at Greta Hall with the Southeys. At Allan Bank, relationships deteriorated as Coleridge's peculiar habits, his continued addiction to opium, his morose and melancholic moods irritated the Wordsworths. Rumblings of the first breakdown in the old friendship had been heard on a Scottish tour in 1803 when Wordsworth hinted that Coleridge's excessive intake of opium was responsible for his troubles and for some years Coleridge had resented Wordsworth's growing reputation as a poet while his own creative powers were patently in decline.

The final split came when Coleridge heard that Wordsworth had admitted to a friend that his guest was 'an absolute nuisance'. Coleridge moved south, even proposing that Sara and the family should join him. She regarded the suggestion with all her experience of a lifetime of her husband's vague and grandiose promises as 'airy nothings'.

Coleridge spent much of the rest of his life in London and the West Country, cared for by friends and finally bringing his opium dependence under control with the help of a generous and patient Dr James Gillman. Greta Hall, 300 miles away, might have been on the other side of the world.

Sara and the children visited him on occasion. She left the Lakes in 1830 to live with her son, Derwent, in Hampstead and proximity to Coleridge resulted in a reconciliation of sorts, mercifully free from the quarrels of the Greta Hall days. Man and wife appear to have remained 'good friends' until Coleridge's death on 25 July 1834.

The few stormy years that Coleridge spent in Keswick contrast sharply with the long and generally happy residence of Robert Southey and his family. Southey was married to Edith Fricker, sister of Sara Coleridge, a union that proved harmonious and peaceful and provided Southey with the permanence and stability necessary for his prolific output of books and articles, poems and reviews, most of which, sadly, are now forgotten.

In April 1801, Coleridge invited the Southeys to Greta Hall. The visit in early September was brief: Southey's heart was in Portugal and his preference was for the warmth and sunshine of the Continent. Keswick was too cold; the lakes were mere rivers; the mountains were pimples compared with the peaks of Portugal.

The birth of a daughter, Margaret, on 31 August 1802 made it essential that the Southeys should have a permanent home. Coleridge urged them to share Greta Hall: there was plenty of room, no furniture to buy, and the two sisters would be a great comfort to each other. Any reservations Southey had about living with his brother-in-law were buttressed by his misgivings over Keswick weather. In a sense, the decision to move was made for him by the sudden death of Margaret, a year old and a victim of hydrocephalus. Southey, living in Bristol, had one paramount wish: to get away from a place so poignantly packed with tragic associations. Moreover, he felt that Edith, distraught as she was, would be 'nowhere so well as with her sister Coleridge'.

On 7 September 1803, the Southeys arrived at Greta Hall, ostensibly for a short stay until the wounds of Margaret's death had healed. In fact, Southey stayed for the rest of his life. His earlier unsettled and restless years were replaced by a permanent home; his yearnings for a place in the sun faded into a deeper affection for colder, wetter Keswick. His somewhat dilettante literary efforts were abandoned in favour of unprecedented industry and concentrated hard labour – a demon for work who accepted his considerable responsibilities willingly and purposefully.

He was aware of the marital conflicts of Coleridge and Sara and knew he would have to shoulder the burden of a household of considerable proportions: his own growing family; Sara and the three Coleridge children; Mrs Wilson, officially Mr Jackson's housekeeper, but, as the much-loved 'Wilsy', the guardian and nurse of the children; a third Fricker sister, the bad-tempered Mrs Lovell. It says much for Southey's moral fibre that he could write to his friend, Grosvenor Bedford, 'there is not a lighter-hearted nor a happier man upon the face of this wide world'.

With Southey in charge, the atmosphere of Greta Hall changed dramatically. Once the grief over Margaret's death had mellowed and Edith May had been born on 11 October 1806, the house bustled with noise and activity. Southey teased and amused the depressed Sara, playing practical jokes and pranks and nicknaming her 'Bumble-cum-Tumble'.

Work was the first priority but the fells pulled. Within a fortnight of arriving at Greta Hall, Southey had walked round the lake and climbed Skiddaw, the first of many ascents to a summit he aptly described as 'bitter bleak, next door to heaven'. In July 1806, he and his brother went off on a three-day walking tour of the district – a mere stroll compared with Coleridge's 1802 marathon.

As Southey's family grew, so financial problems increased. Emma, born in 1808, died when she was just over a year old but Bertha (1809), Katherine (1810) and Isobel (1812) developed into lively, robust children who added yet more noise and bustle to Greta Hall – and further claims on the family budget.

In 1807, Southey was granted a pension of £200 a year: that and the fees from his regular contributions to the newly-launched *Quarterly Review* – the first number was dated February 1809 – were the solid core of his income for many years. He was a model contributor to the *Review:* he made two promises which he never failed to honour – sincerity and punctuality. He emerged as an essayist of some importance and reputation and, though he was never a rich man, he was always able to meet his financial obligations.

Any additional sources of income were welcome but not all were acceptable. The possibility of a university post was precluded by his refusal to subscribe to the Thirty-Nine Articles. The Stewardship of the Greenwich Hospital Derwentwater Estates at a salary of £700 a year appeared an attractive propositon but Southey quickly withdrew when he discovered the post called for a full day's work (and the consequent neglect of his writing) and qualifications in agriculture, surveying and law.

The Poet Laureateship was a different matter. In 1813, it was offered to Sir Walter Scott who declined and generously used his influence in favour of Southey. The salary was only £90 a year but it made a welcome addition to the financial resources of Greta Hall. Southey was in the running for the editorship of the *Times* but that would have meant leaving Keswick – the last thing Southey wanted to do. Over the years, he was invited to apply for various public posts – Historiographer Royal in 1812, Librarian of the Faculty of Advocates in Edinburgh in 1818, a Professorship at Glasgow in 1831 – but he refused all such prestigious and remunerative appointments, presumably because he wanted to stay at Greta Hall.

In 1826, while he was on a continental tour, he was nominated a Member of Parliament for Downtown in Wiltshire without either his knowledge or his approval. In any case, he was ineligible, not having an estate worth £300 a year – a necessary qualification. Back in Keswick, the news and the rumours spread. Southey arrived home to a crowded reception with the town band playing and the citizens celebrating an election that never was. Life at Westminster held no appeal for Southey: 'a seat in Parliament,' he wrote, 'is neither consistent with my circumstances, inclinations, habits or pursuits of life.'

On occasion, he tore himself away from his desk to go on journeys or to visit friends, but most of his days were spent pen in hand in the library he loved so dearly. His annual summer cold forced him to leave Keswick for short periods when the attacks – a kind of virulent hay fever – became increasingly severe. The accompanying sneeze was a sound to be remembered: writing to his brother, Henry, Southey quipped:

Skidda returns, as well he may, the echo of that sneeze,
And folks in Portinscale may say 'God bless us' if they please.

On a visit to London in 1813, Southey met Byron, the *enfant terrible* of the literary world and an outspoken critic of Southey's work. It was an amicable encounter, considering the two men were morally and politically poles apart. By 1821, with Southey's outright condemnation of Byron and his Satanic School, any superficial respect had evaporated. Byron's 'The Vision of Judgement' parodied Southey unmercifully but wisely Southey refused to be drawn into a prolonged public vendetta with a man he had come to regard as 'wicked by disposition'.

In September 1815, Southey visited the Low Countries, mainly to see the battlefield of Waterloo. In Brussels, he called at a hospital to deliver a letter to Richard Carbonell, a Keswick soldier wounded in the war. Unfortunately, he had died six weeks before Southey arrived. One outcome of the journey was 'The Poet's Pilgrimage to Waterloo', an undistinguished set of verses, redeemed by its 'Proem' which is a frank confession of Southey's deep affection for Keswick and the pleasures and satisfactions of home and family.

By the time of the Waterloo trip, his roots were well and truly fixed in Keswick; nothing was likely to tempt him away from the house on the hill, even though there were moments when his busy, happy lifestyle was disturbed. Disorder, rampant in various parts of the country in the winter of 1811-12, penetrated as far as Keswick. Southey wrote to Grosvenor Bedford about his fears of 'ugly fellows' from Carlisle and west Cumberland invading the town and asked his friend to send two pistols and a watchman's rattle for the defence of Greta Hall.

In 1813, Southey reported that nearly all his chickens were stolen in one night. The Whitehaven mail was robbed, the Maryport post-boy was shot at, there were riots about the passage of corn from Cockermouth. Southey concluded that there was 'something very like a Luddite spirit at the bottom of this, originating half in mistake and half in mischief and leading to every kind of evil'.

In 1824, a smashed kitchen window, shattered by a blow from a leg of mutton, woke the Greta Hall household at dead of night. Southey engaged the Town Crier and let it be known that anyone found late at night at Greta Hall would 'take the consequences' – and that included being shot at.

These outbreaks of violence, local and national, helped to convince Southey that a strong Tory government was essential. The radical young revolutionary had not lost his anger against poverty or the employment of children in factories; he still believed the state should provide social services; he hoped for minimal or no unemployment. Lord Shaftesbury described him as 'essentially the friend of the poor, the young and the defenceless – no one so true, so eloquent and so powerful'.

But his political sympathies were soundly Tory, his proposed reforms were along authoritarian rather than democratic lines. One man, one vote was not a policy he supported and order, he insisted, was 'the first thing needful in society'.

His delight in the defeat of Napoleon was celebrated by a bonfire on top of Skiddaw. The first attempt was a sorry failure. It rained so hard that Southey postponed the project: the delay gave the local vandals a field-day, as they scattered and burnt the bonfire. Annoyed and angry, Southey organised a second celebration.

Robert Southey, Keswick's literary lion

On 21 August 1815, a party assembled on the summit of Skiddaw: four of the Southey family, three Wordsworths, Lord and Lady Sunderlin (an Irish peer and his wife who were staying at North Bridge House opposite Greta Hall for the summer), sundry servants and a trail of local 'Rag, Tag and Bobtail'. They feasted on roast beef and plum pudding and sang the National Anthem round flaming barrels of tar. They rolled large balls of tow and turpentine down the fell side and crowned the festivities by sending up a balloon inscribed 'Wellington and Waterloo'.

A torchlight procession left the summit at ten o'clock and arrived safely back in Keswick by midnight. One of the rag-tag overindulged in the punch and descended on horseback, face to tail and supported by his companions who were 'just sober enough to guide and hold him on'. There was only one mishap. While the assembled company were waiting for punch, Wordsworth knocked over the kettle of boiling water. With water in short supply, some of the revellers were quite happy to drink their rum neat.

It was a great occasion, a unique event with everyone in high spirits. The *Cumberland Pacquet* reported that it was the first time carts had been taken to the top of Skiddaw and for many of the locals the first time they had 'been induced to climb its awful height'.

A few months after the Waterloo bonfire, tragedy once more shattered the joy and laughter of Greta Hall. On 17 April 1816, Herbert died at the age of nine. Southey had a particular and intense love for his only son who, by all accounts, was a precocious and charming boy. At the age of six, he was reading *Pilgrim's Progress;* at nine, he was proficient in Greek and had a good knowledge of Latin, French and German. Dorothy Wordsworth described him as 'the perfection of a child, loving books and learning, yet all a child at play'.

Southey never recovered from the death of this much-loved child. The golden hopes for the future died too and, according to de Quincey, so did 'the radiant felicity and the internal serenity of the unhappy father'. He even considered leaving Greta Hall but instead plunged into more and more work. The birth of Charles Cuthbert in February 1819 helped to fill the gap left by Herbert's death and Southey must have felt considerable satisfaction in seeing this second son go to Oxford and launch into a successful career as a parish priest.

Family tragedy seemed to haunt the Southeys and may well have been the prime cause of Edith's sad condition in her last years. In 1826, on his return from a thirteen-week tour of the Continent, Southey found his youngest daughter, Isobel, was dangerously ill. She died within days, a devastating blow, compounding the grief of earlier losses – Margaret, Emma, Herbert...and now Isobel.

For Mrs Southey, the death of a fourth child was overwhelming. She was not a strong woman and for many years she had had to endure ill health and nervous afflictions. Over-anxious and acutely depressed, she felt she was going mad, as indeed she was.

In September 1834, a visitor called at Greta Hall. He was received by a solemn Southey who told him that 'Mrs Southey had, without previous indication or symptom, gone raving mad and to that hopeless degree that within an hour he must take her to an asylum'. She spent some months in a Retreat near York before returning home. She never recovered her sanity and was cared for by her husband and family until her death on 16 November 1837 – a pitiful end for a wife of whom Southey wrote, 'I never knew her to do an unkind act, nor say an unkind word'.

Southey continued to work assiduously, his political writing revealing an ever stronger faith in the more extreme tenets of Toryism and a perpetual condemnation of the evils of poverty. There was little comfort in the offer of a baronetcy in February 1835, a formal recognition of his services to literature and a personal expression from Robert Peel, the Prime Minister, of his gratitude 'for the eminent services you have rendered, not only to literature, but to the higher interests of virtue and religion'.

Southey declined the honour, feeling he lacked the financial means to support it. What did please him was an increase of £300 a year to his pension, a welcome award that roused the objections of his critics but left Southey with enough money to meet the daily expenses of Greta Hall and indulge his unstinting generosity to his friends.

Edith's death, relief though it was, was a severe blow, coming as it did on the heels of several other bereavements: Southey's uncle, Herbert Hill, in 1828; his friend, Sir Walter Scott, in 1832; his brother-in-law, Coleridge, and another friend, Charles Lamb, in 1834. 'At times,' he confessed to Caroline Bowles, 'the burden of loneliness seems to weigh me down.'

Caroline Bowles, an aspiring poet, first wrote to Southey in May, 1818, for help. He agreed to recommend her somewhat mournful verses to Murray, the publisher, and offered advice on their improvement. The obscure writer and the Poet Laureate continued to correspond and it was to Caroline that he turned for comfort and companionship after Edith's death. She was far from being a robust, healthy person and she was twelve years younger than Southey.

The friendship developed and on 4 June 1839 she became the second Mrs Southey. The prospect of consolation and renewed contentment soon evaporated. Within weeks, Southey's mind began to fail: confused and bewildered, he found great difficulty in composing his thoughts and committing them to paper. Such a state of inactivity and perplexity, so alien to his nature, must have been a sore trial. He grew worse. Wordsworth called at Greta Hall and Southey failed to recognise him. The decline continued for a couple of years or so, accompanied by irritability rather than physical pain. Even though he was unable to read any of his 14,000 books, they still brought him pleasure: Wordsworth found him 'patting with both hands his books affectionately like a child'.

He died on 21 March 1843 and was buried at Crosthwaite church two days later – just thirty-five years after his letter of 19 October 1808 to Humphrey Senhouse in which he wrote: 'the sole freehold I am ever likely to possess is a tenement six feet by three in Crosthwaite churchyard.'

Sad though the funeral was, it was overshadowed by family dissension, sparked off by

Kate Southey's dislike of her stepmother. The hostility was fuelled by the strains and stresses of having an invalid in the house. Family and friends took sides and even at the funeral itself refused to forget their differences. Wordsworth was not invited but he went – and he it was who wrote the tribute to his old friend which is on the marble monument in Crosthwaite Church, where Southey had worshipped regularly for some forty years.

With such a prolific output, a lifetime's work in a range of literary genres – forty-five books, hundreds of poems, innumerable articles and reviews – it is sad that Southey is so little read or admired today. With very rare exceptions, his poetry lacks greatness but his prose has earned him a permanent place among the giants of literature. Even his enemies paid their due tributes: Byron called his prose 'perfect' and Hazlitt acknowledged him as 'the best and most natural prose-writer of any poet of the day'.

Among the poems, we remember 'The Battle of Blenheim', 'The Inchcape Rock', 'The Cataract of Lodore' and a few short lyrics rather than the long, ponderous epics. His prose has been more fortunate: the *Letters from England;* the biographies of Nelson and Wesley; histories of Brazil and the Peninsular War; the omnium-gatherum of *The Doctor*, with its immortal children's story of the Three Bears.

In spite of the domestic tragedies, Southey's self-imposed regime of hard labour at Greta Hall had many happy, relaxed moments. The noise and laughter of children were enjoyed as much as the serious business of writing, walks and expeditions as much as the visits of friends. There were, too, the beloved cats, blessed with such fanciful, bizarre names as Madame Bianchi, Pope Joan, Bona Marietta, and His Serene Highness the Archduke Rumpelstilzchen. The essentials of any enjoyable household, Southey declared, were 'a child rising three years old and a kitten rising six weeks'.

The therapeutic comfort of the cats must have been a welcome relaxation from the long hours spent every day at his desk and the bustle of Greta Hall, frequently bursting at the seams with people so that it earned the nickname of 'the Ant Hill' – it certainly had its fair share of aunts as well.

Fortunately, until his last illness, Southey enjoyed sound health and a good appetite, apart from his regular hay fever. 'My skin and bones hardly know what an ailment is,' he confessed and at the age of fifty he admitted to having had only six days of pain – one with toothache and five with a poisoned foot. Routine and order, regular exercise and a sense of humour helped to keep him fit and balanced for the onerous domestic and literary burdens he shouldered for so many years.

The 'Ant Hill' seems to have been something of a little world of its own. The immediate circle in which the Southeys moved was restricted: the Wordsworths, the Calverts at Windy Brow, the Senhouses of Maryport, the Lawsons of Isel, the Peacheys of Derwent Island and the formidable Miss Barker who lived next door at Greta Lodge and was a special friend.

There appears to have been only minimal contact with the ordinary people of Keswick. 'Long as he resided at Keswick,' wrote Southey's son, Cuthbert, 'I do not think there were twenty persons in the lower class whom he knew by sight.' A local summed him up as 'well thowt on but nut a chap as cracked on a deal wi' anybody'.

The trail of eminent visitors to Greta Hall more than compensated for the lack of Keswick society and helped to turn it into one of the most famous literary houses in the country.

Charles Lamb and his sister, Mary, spent three weeks at Greta Hall in August 1802 when Coleridge was in residence. Lamb, an old school friend of Coleridge, was duly impressed, commenting that 'we thought we had got into fairyland'. In spite of his aversion to mountains, he climbed Skiddaw but had no desire whatsoever to settle among the fells. Fleet Street and the Strand were 'better places to live in for good and all than amidst Skiddaw'.

Covent Garden and the shops, the clatter of coaches and the cries of the watchmen, old bookstalls and the Inns of Court – 'for these,' wrote Lamb, 'may Keswick and her giant brood go hang.'

William Hazlitt visited Greta Hall on several occasions to paint portraits of Coleridge and his son, Hartley, and Southey. In December 1803, he left Keswick suddenly and under a cloud. The reasons for this precipitate departure, with unfinished canvases abandoned and the painting of Southey not even started, have never been fully or satisfactorily explained.

It appears he was guilty of assaulting one or more local women and was more or less chased out of town. One version of the story has him pursued by 200 men on horseback as he escaped to Dove Cottage with the connivance of Coleridge who gave him 'all the money I had in the world and the very Shoes off my feet to enable him to escape over the mountains'.

The truth about this Keswick scandal may never be known. Something unpleasant obviously happened and no doubt local gossip embroidered it – were there really 200 horsemen chasing Hazlitt? He may well have alienated Keswickians by his lukewarm attitude to the renewal of hostilities against the French; he may even have been suspected of being a spy, as Wordsworth and Coleridge had been in Somerset in 1797. Was a mild flirtation used as an excuse to drive him away from Keswick? Was he guilty of attempted rape? From Hazlitt himself, not surprisingly, there is silence...

Thomas de Quincey first met Southey at Greta Hall in November 1807, having walked from Penrith and dined at a public house in Threlkeld. The following day Wordsworth arrived and de Quincey was quick to notice that the two men were not on the most cordial of terms. Later they were close friends but in 1807 de Quincey attributed their cool courtesies to their differing values and way of life.

When de Quincey settled in Grasmere, the contacts with Southey continued but not to any great depth. De Quincey claimed that he was 'on such terms for the next ten or eleven years that I might, in a qualified sense, call myself his friend'.

The same could not be said of Percy Bysshe Shelley, who arrived in Keswick in November 1811 for a three months' stay. At nineteen and recently married to Harriet Westbrook, the sixteen-year-old daughter of a London publican, he was hardly the kind of acquaintance the staid Southey was anxious to cultivate. Shelley had an introduction to William Calvert of Greta Bank who was instrumental in securing lodgings for the young couple at Gideon Dare's house on Chestnut Hill.

He was kindly received at Greta Hall but any hero worship began to fade as the two men talked and discussed and argued. The idealistic nineteen-year-old, with all the passionate conviction and confidence of youth, found the thirty-eight-year-old, whose opinions had mellowed and narrowed, something of a disappointment. Southey, wrote Shelley, 'has quite lost my good opinion – his conversation has lost its charm.' The teenage revolutionary was disillusioned with a radical thinker who had degenerated into 'the paid champion of every abuse and absurdity'. To compound his disgust, he found Mrs Southey 'very stupid' and Mrs Coleridge even worse.

Southey, by contrast, was more charitable, seeing in Shelley a vision of his former self – 'he is just what I was in 1794' – and recognising his potential genius. The two men corresponded for some years but never met again. Southey's attitude changed and in a letter of 26 November 1822 he wrote: 'His story, taking it altogether, is the most flagitious and the most tragic which I have known in real life.'

Shelley's stay in Keswick, apart from his unsatisfactory relationship with Southey, was not particularly happy. He was attacked by a gang of ruffians on the doorstep of his cottage. The truth of this episode has been questioned but it is known that on 19 January 1812, the day of the attack, two 'ugly fellows' were in the town and Southey had loaded an old Spanish fowling-piece to defend Greta Hall.

Shelley Cottage, the young poet's home for three months in 1811

In the cottage on Chestnut Hill, Shelley experimented with chemicals and roused the suspicions and objections of his neighbours and his landlord. They were not sorry to see him go; he left Keswick in February 1812 with few regrets.

Southey's other literary friendships were rather more fruitful. Sir Walter Scott was always welcome at Greta Hall and his generosity towards Southey nourished a warm relationship that lasted until Scott's death in 1832. Not that Scott's was an unqualified affection for Southey. 'I like his person,' he wrote, 'admire his genius and respect his immense erudition but...in point of reasoning and political judgment he is nothing better than a wild bull.'

Samuel Rogers visited Southey on several occasions and was particularly impressed with Ormathwaite. 'I think the people of Keswick,' he wrote in August 1812, 'the pleasantest-looking people I ever saw; and the children are beautiful.'

Walter Savage Landor came in 1832, twenty-four years after his first meeting with Southey. The two men corresponded regularly and encouraged each other's literary efforts and political ideas. 'My reverence for his purity of soul,' wrote Landor, 'my grateful estimation of his affection towards me, are not to be expressed in words.'

Other guests at Greta Hall included Jeffrey, editor of the *Edinburgh Review* and Lockhart, editor of the *Quarterly Review;* Dr Thomas Arnold, headmaster of Rugby School; Henry Crabb Robinson, the diarist, who complimented Southey as 'a most amiable man and everything I see in him pleases me'; Canning, a future Prime Minister and Robert Owen, the philanthropist and social reformer; William Wilberforce, the campaigner for the emancipation of slaves, and Dr Bell, the educational pioneer; Sir Humphry Davy, the scientist and John Stuart Mill, philosopher and political economist.

It is surprising to find that Keats did not call on Southey during his brief visit to Keswick in 1818: there is not a whisper of either him or Greta Hall in the letters Keats wrote at the time.

Henry Irwin Jenkinson

10

Cause for Concern

Eminent visitors enjoyed Southey's hospitality at the house on the hill but they appear to have had little effect on the daily life of the ordinary people of Keswick. No doubt that as rumours spread that so and so was arriving a few locals would stand and stare, but the vast majority of Keswickians would be too occupied with the business of daily living to bother much with the comings and goings at Greta Hall.

The population of the town was gradually increasing. The vast parish of Crosthwaite, with Keswick at its hub, included the four townships of Braithwaite, Portinscale, Underskiddaw and St John's and Wythburn, together with the chapelries of Borrowdale, Newlands and Thornthwaite. The total population of the parish in the years 1801, 1811 and 1821 was 3053, 3656 and 4087, with Keswick itself accounting for 1350, 1683 and 1901.

Parson and White's *Directory* of 1829, when Keswick had just over 400 houses, describes it as 'a small but neat market town, consisting of one long street of good houses, delightfully situated near the foot of Derwent Lake'. There were thirteen public houses or inns: at the top of the list, the Royal Oak and the Queen's Head offered post-chaises, ponies and guides for their visitors. Boats were available on the lake and the annual regattas continued to be held at the end of August each year. The noisy battles of Pocklington's day no longer featured on the programme but there was an entertaining selection of horse racing, wrestling, running on land and rowing on the lake.

As the market centre for the district, Keswick held a number of fairs in addition to its regular Saturday market. In May and October, four fairs were arranged for the sale of cattle; rams and cheese were sold at the beginning of November; hirings for farm servants were an excuse for jollifications at Whitsuntide and Martinmas.

The ground floor of the Moot Hall was used as a covered market, selling eggs and butter, meal and poultry. The shambles at the northern end of the building were demolished in 1815. Southey, writing on 31 December 1818, commented: 'The town of Keswick is much improved by the demolition of the shambles. It stands as much in need of moral and magisterial improvement as ever.'

Commerce confined itself to the ground floor of the Moot Hall. Upstairs served as a court room. Here the Lord of the Manor (the Governors of Greenwich Hospital in the early 1800s) held Copyhold Courts and Courts Baron – time-honoured medieval institutions which survived to settle tenancy problems and transfers of property, estate and land disputes.

The Moot Hall, centre-piece of the Market Square

Parson and White's *Directory* details the main manufacturers in Keswick in 1829 as producers of coarse woollen goods, fancy waistcoatings, scythes, edge-tools and black lead pencils. A more comprehensive list of occupations includes the making of gloves, boots and shoes, nails, straw hats, blankets and sheets. The usual trades and professions operated: two lawyers and three surgeons, eleven butchers and seven drapers, three painters and nine grocers, two hairdressers and two stay-makers. Grace Ladyman was designated 'billiard table keeper'; James Ivison combined joinery with auctioneering; Thomas Bailey sold books and patent medicines. Not far away from the town were Clark's woollen mill at Applethwaite, Dover's at Millbeck, Brownrigg's at Braithwaite and two at Thornthwaite. Slate quarries and wad mines in Borrowdale and scattered mineral workings in the neighbourhood added yet other sources of employment and commercial enterprise.

Twenty years later, Mannix and Whellan's *Directory* of 1847 still describes Keswick as 'a neat but small market town, consisting of one long street of good houses'; the range of occupations was substantially the same as that of 1829. Greenwich Hospital Governors were no longer Lords of the Manor: the new owner was John Marshall. In 1832 he introduced a harsher regime into the management of the estate, exercising a much more stringent control over both the workforce and the purse-strings. Southey suggested to him that alders would grow well at the foot of the lake: Marshall's crushing reply was that alders were worth only fourpence a foot. The estate workers found their wages of two shillings and sixpence a day reduced to less than half that figure and tasks were let out at such low rates that labourers could 'scarcely keep their families in bread'.

Marshall continued the Manorial Courts in the Moot Hall. By 1847 a regular magistrates' court sat most Saturdays, with two officials from a list of four: Thomas Storey Spedding of Greta Bank; James Stanger of Lairthwaite; Joshua Stanger of Field Side; and the Hon. John Henry Curzon of Castlette Cottage. Once a month, a County Court, revived by an Act of Parliament in 1846, met at the King's Arms to arbitrate in disputes involving land.

The picture, then, of Keswick at the mid-point of the nineteenth century is that of a pleasant market town, busy with a variety of manufacturing industries – on a small scale but right for the size of the town – and making use of its position in the heart of outstanding natural beauty to develop its tourist trade. It has been estimated that at this period some 8,000 to 10,000 visitors came to Keswick in the summer season. The local population continued to increase gradually: the census figures for Crosthwaite Parish for the years 1831, 1841 and 1851 were 4344, 4759 and 5315 and for Keswick 2159, 2442 and 2618.

Below the surface of bustling prosperity and behind the facade of respectable commercial enterprise, however, another less acceptable face of Keswick was hidden. Opinions about the salubrity of the town differed. Southey, writing on 24 November 1831, told his friend, Mrs Bray of Tavistock: 'For the first time in my life I am taking part in local affairs and am on the committee of a Board of Health for this little, unclean, ill-conditioned town. My reason for doing this is to make the people conclude that a matter must be serious which induces me to come forward in it, and God knows it is fitting that they should think seriously of their danger.'

On the other hand, at a time when a nation-wide epidemic of cholera affected the county, the *Cumberland Pacquet* of 24 July 1832 reported that 'this gay little place, allowed on all hands to be as healthy a town as any in the kingdom, is at present literally filled with strangers...who find a healthy asylum in the beautiful and romantic dale of Keswick'.

In 1848, there was a severe attack of smallpox in a year when the total number of cases of contagious diseases in the town reached 162. The following year there were seven deaths from cholera in only two of the overcrowded yards. It was patently obvious that sanitary conditions were far from satisfactory.

In January 1852, a number of ratepayers, led by James Lynn, the vicar of Crosthwaite, Joshua Stanger, J P, and Joseph Hall, solicitor, petitioned the General Board of Health to apply the provisions of the Public Health Act of 1848 to Keswick. The signatories – 144 out of 622 ratepayers – recognised the benefits of effective sewers and a clean, reliable water supply for the good health of the inhabitants and 'more particularly to the labouring classes residing in the more confined and unhealthy parts of the said town'.

Not all Keswickians were in favour and a counter petition was submitted requesting that the Public Health Act should not be applied to Keswick. It was signed by 452 ratepayers, many of whom had already supported the first petition! It complained that the earlier document had been privately organised and submitted before the ordinary citizens had any information or opportunity to discuss its provisions. What the counter petitioners feared most was the cost of any improvements.

They stressed that there was an adequate supply of good water and that very few houses were without a pump or immediate access to one. Sewers had been installed at considerable expense and it was unjust to impose further taxes to fund an unnecessary project. Population had increased; mortality rates had fallen; and, in any case, those rates were distorted by the number of old and decrepit people in the town. Young Keswickians left their homes for employment elsewhere: as the petition quaintly put it, 'the young and vigorous, attracted by the superior opportunities for the prosecution of business, are lead to increase the healthy population of other towns, thus leaving in Keswick a large proportion of feeble and aged to give an unfair complexion to the bills of mortality.' Healthy paupers, it was claimed, were removed to provide accommodation for the old and dying, distorting the mortality rate even further.

The original petitioners won their case and in April 1852, Robert Rawlinson arrived in Keswick to conduct an 'inquiry into the sewerage, drainage and supply of water, and the sanitary condition of the inhabitants of the town and township of Keswick'.

Rawlinson, a civil engineer, had had considerable experience in the building trade. He had worked out a scheme for supplying Liverpool with water from Lake Bala and had taken part in a civil commission (the first ever sent to an army in the field) to improve sanitary conditions for the troops in the Crimean War. He organised vast numbers of unemployed men in Lancashire in the 1860s into constructing public improvements on a large scale, a programme that earned him the Companionship of the Bath. As one of the first inspectors under the 1848 Public Health Act, he supervised inquiries at many towns from Sunderland to Wigan, Carlisle to Devonport – and Keswick.

With such tested expertise and wide experience at his command, he quickly modified the descriptions of the directories. Keswick may have been 'a small but neat market town, consisting of one long street of good houses' but, Rawlinson pointed out, there were offshoots and lanes, yards and courts, which were far from neat and good. 'Houses and tenements,' he reported, 'are crowded with foul middens and are encroached upon by privies, with large open cesspools, by pigsties, stables, cowsheds, and by slaughter houses.' Refuse from these stagnated or drained away, polluting the subsoil and contaminating the air.

An artist's impression of the Lower Market Place in 1867

Many of the cottages were small, with low ceilings and poor ventilation. Rising damp was common, walls were rotten, drains were foul. Water closets were a luxury: out of sixty inhabitants at Brigham Row, forty-seven had no privy.

Domestic water in the town was supplied by some ninety pumps and wells. Many had been out of order for years; others were unfit for use because of infiltration from surface refuse. The bulk of the poorer inhabitants had no water rights and were obliged to get their supplies wherever they could. The sixty people at Brigham Row relied on the river Greta; at the Forge, workmen apart, seventy people had to share one open trough and one privy.

Rawlinson's limited inspection uncovered a rash of horrifying sores on the face of the town. Near Keswick Bridge there was an outlet which discharged liquid refuse from the gasworks and soil refuse from the town direct into the Greta near a place where people drew water. In James Atkinson's Yard, Rawlinson found a cottage where in summer maggots crawled about the floor. Miss Hutton's Yard had a pump which was said to supply half the town but the drain under the houses was so foul that when Miss Hutton's nephew visited her, 'the effluvium made him vomit'. There were at least four slaughter houses adding further refuse to a primitive and overloaded disposal system

The evidence from James Ivison's property pinpoints the problems. In wet weather, his cellar was flooded and had to be baled out once or twice a day. The pump in his yard was more or less worn out and the water it produced had a brackish taste and was unfit for domestic use. The ashpit and privy were near the well, with consequent danger from overflow and seepage. The privy, serving three properties, eight families and the workmen in a tallow-chandler's manufactory, was 'kept in a most disgusting state, not fit for anyone to enter'.

If Mr Ivison opened the window at the back of his house, everything was covered in soot from the tallow-chandler's chimney and offensive smells drifted in from the rendering of the tallow. He had his own water-closet partly fitted up but he had been refused permission to construct a drain from it and had to suffer the inconvenience of sharing the common privy.

As the water from the pump was so bad, the Ivisons had to get it as best they could from neighbours and other sources, often a quarter of a mile away. On the day he wrote his letter of evidence to Rawlinson, it took the servant girl two hours to carry the day's supply, after she had been refused the use of three pumps.

Inevitably, knowing that Rawlinson was to visit and inspect the town, the locals had made an effort to clean the streets and yards. Channels had been washed out, cesspools emptied and midden refuse removed. The oldest inhabitant said he had never seen the place so free from filth and looking so sweet and comfortable. Rawlinson was not deceived by the show of cosmetic superficiality.

Statistics supplied by Dr Lietch, a local medical practitioner, revealed mortality rates that supported Rawlinson's strictures. Between 1845 and 1850, there were 286 deaths – an average of twenty-three per thousand which contrasted sharply with Brampton near Carlisle at seventeen or Dolgelly in Wales at sixteen per thousand. Moreover, out of the 286 deaths, eighty-two were infants under the age of one year, 130 were men and women under the age of twenty. In other words, a very high proportion of children born in Keswick never reached adulthood.

Not everybody accepted these figures. An anonymous pamphlet by 'A Keswickian', dated 9 March 1853 and based on the 'indisputable correctness' of details for 1852, claimed that the mortality rate was only fifteen per thousand and that the rate of deaths of infants under one year old was one in nine, not one in four. Keswick's rate of mortality at one in sixty-five compared favourably with the southern counties at one in fifty-two, Durham City's one in thirty-one, and that of the country at one in forty-five. The average age at which people died in Darlington and Sunderland, for example, was twenty-four; in Keswick, it was thirty-five. Keswick's working classes lived eighteen years longer than those of Leeds and twenty-two years longer than those of Liverpool. Which set of statistics is right? Perhaps it would be sensible to accept the figures of a qualified doctor as more reliable than those of an indignant and anonymous objector.

Rawlinson also revealed some disturbing details about the five common lodging-houses in the town. Together, they mustered twelve rooms and twenty-six beds: in five years a total of 33,114 (22,546 males and 10,568 females) stayed in these cramped hovels, where beds were within a foot of one another. The proprietors charged from a penny to three-pence a night; their clients were not just the harmless and the unfortunate but also thieves, criminals and professional vagrants – for Southey, writing in 1831, the 'vermin' who carried infectious diseases to and from 'the dens of filth and inquity' where they stayed.

Rawlinson's recommendations were far-reaching. A Local Board of Health was essential to administer and oversee the essential reforms – adequate and efficient sewers and drains, paved streets, a clean and readily available supply of water from local waterworks, the regulation of slaughter-houses and common lodging houses, the provision of baths and wash-houses.

Action followed, though the evils were not swept away over-night and overcrowding in the yards in particular continued for many years. A Ministry of Health report for 1879 still declared that some of the back-courts 'vie with the condemned slums of our large towns and are the nurseries of disease associated with over-crowding'.

A Local Board of Health was inaugurated in 1853. Over the years, a supply of potable water from Skiddaw was harnessed, first by a Waterworks Company formed in 1856 and subsequently in 1879 by the Local Authority. By the end of the 1870s, the mortality rate had fallen to fifteen per thousand: in 1876, the Sanitary Record, the authoritative source of statistics on health, stated that the death rate in Keswick was 'the lowest yet registered in any part of the United Kingdom'.

Apart from its primary purpose, Rawlinson's report includes significant statistics about Keswick a century and half ago. The total number of houses in the town and its immediate environs was 580, made up of 454 private houses, fifty-five shops with houses attached, seventeen inns and beerhouses and fifty-four other dwellings. The rateable value of property on 3 January 1852 was £4,569.8.9; a rate of sevenpence half-penny in the pound produced £142.15.0½. Two burial grounds were available, neither over-crowded: 6,050 square yards at Crosthwaite, 8,016 at St John's.

The local gasworks were established in 1845: four retorts were on site, though never more than three were needed to produce an annual output of about a million cubic feet of gas. There were thirty-three public lamps in the town. The population was about 2,400, with 111 paupers. The police constable, the sole representative of a force set up about 1840, reported that there had been a peak of nearly 9,000 vagrants in 1849: the prospect of some 170 tramps descending on Keswick each week is difficult to believe but presumably the constable's figures were accurate. What crime there was, he insisted, was committed by these invaders, not by the local inhabitants.

Rawlinson's report makes fascinating though disturbing reading. At least it appears to have spurred the leading citizens into action, though there was considerable concern about the cost to ratepayers of any proposed improvements.

The arrival of the next invaders was to transform the town and make it all the more imperative that a clean water supply, efficient drains and adequate sanitary arrangements were available.

John Fisher Crosthwaite

RIBBLE

11

Coaches and Engines

In his evidence to Rawlinson's Inquiry, Mr Frank of the Queen's Head Hotel claimed that up to 15,000 tourists invaded Keswick in a summer season. Most of them would travel by stage-coach, a form of transport that operated in Cumbria from the mid 1700s. The first stage-coach went over Shap in 1763. By the 1780s, the local network was firmly established, both for passengers and freight and in particular for mail. A regular service based on Carlisle, Whitehaven and Kendal linked the other towns in the county, including Keswick. In 1781, a ten-hour journey from Whitehaven to Penrith via Keswick cost 12s, with children on lap charged half-price.

Traditionally, the first local coach service from Keswick to Cockermouth was organised in 1822 by Mr Banks, a tanner who lived at Shu-le-Crow in Penrith Road. The coach was driven over Whinlatter Pass by a well-known local character, Bob McCade or Bob Kegg as he was called. Two years later, in 1824, Jack Cawx claimed the honour of driving the first coach into Borrowdale, a hazardous journey that almost ended in disaster near Grange Bridge.

Parson and White's *Directory* of 1829 lists two regular coaches at Keswick. The Royal Mail left the Royal Oak daily at six in the morning for Cockermouth, Workington and Whitehaven and at six-thirty in the evening for Ambleside and Kendal. The Defiance went to Whitehaven on Mondays, Wednesdays and Fridays, leaving the Queen's Head at noon; an hour later, on Tuesdays and Thursdays, the destination was Penrith.

By 1858, daily runs were scheduled from Keswick to West Cumberland, Penrith and Windermere, Sundays excepted. The *Cumberland Pacquet* of 22 July 1862 reports that twenty-two coaches a day were operating in and out of the town, with a further two added a little later, 'a circumstance that no other town in the kingdom can boast of'.

Some indication of the volume of traffic may be gleaned from a couple of figures. In the year November 1843 to November 1844, just over 11,800 passengers were recorded at the toll-bar at Plumgarths just north of Kendal on the Windermere road. In 1855, a total of 21,480 passengers went through Troutbeck Bridge between Windermere and Ambleside: of these, 15,420 continued their journey to Grasmere and Keswick.

The popular Keswick to Windermere run was operated by several entrepreneurs. Mr Bowden of the Royal Oak had seven four-in-hands on the route each day in the season but the best known operator was Riggs of Windermere Hotel, which dates from 1847. By 1897, this family concern owned almost all the coaches south of Dunmail Raise – fifteen with 150 horses ready to pull them. The brightly coloured black and yellow coaches, driven by 'Robin Redbreasts', as the red-coated and white box-hatted drivers were called, bounced along at a steady twelve miles an hour, a familiar and often very welcome sight on the road to and from Keswick until 1920 when Riggs withdrew their service over Dunmail Raise.

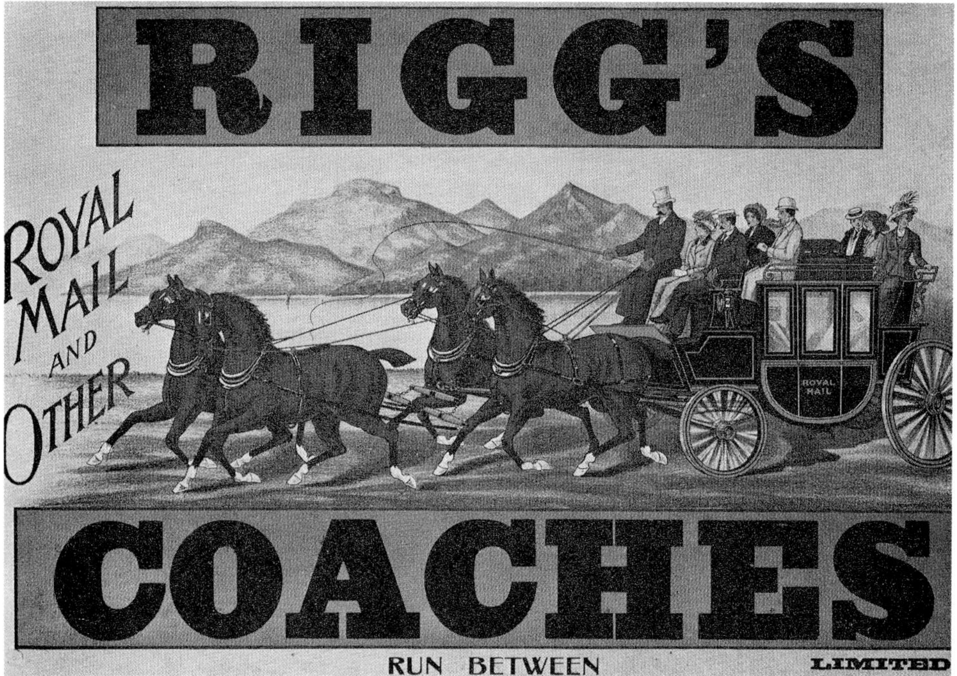

A 'Robin Redbreast' cracks the whip

Fares for the journey of about three and three quarters of an hour from Windermere to Keswick varied from seven shillings for outside seats to nine shillings for inside. The Sportsman, with Ernie Hargreaves at the reins, went for speed and clocked up just under three hours for the twenty-four mile journey. Tom Harrison, a fellow coachman, claimed a grand total of 31,000 miles on the route in twenty-three years.

One minor calamity on the Keswick to Windermere run has gone down in history. A guard named Jim Arnold told the story of an accident at Roughhow Bridge near Shoulthwaite when the Whitehaven mail collided with a pony chaise. The driver of the light vehicle, which was smashed to pieces, was sent flying over the wall into a plantation. Fortunately, he was unhurt: he dusted himself down, vowing he would have the incident thoroughly investigated. The victim of this encounter was William Wordsworth.

Local hoteliers were quick to realise the potential of coach rides for visitors. The trip into Borrowdale from Keswick, over Honister Pass to Buttermere and return by Newlands became a very popular tourist attraction, combining superb scenery and a taste of adventure. On the steeper ascents, passengers got out of the coach and walked; the dangerous descents were treated with great respect. Guidebooks assured nervous clients that 'the drivers attach considerable value to their own necks'.

Coaches for the 'Buttermere Round' left the Market Square at about half past nine and were back in Keswick in time for dinner. The chatter and banter of intending passengers would mingle with the clatter of hooves and the metallic ring of iron-hooped wheels. Short ladders were on hand for climbing into the high seats of the four-in-hand or char-a-banc. Ladies normally wore hats with veils as a sensible protection against the dust that rose in clouds on dry days. The umbrella-basket at the back of the coach was stocked with means of minimal shelter when it rained. Once the seats were full and everybody was settled, there was a toot on the horn, a crack of the whip and they were off.

Jenkinson's *Guide* of 1892 quotes a charge of five shillings for the round trip, plus a shilling for the driver – 'certainly the best and cheapest drive in the Lake District'. A three-hour stop at Buttermere allowed time for a meal at one of the hotels and an excursion to Scale Force by boat at one shilling a head.

Alongside the coaches, four-in-hands and char-a-bancs catering for passenger traffic, Keswick carriers were busy transporting goods. Parson and White's *Directory* of 1829 lists three carriers operating from two warehouses, Robinson's and Walker's, both at High Hill. Slotted into the county-wide network of traffic to and from other towns, Keswick's contribution suggests an adequate provision for the movement of merchandise, supplemented by local carriers whose business was confined to the town and neighbouring villages.

These local horse-drawn deliveries continued for many years but in Slater's *Directory* of 1869 there is no mention of carriers operating further afield. Transport had been revolutionised by another invader: the iron horse.

The railway line from Newcastle to Carlisle was open for traffic by 1838, Lancaster to Carlisle by Penrith and Carlisle to Workington by 1846, and Workington to Cockermouth by 1847. Two factors underlined the logical extension eastwards from Cockermouth to Penrith. One was the invention in 1856 by Henry Bessemer of a new process for converting pig iron into steel; the other was parliamentary approval in 1857 for a line from Darlington to Penrith over Stainmore.

Essential for the Bessemer process were the rich iron ore of West Cumberland and the coking coal of Durham: local Cumbrian coal was unsuitable. The two-way traffic of coal and ore followed the Carlisle-Newcastle route: a direct line from Workington to Darlington by Keswick and Penrith offered an obvious solution to the growing problem of efficient transportation, though no doubt the promoters of the line were fully aware of its future potential for passenger traffic.

The original prospectus issued in 1860 clearly indicated the prime function of the new railway: 'the Line will complete the communication between the Iron Ore Districts and Blast Furnaces of Cumberland and the Iron and Coal Districts of Middlesboro' and South Durham, materially lessening the Railway transit to and from these places – an advantage of the greatest importance in the carriage of heavy materials such as Coke and Iron Ore'.

Various routes were suggested: the one finally adopted was that surveyed in 1859 by Thomas Bouch, engineer of the Stainmore line and for ever remembered as the architect-designer of the ill-fated Tay Bridge.

The first sod of the Cockermouth-Keswick-Penrith line, known locally as the CKP, was cut in a field near Crosthwaite Church on 21 May 1862, a red-letter day in the story of Keswick, celebrated with jollifications reminiscent of a carnival. Shops were closed; a procession of soldiers and clergy, local dignitaries and hundreds of children marched to the ceremony to the music of three bands. A special wheelbarrow and spade were made by local craftsmen: they may still be seen in the Fitz Park Musuem.

The pivot figure was the chairman of the newly formed company, Mr Thomas Hoskins of Higham Hall near Bassenthwaite. His speech and those that followed at the official dinner at the Derwentwater Hotel (twenty-five speeches and toasts) extolled the virtues of the CKP. The line would restore Keswick to its rightful inheritance as the metropolis of the Lake District and bring prosperity to its flagging economy.

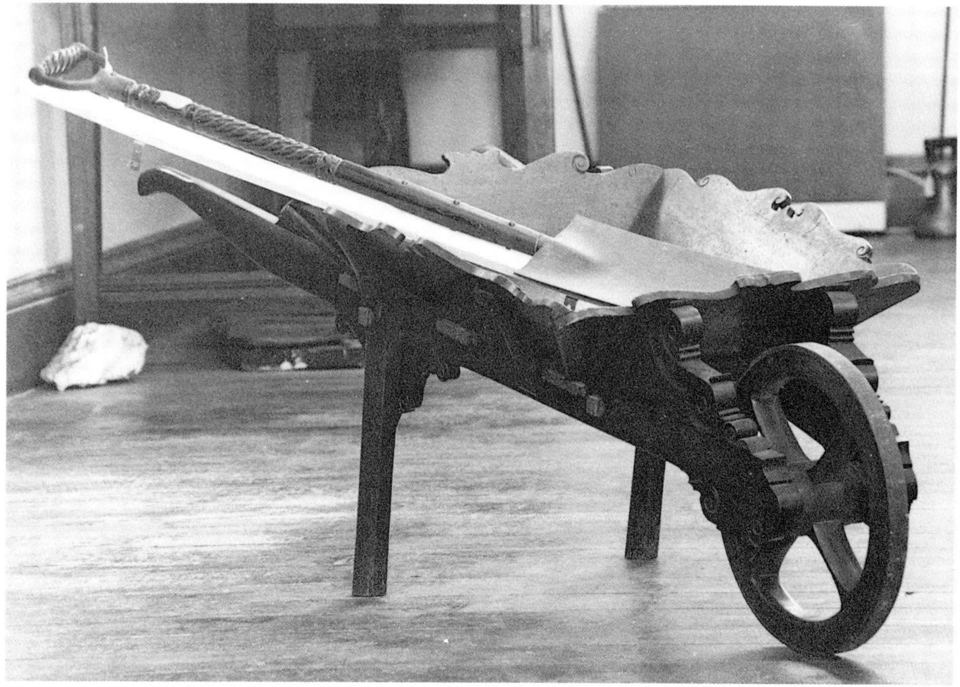

The C K P railway wheelbarrow and spade on display

Work began the following day. The contractors were George Boulton and Son of Newcastle and the estimated cost was some £267,000 or just over £8,000 a mile.

The arrival of the first locomotive in Keswick on 23 July 1863 was another gala occasion. Fourteen horses dragged it through the town, an object of awed wonder for most Keswickians who had never seen a railway engine before. A procession headed for Browfoot Cutting where the iron monster was duly placed on the newly laid rails.

The project took three years to complete. The line was open for mineral traffic on 4 November 1864 and for passengers on 2 January 1865 – six months later than the contractual date and only after a fastidious Board of Trade inspector had discovered a dozen faults that had to be rectified before the line could be officially authorised as safe for passengers.

The thirty-one miles of track were single throughout, with passing loops at Bassenthwaite Lake, Keswick and Penruddock. 135 bridges had to be built, the longest being the Mosedale Viaduct of 404 feet and twelve arches. Between Cockermouth and Penrith, there were eight stations: Embleton, Bassenthwaite Lake, Braithwaite, Keswick, Threlkeld, Troutbeck, Penruddock and Blencow.

Pressure from various sources, including the County Council Education Committee and the redoubtable Canon Rawnsley, was responsible for a special halt at Highgate, a remote farm between Threlkeld and Troutbeck. Here, on 17 August 1908, a service was inaugurated, exclusively for a dozen or so children from nearby farms, taking them to and from school in Threlkeld. It lasted for twenty years, until January 1929, when the children began to travel by bus.

A second special halt at Briery, a mile east of Keswick, was built in the early 1920s for workers at the Bobbin Mill. Along with the mill, it closed in November 1958, but its truncated, sturdy remains can still be seen as part of the holiday cottages and caravan complex known as Low Briery Village.

Mindful of the serious riots which had disturbed the construction of the Lancaster to Carlisle railway in 1846, the directors of the CKP appointed the Rev. G Trueman of Wythop and the Rev. W Whitelegg of Threlkeld as chaplains to the large work-force of navvies in the hope that the active presence of the two clergymen would help to avoid violence. A temporary chapel was provided at Embleton and in Keswick meetings were organised for the social and moral welfare of the men. In December 1863, for example, over 150 workmen sat down to tea in Brigham School, fussed over by a group of local ladies and subjected to several addresses 'on various topics suited to the capacities of men in their station of life'.

Within a few years of the line being completed, problems arose. False economy had decreed that only light iron rails were used for the track. They proved inadequate and in the 1870s were replaced by steel rails and heavier 'chairs' to carry them. The considerable cost meant that any plans for the essential doubling of the line had to be cancelled. There were sections of double track from Troutbeck to Penruddock and Blencow to Redhills Junction near Penrith but the prohibitive outlay for two lines over a route with so many cuttings, tunnels and bridges precluded any scheme for improvement throughout its full length.

From time to time, alterations were made to Keswick Station. The subway, built in 1873, was extended twenty years later; platforms were lengthened and refurbished in the 1890s; loops were added to the tracks and a locomotive turntable installed. A prominent water-tank dating from 1864 was enlarged in 1880. An attractive glazed roof protected much of both Up and Down platforms; the provision of electric light made Keswick unique on the CKP for many years; telephones arrived in 1910. The weigh-house in the adjoining goods yard was a distinctive feature, its tall finials giving the appearance of a miniature pagoda.

The stationmaster's house was built in 1865. In 1898 a small suspension bridge spanned the Greta opposite what is today the Millfield Retirement Home: it provided a convenient and popular short cut to the station but had to be closed some years ago on grounds of safety.

From about 1865 to 1873, a refreshment room was available on the station. W.H. Smith and Sons opened a bookstall in 1871: it was taken over by their rivals, Wyman and Sons, from 1909 to the 1950s, except for a period of ten years in the 1920s when it was run by Chaplin's, the well-known Keswick stationer and bookseller.

The station forecourt was always a busy area. Passengers emerging from the arrival platform were faced with a row of horse-drawn conveyances belonging to the various hotels in the town. The major establishments were allowed to have a representative on the platform itself but by the 1930s this privilege was restricted to the Keswick Hotel only.

Keswick Hotel, still the largest in the town

This impressive hotel, with all the solid elegance of local stone and Victorian standards of comfort, dominated the forecourt. Built in the 1860s and administered by a subsidiary of the CKP company, it was strategically sited and even incorporated a covered way on to the station platform – a most welcome refinement protecting guests from the vagaries of Keswick weather. From the 1880s, the hotel was in the hands of the Wivell family, first as managers and later as proprietors; since 1945, it has changed hands several times. Among its many distinguished guests, who have included royalty and celebrities from all over the world, were the girls of Roedean School, who were evacuated to Keswick during the Second World War.

Keswick, suitably located midway between Cockermouth and Penrith, was ideally situated as the CKP headquarters, and here, from the 1860s, the Board of Directors used to meet. The station building not only provided the essentials for working the line – platforms, ticket office, waiting rooms; it also incorporated a Board Room and offices for the secretary, the traffic manager and the accountant.

The station staff were very conscious of their unique position on the line. For many years, the stationmaster adopted a uniform of frock coat and top hat, letting the world know that Keswick was every bit as important as Carlisle or Euston.

Apart from its original function as a carrier of coke and iron ore, the CKP rapidly expanded the range of materials it handled: granite and roadstone from Embleton and Threlkeld quarries; lead from Braithwaite and Threlkeld mines; limestone from Blencow and Flusco; slate from Honister; pit props from Bassenthwaite Lake; sheep and cattle from Cockermouth and Troutbeck; and from 1870 the mail, which was carried from Keswick to Penrith for an annual charge of £225.

The volume of freight traffic was closely linked with the fluctuating fortunes of West Cumberland and its industries. Competition from the coastal route to Carlisle, strikes, slumps in demand, the production of suitable local coking coal, the great depression of the 1930s: all contributed to a variable amount of traffic and eventually to the decline of the railway itself.

From its inception and particularly later when goods traffic decreased, the CKP was seen as a line for passengers. Its popularity was immediate. On Easter Monday 1865, just three months after the first passenger train, 1200 visitors arrived at Keswick station. In May 1866, the first excursion trains of the season brought between 3000 and 4000 people from Preston for the equivalent of 15p return.

Local clergy condemned Sunday excursions, a restriction no doubt strongly supported by Mr Peter Thompson, secretary and manager of the CKP from 1870 and a Board member from 1913. He was a man of strict non-conformist principles and regarded Sunday as a day of religious observance and obligations, not an opportunity to cavort in the Lake District.

By the early 1900s, eight or nine daily trains were running on the CKP. In the summer months, the 'Lakes Express' ran daily to and from Euston and regular excursions from the conurbations of northern England and southern Scotland ensured the continuing prosperity of the line.

The arrival of the internal combustion engine and the upgrading and extension of the local road network began to gnaw away at the fortunes of the CKP. The introduction of diesel units in 1955, among the first in Britain, provided a change of emphasis and something of a temporary boost, though steam fans resented the passing of their beloved locomotives and in particular the distinctive 'Cauliflower' engines that had run on the line for so many years.

By the 1960s, British Rail claimed that the CKP was losing up to £56,000 a year and urgent repairs and renewals would cost nearly £90,000. Passenger statistics were depressingly low: on a typical summer day, 262 people alighted at Keswick from Penrith and eighty-nine travelled from Keswick to Penrith. In winter, the corresponding figures were ninety-nine and forty-three. At Troutbeck, only fourteen passengers a day used the station.

The solution was obvious but painful. Economic factors triumphed over local protests and in 1963 the Beeching Report recommended closure. Goods traffic came to an end in 1964; the last passenger train from Workington to Cockermouth and Keswick ran on 16 April 1966. On 6 March 1972, Keswick and Penrith Round Tables organised the final rites for the line between the two towns. Some 450 enthusiasts packed the 'Farewell Special'; Keswickians in large numbers waved the train away on its final journey – a sad occasion described by the Chairman of the Urban District Council as rather like an Irish wake, with the mourners putting on a brave face to hide their sorrows. Short term economy had triumphed and one of the most attractive railways in Britain disappeared. There would be no more views through carriage windows of thirty miles of superb scenery; no more gasps of admiration at the colourful gardens of Bassenthwaite Lake and Braithwaite stations; no more Sunday services, complete with resident harmonium, in Troutbeck station premises; no more sounds of the bagpipes at Blencow as stationmaster George Gaskarth marched up and down the platform in full Scottish regalia.

The closure of the CKP also put an end to a proposal that had been aired from time to time since the line opened. A railway had reached Windermere in 1847: the logical plan was to extend it to Ambleside and Keswick to link with the CKP. Opposition was strong. As early as 1844, Wordsworth had condemned the Kendal to Windermere line: 'Is there no nook of English ground secure From rash assault?' his famous sonnet questioned.

In the 1870s, Robert Somervell, a Kendal business man, spearheaded the attack on the suggested extension to Keswick. Ruskin, then resident at Coniston, was roused to fierce indignation. For him, railways were 'the loathsomest form of devilry...carriages of damned souls on the ridges of their own graves', and he envisaged 'stupid herds of modern tourists' being deposited like coals from a sack at Windermere and Keswick.

A bill before Parliament in 1877 to promote the building of a line from Windermere to Ambleside was welcomed in Keswick as the first step in a railway over Dunmail Raise. Later ideas suggested an Ambleside Light Railway, a narrow gauge tramway, and in 1921 the use of special locomotives to minimise noise and smoke emission on the Ambleside to Keswick route. Can we be sure that the dream is dead? Serious proposals to help in solving the growing problems of road traffic congestion hint at the introduction of light railways. Ratty serves Eskdale well, so why not a miniature railway in Langdale or Borrowdale...or over Dunmail Raise?

The streams of cars that rush over the Raise today are the prolific descendants of an invader that nosed its way into the Lake District a century ago. The internal combustion engine has changed the face of the area even more decisively than the railway did.

In 1900 it was estimated that there were only 800 motor cars in the whole of Britain – frail, awkward-looking contraptions, with narrow wheels and minimum protection against the elements...a world away from today's sleek and speedy models. In that year, the Thousand Mile Motor Trial passed through Keswick. Sixty-five vehicles left London for Edinburgh and back: twenty-three completed the Trial. The message of this venture was clear: the car was capable of travelling long distances and was here to stay.

Not surprisingly, there is some debate about the owner of the first car in Keswick. It is generally accepted that George Abraham's Sunbeam Mobley, which appeared on the streets in 1902, was number one but claims have been made for a car owned by the Blacks of Underscar as the first and for Dr Crawfurd's De Dion as the second. In 1904, Edwin Quirk was driving his eight-horse-power Darracq: until a few years ago, it was given an airing now and then – and a fine sight it was, with paint-work gleaming, polished metal shining and hardly a speck of dust in evidence.

The age of the motor car has arrived

These primitive vehicles were not universally welcomed. Their noisy engines frightened horses as the cars sped along, sometimes at over twelve miles an hour, churning up clouds of dust on the unsurfaced highways. By 1905, Cumberland County Council was receiving complaints about the damage that cars were causing. 'Our beautiful roads,' wrote one objector, 'are being ruined by the sucking action of motorists' rubber tyres.'

Other locals saw a new public transport age ahead. The *Westmorland Gazette* reported in January 1905 that 'the experiment made last season in the employment of motor cars between Windermere and Keswick is stated to have proved so successful as to encourage those who undertook the enterprise to place orders for numerous steam motor cars to be employed during the coming season on this route'.

Public bus services were soon introduced. By 1910 Quirk's garage in Keswick was advertising daily Red Motor Charabanc trips round Bassenthwaite, Derwentwater, Thirlmere and along Applethwaite Terrace. In 1912, the Whitehaven Motor Service Company was set up; in 1921 it expanded into the Cumberland Motor Services Ltd. and increased the number of its routes, among them Whitehaven to Keswick via Workington and Cockermouth. Keswick to Penrith followed in 1928 and Keswick to Carlisle in 1929. The Kendal to Keswick service, particularly important for tourists, was inaugurated by Ribble Motor Services in 1927.

Keswick Bus Station, a well-built and adequately equipped complex with superb views of the surrounding fells, was opened in June 1933. As well as garaging for nine buses, it had offices and staff accommodation, two shops and a cafe. For many years, it was a bustling, busy centre, with buses to and from county destinations supplemented by long distance coaches and excursion traffic from many parts of the country. With a dramatic decline in bus usage in the 1980s, it was sold as a site for a supermarket, with minimal provision for the skeleton public bus service that continues to operate.

The Borrowdale service has always been something of a unique enterprise. A bus of sorts ran before the First World War; in 1920, John Woodend of Seatoller found his old chain-driven Daimler was challenged by Mr W F Askew's strange contraption – the body of a horse-drawn wagonette hitched on to a Ford chassis.

By 1928, five companies operated in the summer months. The first bus for Seatoller left Keswick at seven o'clock in the morning, the last at 8.50 at night, with a twenty minute service in between and a special 'pictures' bus at 9.50 every Saturday to cater for cinema goers. Many travellers will remember journeys when the bus was packed tight and the load was reduced to legal limits on the outskirts of the town.

The narrow, twisting valley road, snow and floods, tested the skill and patience of the drivers of the Borrowdale buses. A record free of any serious accidents is proof enough of the competence of men like Sid Simpson (one of the first men in the north of England to drive a vehicle with pneumatic tyres) and genial John Atkinson, who reckoned he had driven about 900,000 miles up and down the valley on an estimated 55,000 round trips since 1929.

On Whit Sunday 1915, a traffic census at the Royal Oak corner in the centre of Keswick recorded 547 cars, 371 motor-bikes, 841 bicycles and 258 horse-drawn vehicles. Twenty years later in 1935, a report concluded that 'some believe that Keswick loses a good deal of business during the season owing to the congestion both in and around the town and that many motorists avoid Keswick because of the difficulty of moving about the town and in and out of it during the busy times'.

It is a comment that could have been written in any year since 1935 as the flow of traffic has grown to almost unbearable proportions. The M6 and A66 have brought ten million people within a three-hour drive of the Lake District and there are days when they all seem to have converged on Keswick!

12

Call to Arms

The effects of the rapid increase of visitors, as rail and road transport improved, were compounded by the demands of industry and the pressures for enhanced amenities for the country's growing population. The Lake District was menaced by invaders who threatened to destroy the landscape and the rural peace which the visitors came to enjoy.

Between 1851 and 1864, the demand for water in the city of Manchester trebled: where better than the lakes of Cumberland and Westmorland to satisfy this ever-increasing thirst? Ullswater and Haweswater were considered and rejected; in 1876, Alderman Grave, born in Cockermouth and owner of a house in Portinscale, suggested Thirlmere.

The old bridges spanning the narrows of Thirlmere

At 533 feet above sea level, it was high enough to feed water to Manchester by gravity. Some 11,000 acres drained into the lake and eighty-one inches of rainfall annually ensured water in plenty. There were few problems in building a dam in the ravine at the northern end of the lake.

The surface area of about 330 acres was in two parts, pinched to a narrow gap near the middle. Here an old-fashioned bridge of stone piers connected by wooden walkways and variously identified as Celtic or Roman spanned the water, carrying a track from Dale Head Hall on the east to Armboth House on the west.

The proposed reservoir would more than double the surface area to nearly 800 acres and the capacity would increase to over 8,000 million gallons. A ninety-five mile aqueduct through tunnels, pipes and 'cut and cover' would carry fifty million gallons a day to Manchester.

Owners of the affected property were not in favour of the scheme until carrots of cash were dangled before them. The most protracted and troublesome dispute was over the 1,550 acres and five farms owned by Countess Ossalinsky, who had inherited the land and property of her grandfather, Mr Jackson. Manchester estimated her estate at a maximum of £25,000: The Countess's valuers produced a figure of £100,000. The case went to arbitration and she was awarded £70,000.

The other principal objector was Thomas Leathes Stanger-Leathes, Lord of the Manor of Legburthwaite and owner of both Thirlmere and the Dale Head Hall estate. The property had belonged to the Leathes family since 1577, a claim to possession enshrined in the old name for the lake of Leathes Water. There used to be an inscription on a stained glass window at Dale Head Hall (now a hotel) which read: 'Cristopherus Laythes, hoc Dom. Aedif. AD 1623'.

The death of Thomas Leathes in 1876 conveniently left the way clear for purposeful negotiations between his son and heir, George, and Manchester. After twenty years in Australia, he was not restricted by any obstinate family pride and Manchester, in spite of vigorous opposition from other members of the Leathes family, succeeded in buying the estate.

Negotiations with Sir Henry Vane for the Manor of Wythburn and property adjoining the lake proceeded much more smoothly; other owners, like those at the 'City', a tiny hamlet that belied its name, were less amenable and their houses and acres on the lake shore were bought only after protracted and hard bargaining.

As Manchester's proposed intentions became clearer, there was considerable opposition to what many people, locally and nationally, regarded as desecration of a unique and beautiful landscape: the *Spectator*, for example, found the Thirlmere development 'very big, very ugly and very revolting'. A Defence Association was formed, with Robert Somervell as secretary, men of the stature of Ruskin and Carlyle as committee members and a formidable phalanx of ecclesiastical dignitaries, academics and others in support.

Alderman Harwood, chairman of the Waterworks Committee, succeeded in persuading many local people of the economic advantages of the scheme. The temptations of financial gain were great, so great that even the secretary of the Defence Association resigned and signed the memorial in favour of the reservoir. On the other hand, some Keswick residents feared that the town might be flooded when the sluice gates were opened – and there was always the danger of the dam bursting.

The parliamentary bill authorising the works received the Royal Assent on 23 May 1879. The negotiations of wayleaves with some 200 owners and 400 lessees and tenants, plus a trade depression in the city, meant that construction did not begin until early in 1886.

On 22 August 1890, using his specially inscribed silver trowel, Alderman Harwood laid the foundation stone of the Thirlmere Embankment. A new road, warmly welcomed in

Keswick, was built on the west side of the lake and opened for public use on 3 February 1894. To accommodate the army of workmen, some forty temporary huts were erected at Legburthwaite, Armboth and Wythburn; one building served as school, chapel and recreation room; a cottage was converted into a small hospital with a resident nurse. Trade in Keswick certainly increased, particularly in the public houses. Some horrendous cases of drunkenness, including fatalities, came before the magistrates but, considering the numbers involved, good order prevailed and petty crimes were few.

The works were officially opened on 12 October 1894 by Alderman Sir John Harwood. Among the large crowd of eminent supporters was the Rev. Hardwicke Rawnsley. The fiery opponent of any unsympathetic development in his beloved Lakeland had been persuaded that the Thirlmere project was of sufficient benefit to the citizens of Manchester to override any other considerations. His capitulation was clear from the opening words of his prayer at the ceremony: 'We bless Thee, O Heavenly Father, for the love that inspired this vast design, the wisdom that planned and oversaw, the patience that endured to its completeness...'. There must have been many a wry smile from the city fathers to hear Lakeland's doughty champion bestowing so fulsome a tribute on their efforts.

The Rock of Names

Rawnsley deserves a word of credit for his attempt to salvage 'The Rock of Names'. In 1802, Wordsworth, his sister Dorothy, his brother John, his wife Mary, her sister Sara, and Coleridge carved their initials on a rock at Black Crag by the side of the old turnpike road. The rock was blown up but Rawnsley managed to collect the fragments and had them built into a cairn which was located in the wood above the new main road just north of the straining well. The site was seldom visited and the stone was preserved from further vandalism: with perseverance, it was possible to decipher the initials. In 1984, not without opposition, the rock and its inscription were removed to the garden of Dove Cottage at Grasmere.

Even after water began to flow from Thirlmere in October 1894, objections continued. The ugly exposed rim as the level of the lake fluctuated was roundly condemned but little could be done to alleviate the eyesore of a permanent scar that, in times of drought, expanded into acres of arid moonlike landscape.

Although footpaths to Helvellyn and the Armboth fells were open to walkers and two trails, Swirls and Launchy Gill, were available, access to the shore of the Lake was prohibited for nearly a century. Only in recent years, with more enlightened attitudes to recreational facilities and the installation of more sophisticated methods of filtration, have opportunities for walking on the lake shore been provided. Fortunately, powered craft are not allowed on the lake and the peace of Thirlmere – a comparative term in view of roads and traffic on both sides of the lake – remains one of its most attractive features.

The blanket planting of some 2,000 acres of conifers from 1908 aroused considerable disquiet but trees were essential to stabilise the gathering-grounds – and Manchester opted for a quick-growing cash crop. For a century no-one thought of challenging the authority's right to grow whatever trees they wished. But in January 1985, a surprising attack was made by a private individual. It was a David and Goliath contest in which one woman, alone and unrepresented, took on the might of the North West Water Authority, successors to Manchester Corporation, together with its lawyers and technical experts.

Before Keswick magistrates, Mrs Susan Johnson accused the authority of failing to comply with the Waterworks Act of 1879 which required that 'all reasonable regard shall be had to the preservation, as well for the public as for private owners, of the beauty of the scenery' and that the margin of the lake and its associated works should be planted with indigenous trees. Mrs Johnson submitted that these provisions had been ignored by the extensive use of conifers.

She won her case. The lawyers and experts were routed: the Authority promised to increase the planting of broad-leaved species and native shrubs and to soften the lines of the existing forest. It was an astonishing and singular triumph for a private individual: but Mrs Johnson was the daughter of the Rev. H H Symonds, the founder of the Friends of the Lake District, and fighting for conservation was in her blood.

About the time that the early preservationists were challenging Manchester's plans to convert Thirlmere into a reservoir, another battle was fought. In 1882, the Buttermere Green Slate Company was anxious to expand. It felt that any plans for growth were thwarted by the slow and laborious methods of transport they were forced to use – horse-drawn carts from the quarries at the top of Honister Pass to the railway station at Keswick.

They proposed the building of a single line from Braithwaite station, running along Catbells and over the narrow gap between Castle Crag and Lobstone Band to the top of Honister Pass.

Opposition to this defacing of Newlands and Borrowdale was immediate and unequivocal. It was led by the Rev. Hardwicke Rawnsley, the first example of his many fights to defend the Lake District from unsuitable development. He saw the dispute not as some parochial squabble but as a challenge to the thousands who came to the Lakes for peace and freedom from an urban environment. 'Let the slate train once roar along the western side of Derwentwater,' he thundered; 'let it once cross the lovely vale of Newlands, and Keswick as the resort of weary men in search of rest will cease to be.'

The battle seized public imagination and newspapers all over the country carried letters and articles in support of the objectors. The promoters of the scheme were not without a voice. Was a single line of narrow gauge railway any more disfiguring than a carriage road, they argued? Would it not benefit the economy of the district? Could it not be used for tourist as well as slate traffic?

The opposition carried the day and the parliamentary bill was withdrawn on the grounds of expense. Whatever else the Braithwaite-Honister railway dispute did, it plainly and forcefully singled out Rawnsley as the key figure in the struggle to protect the Lake District, a fearless, articulate, impassioned St George, ready and eager to take up arms against any dragon that dared to threaten his much loved Lakeland.

It was not long before he was once again spurred into action. Disturbed by the closure of footpaths in Scotland and around Ambleside, he proposed the revival of the Keswick and District Footpath Preservation Society. He was elected president, with H I Jenkinson as secretary and John Postlethwaite as treasurer. The presidency was offered to Mr J J Spedding, chairman of the Keswick magistrates, but he refused, declaring he wanted nothing to do with such 'socialistic societies'.

The crisis that persuaded Rawnsley to re-form the Footpath Preservation Society was the closure by Mrs Spencer Bell of Fawe Park of a right of way that ran from Nichol End beside her house to the foot of Catbells – once an old packhorse route but in 1886, as now, a popular footpath. Mrs Bell was adamant and took no notice of requests, deputations or remonstrances; she refused arbitration and had her gardener fasten a gate across the track, reinforced by barriers of brambles and bundles of sticks.

The time for action had arrived. On 30 August 1887, an attacking party of the Footpath Preservation Society headed for Fawe Park. Mrs Bell's emotional appeal was undermined by her accusation that the Association was hounding her unmercifully and that Keswick people were 'a lot of hungry sharks'. The protestors moved in and removed the gate and its attendant barriers, wire and thorn bushes, and seven large oak tree trunks: a horse-drawn carriage drove along the track, followed by an entourage of supporters on foot.

Mrs Bell was no craven foe. Stronger barriers were built; solicitors were engaged. The skirmishes continued, a ding-dong altercation with determined Keswickians tearing down the blockades until Mrs Bell finally capitulated.

The Fawe Park dispute roused local anger: the Latrigg Footpath closures earned national headlines. There were two routes to the summit of this popular fell. One was by Spooney Green Lane; the other was over Calvert Bridge and along the terrace above Greta Bank Farm. The owners of Latrigg, Miss Spedding and Mr J J Spedding, claimed it as their freehold under an Enclosure Act of 1814 and declared it to be private land.

When Spooney Green was reopened in 1864, the then owner of Latrigg, Mr Anthony Spedding, tried to close the terrace. The attempts rumbled on until the mid 1880s when locked gates, notice boards and wire fences began to appear and trees were planted over existing footpaths.

Keswick people were dismayed and disgusted with this interference with what they regarded as established rights of access. The crisis came in May 1887 when five youths were prosecuted for wilful damage to the extent of one shilling. The case was withdrawn in favour of more forceful action: Mr Spedding invited a deliberate trespass on the disputed path to engineer a legal confrontation which would settle the dispute. The Footpath Preservation Society agreed without hesitation: Henry Jenkinson saw the affair as a national test case for public access to the mountains.

The view from Latrigg in 1906

A preliminary assault on the gates and tar-soaked rubbish barriers in August 1887 was followed by a mass protest on 1 October 1887. 2,000 people, among them Samuel Plimsoll, MP, marched behind Jenkinson, singing 'Rule Britannia' and disposing of any obstructions on their way to the top of Latrigg. Rawnsley did not join the objectors. He appears to have been away from home at the time but his absence from any of the major footpath demonstrations is somewhat surprising for so fearless and forthright a campaigner.

As anticipated, Mr Spedding took the Association to court and on 6 July 1888 Rawnsley, Jenkinson and six other defendants appeared in Carlisle before Mr Justice Grantham and a special jury on charges of committing trespass. A number of local people with long memories gave evidence, among them the Rev. Cuthbert Southey, Robert Southey's son, who recalled that during his years at Greta Hall from 1819 to 1842 there were no restrictions on the use of the terrace path. The prosecution sought an injunction to stop further trespass: the defendants maintained their right to freedom of access. Judge Grantham suggested both sides should meet and an hour later the battle for Latrigg ended in compromise.

The Footpath Society abandoned its claim to the terrace path, even though they had produced overwhelming proof that it was a right of way: Mr Spedding conceded the route to Latrigg by Spooney Green was for public use. This final solution, tame whimper though it was after so vigorous a campaign, established a principle: it was a victory for freedom to roam on mountains and open spaces, a freedom cherished and defended in our own day.

Rawnsley's involvement in the Thirlmere reservoir and the Braithwaite to Honister railway disputes undoubtedly inspired his proposal for some sort of protective organisation. On 2 May 1883, just twenty days after the Braithwaite-Honister Railway Bill was withdrawn, he spoke at the fourth annual meeting of the Wordsworth Society. This august body of academics and eminent national personalities was formed in 1880 to promote the study of the poet's work and to unite those in sympathy with his ideas: with Matthew Arnold in the chair, it included among its members not only Worthsworthian scholars such as Professor William Knight and Professor Edward Dowden but also Robert Browning, Matthew Arnold, Lord Coleridge, John Ruskin and the Archbishop of Canterbury.

Such a group was certain to support Rawnsley's impassioned plea for the formation of a society 'to protect the Lake District from those injurious encroachments upon its scenery which are from time to time attempted from purely commercial or speculative motives, without regard to its claim as a national recreation ground'. He warned the meeting that there would be 'more invasions and desecrations of Lakeland': the ensuing century proved the truth of his prediction.

Within weeks, the newly-formed Lake District Defence Society was fighting the construction of a railway in Ennerdale. Other threats to scenery and freedom followed: the extension of the Kendal-Windermere line to Ambleside; the Keswick footpath disputes; a dam on the river Duddon; the opening of a quarry by Rydal Water.

The Society was in the van of the forces that opposed such harmful schemes but in 1893 there was a crucial event which marked a turning point in the battle to conserve the unique landscape of the Lake District.

Several important properties were for sale, Lodore Falls and the island on Grasmere among them. Rawnsley realised that these were just the sort of property that ought to be owned and preserved by some kind of national body as a public asset – his own small local Defence Association was inadequate.

Fortunately, other amenity-minded campaigners were thinking along similar lines: Hugh Lupus Grosvenor, Duke of Westminster and an enlightened aristocrat; Octavia Hill, a vigorous social reformer whom Rawnsley had known since 1875 during his days as a Soho lay chaplain; and Robert Hunter, a brilliant lawyer committed to what has become the conservation movement.

Rawnsley turned to this trio for support. The idea of a national public trust grew; the Duke of Westminster confided to Octavia Hill 'Mark my words, Miss Hill, this is going to be a very big thing.' He can hardly have realised just how big the proposed organisation was destined to become, how vital its work was to be in protecting both landscape and buildings of historical and architectural interest.

Interest and commitment grew. In January 1895, a meeting at Grosvenor House formally inaugurated the establishment of the National Trust for Places of Historic Interest or Natural Beauty with Rawnsley as honorary secretary, a post he held for twenty-five years until his death in 1920.

He was directly responsible for the Trust's first acquisition a short while after its foundation. He was staying with Mrs Fannie Talbot at Barmouth when he received the Trust's draft articles of association. Mrs Talbot read them and immediately offered a small piece of land called Dinas Olen to the infant Trust. It was less than five acres, a steep, gorse-clad area overlooking Cardigan Bay: Mrs Talbot wanted the public to enjoy this tiny haven, free from 'the abomination of asphalt paths and the cast iron seats of serpent design'.

Of more significance to Keswick was the Trust's acquisition of its first Lake District property in 1902, a piece of prime landscape on Rawnsley's front doorstep. The Brandelhow estate on the west shore of Derwentwater, 108 acres of pasture and woodland nestling under the slopes of Catbells, came on the market for £6,500. Rawnsley got to work, launched an appeal and within five months over £7,500 was raised from donations large and small. One subscriber wrote: 'I am a working man and cannot afford more than two shillings but I once saw Derwentwater and I can never forget it.' A guinea arrived with a note: 'I am blind and I am dying, but I remember my days on Derwentwater.'

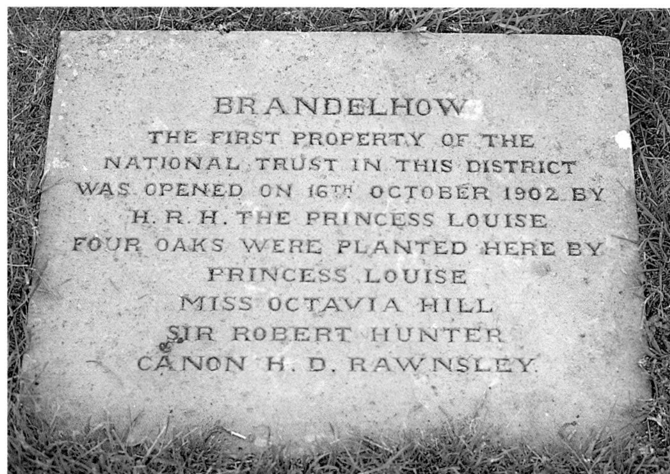

Brandelhow, the commemorative plaque

The opening ceremony was performed by H R H the Princess Louise on 16 October 1902, a day when Keswickians painted the town red, white and blue in honour of the royal visitor, with bunting criss-crossing the streets, and shops and houses decorated with flags and banners.

The weather was unkind: a strong wind whisked away the specially erected marquee and the Princess had to contend with a cold north-westerly that 'played mischievous pranks with the fantastic headgear of the ladies and the "tiles" of the gentlemen'. The boys of Keswick School formed a guard of honour; the Band of the First Volunteer Brigade, Border Regiment, played appropriate music; speeches were made and commemorative gifts were presented...and, of course, Rawnsley wrote a sonnet, as he invariably did for such occasions. The dignitaries planted trees: one by the Princess and one by the Duke of Argyll, one by each of the three founders of the National Trust (the Duke of Westminster had died in 1900).

Octavia Hill wrote to her mother: 'I have just come back from the great opening...it was very successful, very simple, real and unconventional...the simple little red dais was out in the open under the free sky, with the great lake lying below, and the golden fern clad slopes of Catbells above.'

It was a memorable day and an auspicious beginning for the work of the Trust in the Lake District. Today, the tiny acorn has burgeoned into a mighty oak: the Trust's Lakeland holdings include 130,000 acres of land, with a further 20,000 on lease and 12,000 covenanted, together with eighty-five farms and over 200 houses and cottages.

Eliza Lynn

ARCADE

13

Social Conscience

The twin invasions of railway and motor vehicle transformed Keswick from a small market town into a busy, thriving tourist centre. The early visitors, few in number, were those who could afford the time and money to indulge their fancies: the advent of cheap excursion trains and easy access by road meant that all sections of the population descended on Keswick in ever-increasing numbers.

The town responded. Its population grew; its facilities expanded; its housing and commercial stock developed. The table of resident population over two centuries shows a marked upward curve, with a 60% increase between 1871 and 1921 and a fairly stable figure in the present century:

1801 – 1350	1901 – 4451
1851 – 2618	1951 – 4867
1871 – 2782	1991 – 4836

More residents and more tourists brought golden days for the building trade from the 1870s onwards, meeting the demand for houses for local people, accommodation for visitors and facilities for both.

The area east of the town centre, particularly Leonard's Field, was developed. A walk along today's Blencathra Street, for example, shows the pattern of building blocks of named houses until eventually the street was complete. Plaques on the walls record: Abbotsleigh Terrace 1878; Stanley Terrace 1883; Thorp Villas 1892; Princess Terrace 1894; Albert Terrace 1897.

For the residents, the 1880s and 1890s were a period of expanding activities – social and sporting, educational and leisure, ranging from agricultural shows and athletic contests to circuses and concerts, from cricket and rugby to table tennis and figure skating.

On the football field, Southey Hill Wanderers took on Brigham Rovers; on the lower slopes of Latrigg, near Spooney Green, members of the Golf Club played their nine holes. In 1886 the Derwentwater Bathing and Swimming Club began to use the lake, providing changing rooms and a spring-board at the Isthmus. Lawn tennis was firmly established by 1888 when the first Keswick and Lake District Tournament was held, a four-day jamboree that was judged 'a splendid success from every point of view'.

Horses were raced on the Howrahs; the annual Bank Holiday Sports and Gala organised by the United Friendly Societies and Clubs attracted large crowds – some 5,000 on 1 August 1898. The Curling Club, inaugurated in 1875, made sure their sport was not dependent on a frozen Derwentwater by negotiating the purchase of a site for a permanent pond in the Tile Kiln Field in 1891 – now a caravan site near the Crosthwaite roundabout.

The town had two main venues for indoor entertainment. The Oddfellows' Hall staged an astonishing variety of attractions, from Miss Nellie White, the African nightingale, and the Farningham Boys' Military Band to the mirth and magic of Houdini and the curious antics of General Tom Thumb.

Arctic conditions on the river Greta outside the Pavilion

The Queen of the Lakes Pavilion in Station Road was opened in 1895, an amenity that served the town until it was demolished in 1988 and replaced by Riverside Lodge flats. In its day, it acted as host to pantomime and dances, roller-skating and exhibitions, church teas and whist drives, amateur dramatics and professional opera.

Temperance societies flourished. The Temperance Reform Society, formed in 1849, held weekly meetings and regular open-air public gatherings which swelled the ranks of those who took the pledge or were strongly opposed to the Sunday opening of public houses. At the Society's annual tea meeting on 12 November 1877, for example, there were so many people to be catered for that two sittings were necessary: in 1884, the St John's branch of the Band of Hope boasted over 200 juvenile members.

Temperance apart, other societies, many inspired by Victorian seriousness and philanthropy, satisfied a range of interests: the Young Men's Mutual Improvement Class, the Choral and Harmonic Society, the Discussion Class, the Horticultural and Cottage Gardeners' Association, the Sketching Club.

Most of these organisations no longer exist but one does survive and still flourishes. The Literary Society, founded in 1869, changed its name to the Literary and Scientific Society in 1874 and in 1948 to its present label of Keswick Lecture Society. As well as providing an annual programme of lectures, it also arranged university extension courses, the forerunner of today's evening classes. A series of six meetings on 'Shakespeare's Tragedies' in 1900 attracted an average attendance of 102 each night.

In that same year, 1900, the Society's membership reached 157. It has, with a few hiccups, continued to grow, reaching a peak of 321 in 1975. Today it maintains its tradition as one of the oldest lecture societies in the country, with a fairly stable audience of about 200.

In a different field of entertainment, travelling circuses were always a sure draw; local amateur groups like the Christy Minstrels or the Garrick Club supplemented the regular visits of professional performers. The one group of musicians that was certain to pull in a large and enthusiastic audience was the Rock Band. The story of this unique instrument goes back to the musical stones of Peter Crosthwaite. In June 1785, he found six stones in the bed of the river Greta; he chipped and shaped them so that they produced pure sounds on being struck. He added another ten to make a primitive two-octave xylophone, later described as 'the first set of musical stones that ever was in the world and one of the great curiosities of the kind in England'.

Imitations and refinements followed. Two local families, the Richardsons and the Tills, helped to make Keswick's sound of music known far and wide.

To their sixty-one 'keys' quarried from Skiddaw slate, the Richardsons added steel plates, drums and bells and used muffled mallets or hammers to strike the stones: their 'Rock Harmonicon' is still on view in Fitz Park Museum. The family travelled widely in Britain and on the Continent and in 1848 gave three performances at Buckingham Palace for Queen Victoria.

The Till family and their Rock Harmonicon

The Tills gave their first public concert on the 'geological piano' in the Oddfellows' Hall in October 1877 and rapidly established themselves as popular entertainers for locals and visitors alike. A full performance by the two sisters and two brothers included songs and recitals on a variety of instruments – ocarinas, zithers, musical glasses and fairy bells. Their fame spread: they were warmly received in America by large audiences – over 2,000 in Philadelphia in 1885, for example.

Yet another instrument was made by Mr G P Abraham and his two sons. Along with the illustrated lectures of this famous photographic trio, the rock band added a further treat for the growing number of tourists ready to be entertained in the evenings.

Both local residents and visitors were plainly well catered for by a wide selection of indoor leisure activities. The need for some form of outdoor recreational facility grew in the latter half of the nineteenth century and it was in 1880 that the idea of a park was first mooted. The moving spirit was Henry Irwin Jenkinson, whose efforts on behalf of the Footpath Preservation Society have already been noted. In April, 1880, he alerted his fellow townsfolk to the fact that the land between the railway and the Greta – the Fitz – was being offered for sale as building plots.

Along with the Rev. T K Richmond, vicar of Crosthwaite, Thomas Hodgson, builder and architect, and John Fisher Crosthwaite, postmaster and bank manager, Jenkinson negotiated with Mr S H le Fleming of Rydal Hall, owner of the land, who agreed to sell for £7,500.

Mr Crosthwaite had received an enquiry about the proposal from Mr Thomas Hewetson, an ex-Keswickian living in Devon. Thomas's father, John, variously described as cobbler, cordwainer and innkeeper, died in 1836 at the age of forty-four. His widow was faced with the formidable task of supporting her large family of three boys and five girls.

Henry, the second son, left Keswick in 1836 when he was only fifteen years old. He lived with his uncle in London, working as an apprentice in his prosperous business which dealt in leather, sail cloth, sacking and linen. Henry was so successful that by 1848 he was joined by his elder brother, Thomas, and his five sisters. In 1867, when his uncle died, Henry took over full control of the business and eventually retired, a rich man, to Tunbridge Wells in Kent.

The brothers never forgot their native town. When Jenkinson sent Thomas the plan of the proposed park, he and Henry immediately offered £500 each towards the cost of buying the land, including the six-acre field on the opposite side of Station Road, which belonged to the Keswick Hotel. Henry Hewetson strongly urged Jenkinson and his colleagues to snap up the Fitz before it was too late. He supported his advice by more generous financial gifts: of the total cost of around £9,800, the Hewetson family provided £5,250.

The conveyance was completed by August 1882. To mark the Queen's Jubilee in 1887, a final effort was made to clear the outstanding debt of £600: Keswick was almost buried in a riot of bunting and banners as a long procession marched to Fitz Park to hear John Fisher Crosthwaite announce the good news that all bills had been paid and that the Park was dedicated to the people of Keswick for ever. Henry Jenkinson, his dream crystallised into reality after seven years' hard work, 160 committee meetings and 16 hand-written books of minutes, could be forgiven for his rather fulsome declaration: 'This is a great day in the history of England and of the world and I am happy to say it will also be for ever memorable in the history of Keswick.'

In 1923, the Park was extended by a gift from Mr and Mrs J B Wivell. A triangle of land between the Greta and Penrith Road, incorporating the War Memorial, was donated in memory of their son, George, who was killed in the First World War, and their daughter, Mary Elizabeth, who had died some years previously.

When the Park was opened for public use, a formidable list of thirty-two bye-laws was drawn up, aimed at preserving and protecting its amenities. All buildings were prohibited except those specifically linked with exercise or recreation; no intoxicating drink was to be sold; shows, agricultural exhibitions, training by the local Volunteers and similar functions were allowed up to a limit of nine days in any one year.

Facilities were available not only for cricket and football, tennis and bowls, but also for croquet and quoits, archery and pole leaping.

The central aim of the Park was clearly defined and has remained ever since – 'the general enjoyment of the grounds by the public shall be the principal object'. After a century of constant use, both Upper and Lower Fitz are in excellent condition in spite of continuing financial problems. A succession of committed Trustees has battled against lack of money but somehow managed to keep the two areas trim and bright with flower beds or readily available for sports and other activities. Bowling greens and tennis courts are popular with residents and visitors alike; a new cricket pavilion in 1994 has added considerably to the facilities of the club.

By 1992, it had become overwhelmingly obvious that financial difficulties had reached crisis point. Lengthy negotiations resulted in a transfer of trusteeship to the Keswick Town Council in April 1994, a management arrangement which should ensure the future stability and local control of the Park.

Henry Hewetson died on 30 May 1895 and a handsome memorial tablet was placed in Crosthwaite Church. Local opinion, however, favoured some form of official tribute to the Hewetson family for their generosity, some permanent and substantial recognition of their liberality.

The story of what eventually became the Hewetson memorial goes back to 31 March 1873. On that date, a meeting of the four-year-old Keswick Literary Society resolved that steps should be taken to form a museum. There was a strong tradition in the earlier successful museums of Peter Crosthwaite and Thomas Hutton.

In charge of the project were three men: Canon Harford Battersby, incumbent of St John's church; Dr Knight, a local medical practitioner; and Mr Clifton Ward, a geologist who came to the Lake District in 1869 as a working scientist of the Geological Survey.

The three began to collect suitable material: Clifton Ward's expertise and contacts ensured a supply of rocks and minerals. It soon became obvious that the growing number of items could not be accommodated in the show cases in the Reading Room of the Battersby Hall, the parochial meeting building of St John's church. A permanent home and more space were needed and in 1875 a room was rented in the Moot Hall and the Society's exhibits were put on show – 1,319 in all, including over 700 rocks and minerals and 260 moths and butterflies. Clifton Ward and John Birkett assumed the responsibilities of voluntary curators. Admission, except for occasional open days, was for members of the Literary and Scientific Society only.

In 1878, the Society bought Flintoft's relief model of the Lake District for £160, a museum piece if ever there was one. Built on a scale of three inches to the mile, it covered 1,200 square miles – a meticulously fashioned replica of fells and valleys, rivers and roads, still on show in Fitz Park Museum.

With the major attraction available, the Society leased the Museum to Mr Thomas Mayson and opened it to visitors. From 1883, when Mayson's contract ended, the Society appointed William Greenip, a local postman and ornithologist, to take charge. The Museum was firmly established on the tourist trail but in 1896 a crisis loomed.

The Urban District Council gave notice to the Society that the Museum must be removed from the Moot Hall. A sub-committee explored several possible solutions, finally deciding to approach the Fitz Park trustees to ask whether they 'would view with favour the suggestion that had been made of a building being erected in the Lower Fitz, in connection with the Hewetson Memorial, which would serve the dual purpose of housing the Museum and affording accommodation for a Park Keeper's Lodge...and whether the Fitz Trustees would accept the care of the Museum (including Flintoft's Model) as a public Trust'.

To their eternal credit, the Trustees and the Hewetson Memorial Committee agreed. The Lodge and the Museum were built at a cost of just over £1,000 and officially handed over to the Trustees on 4 August 1898 – and appropriately dedicated to Henry and Thomas Hewetson, Keswick benefactors extraordinary.

Fitz Park Museum a century ago

The Museum, perpetually struggling with insufficient funds, still continues to attract a steady flow of visitors. Part of its charm lies in its Victorian ambience, its lack of modern gimmicks; part of its importance lies in a number of unique and valuable items: manuscripts of the Lake Poets and Sir Hugh Walpole, the Musical Stones, the Flintoft Model, a large collection of minerals and rocks, local antiquities and the ever-intriguing 500-year-old cat.

The future of the Museum and Art Gallery came under official discussion in 1992. The outlook was bleak: structural improvements and repairs were essential, expenses were increasing, income was meagre. Only support from Allerdale Borough Council kept a prime tourist attraction and educational display open.

After considerable negotiations, an agreement was reached and Allerdale Borough Council took over the trusteeship from April 1994. The Keswick building and its contents were taken into the network of Allerdale's museum service, with professional advice and supervision available and a much greater measure of financial security promised for the years ahead.

Two further memorials nearby commemorate the local personalities who were mainly responsible for the creation of Fitz Park. Opposite the Museum are the ornamental gates which serve as the main entrance to Upper Fitz Park. These are dedicated to Henry Irwin Jenkinson, a man described by Mr W Routh Fitzpatrick, a fellow Keswickian, as one 'who may be said to have sacrificed his life to the good of his fellow townsmen and others'. They were formally opened on 6 July 1893 as the first item in a programme of events celebrating the marriage of the Duke of York and Princess May – a worthy occasion for remembering a conscientious philanthropist. John Fisher Crosthwaite's contribution to the creation of Fitz

Park was recognised by the dedication of a gate exactly opposite Jenkinson's, giving access to Lower Fitz Park and completed in June 1898.

Memorials apart, the Art Gallery was added to the Museum building in 1905 and officially opened to the public for the first time in July of the following year – a lofty, spacious room which still houses a permanent collection of paintings and other treasures and acts as a venue for changing monthly exhibitions from April to October each year.

In 1872, Jenkinson, ever anxious for the welfare of his fellow Keswickians, suggested an annual dinner and entertainment for the old people of the town. The idea was warmly received and the first 'Old Folks' Do' was held in the Oddfellows' Hall on 31 December 1872. The pattern has persisted to the present day, though the entertainment has become more sophisticated, ranging from church choirs and local bands to films and operettas. There have been occasional snags. In 1908, for example, Canon Rawnsley thought it was unsuitable for a troupe of 'nigger' minstrels to perform and asked for them to be transformed into white minstrels. The leader refused and the act was withdrawn.

For many years, Rawnsley contributed a dialect poem, always well received and often about some local person or event, but it is not difficult to imagine the baffled reactions of a group of Belgian refugees at the 1914 dinner as they listened to 'Hoo Jossy went to t'War'.

Although the 'Do', possibly the oldest of its kind in the country, has been threatened on a number of occasions, it continues to be a much appreciated get-together for the older inhabitants of the town. Rocketing costs and problems of raising the necessary funding have caused the organisers considerable headaches in recent years but it is to be hoped that this old tradition will not be allowed – or forced – to fade away.

Among Rawnsley's many contributions to the life and welfare of Keswick at a time when so much was happening in the fields of social and recreational provision was the establishment of an organisation that lasted for a century and became known all over the world.

He was appointed vicar of Crosthwaite in July 1883. Just over a year later, the people of Keswick were surprised to receive a circular carrying the names of Rawnsley and sixteen other local worthies announcing the opening on 1 November 1884 of a school for the teaching of 'art industries'.

The project was the brain-child of Rawnsley and his wife, Edith, instigated by the sincerest of motives. There was considerable unemployment in the town, particularly in the winter months, and the new school would help to reduce the numbers of idle workmen. Craftsmanship was deemed more important than monetary rewards; only hand-made articles would be produced. An incidental aim was the encouragement of temperance: if men were busy at classes or exercising their skills at home, they would not be drinking in the public houses.

Mrs Rawnsley assumed command. The classes met in the Parish Room, concentrating on wood carving and metal work under the supervision of a professional from South Kensington and a local designer. By 1888, nearly seventy men were turning out trays and lamps, bowls and finger plates. Tanners and coach drivers, pencil makers and shop assistants turned their hands to new, practical skills: one keen craftsman walked three miles from St John's in the Vale – and he had only one leg.

By 1889, a new craft had been introduced for the women of the town. Some years previously, the spinning and weaving of flax to make linen for embroidery had been revived in the Langdale valley, with the blessing and support of John Ruskin. The key figure was Miss Marion Twelves: she was persuaded to come to Keswick and 'The Ruskin Linen Industry' was established as an essential part of the Rawnsleys' scheme. Miss Twelves first held her spinning and weaving classes in an old woollen mill in Penrith Road that was demolished some years ago: in 1894, she moved to the seventeenth century cottages at High Hill, variously known as St George's Cottages or Ruskin and Porch Cottages.

Miss Twelves at her spinning wheel

Here Miss Twelves lived and worked for nearly thirty years: the embroidered linen of her school was sold all over the world. Among its more prestigious productions were the palls which covered the coffins of Tennyson and Ruskin.

There appear to have been some clashes of personality between Miss Twelves and the Rawnsleys. With the move to High Hill, she broke off her official connexion with them and operated her own successful business independently, working in association with Ruskin's St George's Guild and using Ruskin's motto 'Today' as a trade mark.

Few memories of this enterprising woman and her achievements remain. She died in July 1929. The High Hill cottages, somewhat altered, are still there; opposite, over the wall and by the river, are some steps, replicas of the original steps used by the workers for retting – soaking the flax in the Greta to break down the cellulose coating and expose the fibres before spinning.

The popularity of the Rawnsleys' school continued to grow until it became obvious that the Parish Room was much too small and inconvenient: a permanent, purpose-built and self-contained building was necessary.

With typical zest, the Rawnsleys set about yet another demanding project. A site near Greta Bridge was acquired and within two years nearly £1,200 was subscribed. Work began in May 1893 by two local contractors – T and I Hodgson, builders, and F. and W. Green, joiners and carpenters, two firms responsible for much development in Keswick and still serving the community. A year later, on 4 April 1894, the new Keswick School of Industrial Arts was officially opened.

The workshops were on the ground floor. Upstairs were a showroom, reached by an outside staircase, and a balcony decorated with a legend that epitomised the original ideals of the school: 'The loving eye and patient hand shall work with joy to bless the land'.

On the door-plate of the showroom were inscribed two lines by Robert Browning:

Oh, Earth, as God has made it, all is beauty!
And knowing this is love, and love is duty.

A third quotation, by Rawnsley himself, graced a doorway from the metal room to the wood-carving area:

The makers are the poets! Ply your skill!
Beat rhythmic hammers! Work, harmonious will!
Coleridge and Southey watch from yonder hill.

For nearly a century, the School was a magnet for visitors, a source of employment for local residents and an institution whose products reached an international market. Stainless steel took over from the more expensive brass and copper. Bowls and trays, cooker hoods and work tops, crosses and trophies have found their way into palaces and cottages, cathedrals and village churches, sports clubs and school halls – much admired, much appreciated.

Sadly, by the 1980s, the School was facing an economic crisis, sparked off by the narrow range of goods, cheaper rival products and an inadequate system of marketing in an increasingly competitive economy. In spite of determined efforts by the Trustees and a good deal of local sympathy, the School was closed in 1984. The building, tastefully adapted and extended, remains much as it was, externally, in its new role as an up-market restaurant.

As the town expanded, the population increased and more visitors arrived, so the need for community services became more urgent. Once again the generosity of the Hewetsons was on offer.

In his quarterly report to the Local Board on 31 December 1881, Dr Black, the Medical Officer of Health, brought to the Board's notice the desirability of a cottage hospital in the town. Henry Hewetson strongly supported the idea and offered to donate the small farm of Monk Hall and fourteen acres of land as a site for a hospital providing a range of services – medical, surgical, therapeutic, emergency – mainly for the poorer people of Keswick. His motives, as always, were wholly philanthropic and in addition he wished the hospital to be 'a memorial of the beneficient nature and life' of his sister, Mary.

Work on dismantling Monk Hall began in June 1890 and the hospital was officially opened on 19 August 1892. It remains basically the same today, though extensions and improvements – the Lady Randles operating theatre in 1932, a new wing in 1988, for example – have widened the range and increased the effectiveness of patient treatment to meet the more rigorous standards of modern medical practice.

The Mary Hewetson Hospital, long before the NHS

While the hospital was being built, another group of workmen was busy in the town constructing a new post office on the site of the old poorhouse. The schedule included a thirty-five foot wide street between the new premises and the old post office and former Cumberland Union Bank, built in 1864. The thoroughfare was appropriately named Bank Street.

The Post Office was opened for business on 2 February 1891 but the story of Keswick's postal service goes back at least a century before that date. In 1789, Mary Southward was paid £23 a year as postmistress and an allocation of £158.5.0. for 'riding work' – expenses incurred in carrying mail to and from Penrith. Before coaches were in general use, the mail was transported on horseback in saddlebags – an open invitation to thieves lurking on the lonely stretches of Troutbeck Moor. There is a tradition that at least one robbery took place near Dacre road-end, where the postman was left tied to a tree overnight.

Mary Southward was the widow of the landlord of the Royal Oak Inn and it seems reasonable to suppose that he had been postmaster before Mary took over the duties. In 1790, she married John I'Anson, who not only became the new landlord of the Royal Oak but also the town postmaster. In 1797, a bye-letter office was opened at the inn, giving Keswick its first, though small, post office. When the I'Ansons retired in 1808, they lived in a new house in Ambleside Road called Acorn House – an appropriate name coined by Mary because the house had been built from the profits of the Oak.

The office was transferred to Museum Square (the present Herries Thwaite shopping complex) opposite Peter Crosthwaite's Museum. James Atkinson was postmaster from 1808 to 1846, when John Fisher Crosthwaite began his forty year stint.

One of his first duties was to set up sub-offices in some of the neighbouring villages: Braithwaite, 1846; Bassenthwaite, 1848; Rosthwaite, 1854; Threlkeld, 1856. During his long term of office, business increased dramatically: in the 1840s, the staff comprised Crosthwaite himself and his family and one female letter-carrier; in 1888, a total of thirty-five people was employed, which included four clerks, seven sub-postmasters, seven rural postmen, five town letter-carriers and six telegraph messengers. It is a salutary thought that in the 1880s the town had four deliveries of mail in the summer months and a letter posted in Keswick before seven o'clock in the morning was delivered in London the same evening.

Stories about the pioneering postmen abound. Joe Littledale, who died in 1836, once told Southey the reason for Keswick's ample rainfall: 'I have observed that when the moon is turned upward, we have fine weather after it; but if it is turned downward, then we have a wet season. And the reason I think is that when it is turned down, it holds no water, like a basin, you know, and then down it all comes.'

William Greenip and his son, also William, delivered mail in Braithwaite and Newlands for over thirty years and both gained a reputation as local naturalists, mineralogists and antiquarians. Old Jimmy Langhorne the Borrowdale postman, reckoned he had walked the equivalent of at least five times round the world.

The first telephone in Keswick appears to have been a connexion between William Wilson's Keswick Hotel and his coaching office in St John's Street, a distance of about half a mile. The first message on 12 May 1884 was 'distinctly heard and immediately responded to'. By August 1901, the installation of a basic telephone system was nearing completion and lines were being built between Keswick and Penrith.

Gas was available by 1846 when the Gaslight Company was formed and the gasworks were built. By 1882, the town had sixty-seven street lamps; by 1889, only seventy cookers were in use, a figure boosted by reducing the cost per 1,000 cubic feet to 3s.3d. in 1892 and the introduction of penny-in-the-slot meters in 1894. The conversion of the system to North Sea gas meant that the locally produced supply was no longer needed and the familiar works and gasholders on Greta Side were demolished in the 1980s.

With the water of the Greta so readily and conveniently available, it is not surprising that Keswick was an early pioneer in the use of hydro-electric power for a public supply. The Keswick Electric Light Company was registered in 1889 – the first public electricity supply in the north-west – and a generating plant was built at Brigham Forge, where the existing weir and races of an old woollen mill were harnessed.

In January 1890, power (100 volts DC) was switched on for the Company's first customers which included the Keswick Hotel, the railway station offices, Crosthwaite and St John's churches and a handful of private homes. Within a year, demand had risen to over 700 lamps and a stand-in engine had to be brought into use. In 1898, the overhead wires were replaced by underground mains and a new steam engine and turbine were installed at the Forge. In 1899, the Company's shares and debentures were taken over by the Windermere and District Electricity Supply Company, though the Keswick unit remained a separate entity until 1938 when supplies became the responsibility of the Central Electricity Board. Little remains today as a reminder of the original generating station at the Forge, which closed down in 1941. The building has been converted into holiday flats but the head and tail races of the Greta may still be seen.

Another vital public service, a fire brigade, was initiated during the period of Keswick's rapid and extensive development. In May 1885, a voluntary group of fire fighters was formed, with Joseph Hall, a local solicitor, as superintendent. The Local Board was given permission to borrow £300 to buy a fire engine and appliances and to provide a building to house them. The first horse-drawn engine was christened 'Derwent', the forerunner of successive vehicles, each more sophisticated and more efficient than its predecessor. The engine bought in 1931 was probably the first motorised model.

Keswick is still served by a volunteer fire brigade and today's team is well equipped and well organised. Whether its facilities are required for dealing with a blaze, a rescue or pumping out flooded houses, the response is rapid, the effort unstinting, the service effective.

As early as 1819, William Green's Guide records a Mr Robert Stubbs as the organiser of a circulating library. Thirty years later, the town's first public library was founded by the Rev. Frederick Myers, vicar of St John's Church, with the proceeds of a legacy from his mother-in-law, Mrs John Marshall. Its aim, as a plaque inside the building reminds us, was 'to encourage the spirit of self culture and to promote the combination of secular and spiritual instruction in this district'.

The building still stands, as sturdy and four-square as ever, on the corner of Church Street opposite St John's church. In 1855, two small rooms were added and, on the first floor, a lecture hall named after the Rev. T D Harford Battersby, with seating for up to 250 people.

The library complex soon became the cultural and educational heart of Keswick. The class rooms and the Battersby Hall were the meeting places of many organisations and for some years Mr Blackman taught older pupils in the back room, still sometimes referred to as 'Blackman's Room'.

In 1926, it became a Reading Room, largely financed by a generous donation from Hugh Walpole, who was a member of the Library Committee. In more recent years, the whole block has been used for the teaching of junior and nursery children from St John's School over the road.

The library itself seems to have been more popular with visitors than with locals – a refuge on rainy days, perhaps. In 1878, when both book stock and annual issues stood at 2,500, only ninety-four townsfolk were subscribers. Finance was a perpetual problem and funds were boosted by the time-honoured methods of sales of work and bazaars, public appeals and that peculiarly Victorian jollification, the 'Conversazione'.

By 1958, declining membership, rising costs and lack of funds seriously affected the efficiency and facilities of this independent subscription library and it was absorbed into the county system which had been operating on a small scale on a shop site in Bank Street for some twenty years. The St John's building was refurbished and redecorated; stock was reorganised and brought up to date. By 1972, the annual issue figures had reached 100,000 and the St John's accommodation was clearly quite inadequate.

A new, purpose-built library in Heads Lane was opened on 25 June 1973 by Mrs E S Raven, whose late husband, Stanley, a Keswickian born and bred, had been County Librarian for a number of years. It cost £47,300 and houses some 20,000 books, including an excellent local history collection whose nucleus is a gift in 1945 of about 300 books from Sir Hugh Walpole's library.

Canon Thomas Dundas Harford-Battersby

14

Sermons in Stone

For a town of its size, isolated in the only mountainous area of England, Keswick has a surprisingly rich religious history.

At the heart of this ecclesiastical evolution is Crosthwaite Church, mother church to five chapels – Borrowdale, Newlands, Thornthwaite, Wythburn and St John's in the Vale – in an ancient parish of at least 150 square miles that extended from Dunmail Raise to Skiddaw, Bassenthwaite to Threlkeld.

The authentic history of St Kentigern's, Crosthwaite, begins with the 'basilica' of the twelfth century: traces of the original stone walls may still be seen in the north aisle. In the early 1190s, Alice de Rumelli the Second gave the advowson – the right of presenting clergymen to a benefice – to the Cistercian Abbey of Fountains. Along with the advowson went land and certain privileges – offerings, fees, revenues and tithes – annual contributions which continued for centuries. Elizabeth Lynn in the nineteenth century remembered her childhood at Crosthwaite vicarage when 'our place used to overflow with produce at tithing times. At Easter, eggs came in by the hundred and at "shearing time" wool by the cart-load. Everything else was in like quantity'.

A revaluation of Crosthwaite in 1291 rated the church at £30.13s.4d. and the vicarage at £20. In 1318, these figures were drastically reduced to £10 and £4, due, it has been suggested, to the incursions and depredations of Scottish invaders – an explanation arguably applicable to parishes in north Cumbria but of doubtful validity for a parish deep in the fells.

By the early 1500s, extensions and additions had transformed the church into more or less the design we see today. The area at the east end of the south aisle appears originally to have been the Chapel or Chantry of St Mary Magdalen, an identification supported by a piscina, now hidden under a seat, and the image of the saint in a window. It is likely that the chantry was established by the Derwentwater family: the will of Sir John Radcliffe, who died in 1526, 'ordained that a priest should say mass and sing daily for his soul and the soul of his wife before the altar of our Lady of Pity in the Church of Crosthwaite'. A chantry survey of 1534 names John Steyle as the priest of St Mary Magdalen's chapel 'within the parish of Crosthwaite'.

Details of a visitation in 1571 ordered by Bishop Barnes reveal a considerable stock of Catholic items. Instructions were given to 'sell, alienate and put away...all and every such popish reliques and monuments of superstition and idolatry as presently remain'. The offending objects included communion vessels and vestments, twenty-nine candlesticks, handbells and 'the painted cloths with pictures of Peter and Paul and the Trinity'.

Church, school and an interested bystander

The importance of Crosthwaite in the life of the town is indicated by the visit of Bishop Nicolson on 9 September 1702 when he confirmed over 400 people. A year later, his diary entry for 15 September 1703 noted that 'the Quire wants Glazeing and Care to be taken of the Roof and that seats crowded the chancel 'even to the very side of the Communion Table; which has no rails about it, nor is (hardly) an Inch above the Floor'. He complained about the rough unevenness of the nave floor, which was frequently disturbed by burials. Between 1626 and 1650, for example, 555 people were interred in the body of the church and twenty-one in the chancel – an average of twenty-three a year, many of whom no doubt were children.

In 1812, the leaking lead roof was removed and replaced by slate. Maintenance of the windows appears to have consisted of the glazier removing pieces of the ancient glass which he sold or gave to his friends. In the earlier part of the nineteenth century, Eliza Lynn tells us, the interior of the church was 'more like a huge whitewashed cattle pen than a decent church': broken windows, decrepit pews, the crumbling whitewash of centuries called for drastic action. Southey, writing to Charles Wynn on 30 August 1825, had harsh words to say about the Bishop and the state of the church: 'Our bishop is a sleeping one and this place has been shamefully neglected. No confirmation has been held here within the living memory of man.' In spite of his name, Bishop Goodenough was obviously no Nicolson.

The great restoration of 1844 was financed by James Stanger, a local philanthropist, and supervised by Gilbert Scott, the architect, best known as the designer of the Albert Memorial, St Pancras Station and Glasgow University. A vigorous, perhaps too vigorous, refurbishment destroyed some of the ancient features of the building: the organ gallery, pews, alter table, rails and reading desk were removed and sold; the 1610 pulpit was transferred to Newlands Church.

The ossuary or bone-house at the west end of the north aisle was cleared; the flags of the rest of the church were raised; the remains of buried corpses were excavated and decorously interred in the churchyard. The interior walls were stripped of their whitewash and replastered; stone work was re-dressed and the outside was covered in grey roughcast. The porch was built, the old oak door removed and burned. Imbedded in it were several musket balls and signs of other perforations: their origin is unknown but popular tradition assigns them to Cromwell's day.

The church reopened for divine service on 3 August 1845. Eliza Lynn no longer saw a whitewashed pen but 'a country cathedral, one of the most beautiful churches in the country'.

It is not surprising that during Rawnsley's incumbency from 1883 to 1917 some further changes were made: that energetic cleric was hardly likely to sit back and meekly accept his predecessor's efforts.

In 1885, the organ at the west end was removed from its gallery and rebuilt below in the space previously occupied by a substantial singers' gallery. In 1889, a handsome reredos was installed, its bosses carved with the initials of some twenty benefactors of the parish, from King Richard I to the Hewetsons. New, too, were the altar rails, the east window and the marble mosaic pavement incorporating the emblems of St Kentigern – a sanctuary of considerable beauty and dignity.

A slab gravestone in front of the communion rail marks the burial place of Edward Stephenson. Born in Keswick in 1691, he achieved the temporary honour of acting as Governor of Bengal for thirty-five hours in September 1728. 'Governor's House' in St John's Street, the present premises of the Derwent Club, is a reminder of the several properties he built or bought on his return to England as a very wealthy man.

Rawnsley's repair work on the walls uncovered a number of consecration crosses to add to those already visible. Etched into the stone, these ancient carvings, varying from five to six inches in diameter, mark the places where the bishop anointed the walls during the service of consecration. In all, Crosthwaite boasts twenty-one of these crosses – twelve outside and nine inside – and claims to be the only church in England with a complete set of external crosses.

Rawnsley's twenty-five years' work in the parish was acknowledged in 1909 by the creation of the baptistry. Situated on the left immediately inside the main entrance, it incorporates several unusual features: a piece of rare marble from Carrara, uncovered after an avalanche; the largest single slab of purple-red Rondona breccia in the country; a fourteenth century font, richly and elaborately carved with leaves and flowers, shields and emblems, delicate tracery and a Latin inscription, with a dedication to Thomas de Eskhead, vicar of Crosthwaite in the late 1300s. A tribute to Rawnsley is traced in Gothic script round the baptistry panelling.

Records of the church bells go back to 1699 when the churchwardens' accounts include 4s.6d. for 'ringinge', 5s. for a bell rope and a charge for 'oyle'. In 1775 a ring of six new bells costing £196 was installed. They were delivered by sea to Workington along with a set for St Michael's Church in Workington. Tradition has it that the Rev. James Lushington, vicar of Crosthwaite, hearing that one set was inferior, bribed the captain of the ship to let him have the better of the two rings – a nice story of local loyalty and ecclesiastical misdemeanour that unfortunately has no evidence to support it.

A list of rules for the bellringers, drawn up in 1826 by eighty-six year old Thomas Martin, writing master of Crosthwaite School, still hangs in the tower. It displays, in rhyme, a range of penalties: a shilling for ringing without consent or for swearing; a quart of ale for interrrupting a peal; a penny for stopping before the bellmaster's signal. It ends with this exhortation:

You Ringers all take care, you must not fail,
To have your forfeitures all spent in Ale.
With Heart upright let each true Subject ring
For Health and Peace, to Country, Church and King.

A fire in the tower on 23 January 1882 caused considerable damage to the framework on which the bells were hung and to the beams supporting the belfry floor. Enough funds were raised by the parish to repair the damage, add two more bells to the peal and buy a set of handbells for the Crosthwaite Handbell Ringers, who, a century later, continue to entertain audiences and raise money for church funds and charities.

There used to be a small medieval bell on a window sill in the south aisle. It came originally from the old chapel at Loweswater and, so the story goes, was rescued from a Maryport scrap dealer by Rawnsley. He hung it outside the Parish Room in Main Street, later replacing it with a more modern bell and transferring it to the inside of the church. There it remained until 1972, when it was returned to its rightful owners at Loweswater.

The interior of Crosthwaite Church has a proliferation of memorials – windows, tablets, brass plates, tombs. Three deserve a special mention: the fifteenth century alabaster effigies, almost certainly of Thomas and Margaret Radcliffe; the sixteenth century brasses of Sir John and Lady Radcliffe; and the white marble recumbent figure of Southey, with, carved on the plinth, the poem Wordsworth wrote to honour his friend.

The ancient 'bolster' stone or 'pillow' near the Southey tomb, dug out of the churchyard on 8 November 1875, has various markings, including a cross. It may have come from the grave of some ecclesiastic but there are no grounds for its suggested association with St Herbert.

The church clock, one-handed like that of the Moot Hall, was probably installed about 1720. William Gascoigne was paid 5s. in 1784 for cleaning it and in 1841 it was put into working order by Jonathan Otley and John Musgrave after being out of commission for more than fifty years.

The vicarage has a history of its own. It goes back to at least 1250 – it is mentioned in the church endowment deeds – but we can only assume that it was on the site of the present building. A survey by the Commissioners of Henry VIII in the 1540s identifies the vicar, John Herynge, as having 'a mansion and glebe pertaining to the said vicarage, which, one year with another, is worth £0.4s.0d'.

Thomas Christian, vicar from 1728 to 1770, built 'a very neat convenient house'; it was extended in 1821 – ten bedrooms were just about adequate for Parson Lynn's large family – and Rawnsley's study, added in 1903, was positioned to catch the day-long sunshine. In 1989 it was vacated for a modern vicarage at the bottom of the garden, and is now a private dwelling, rechristened 'Crosthwaite Grange'.

The story of Crosthwaite's sister church, St John's, is less complicated, if only because it has a mere century and a half to record.

In 1832, when the population of Keswick was over 2,000, John Marshall bought the Derwentwater estates from Greenwich Hospital. He recognised the need for a second church and abandoned plans for a house on Broomhill Point in favour of a new church. The foundation stone was laid in 1836, a few months before Marshall died on 31 October 1836 at the early age of thirty eight. The family carried out his wishes and the church was consecrated by Hugh Percy, Bishop of Carlisle, on 27 December 1838. Nearly twenty years later, in 1856, St John's was designated a separate parish.

Over the years, extensions have transformed the original church into a spacious and elegantly proportioned building: the north aisle in 1862, the south aisle in 1882, the chancel enlarged in 1889. Several memorials commemorate members of the Marshall family along with other Keswick worthies such as Dr Knight, a local medical practitioner; the Rev. J. Clifton Ward, geologist and philanthropist; Thomas Highton, headmaster of Brigham School for many years. Visitors drawn by the grave of Sir Hugh Walpole on the terrace enjoy a superb view of Derwentwater and the Borrowdale fells.

St John's organ, first installed in 1889, replaced in 1912 and refurbished in 1990, continues to be admired for its rich tones and flexible combinations and recognised as a fine instrument by its makers, the organists who have played it and the congregations who have listened to it.

St John's Church and Parsonage

In 1985, a new chapter was opened in the story of St John's. The vicarage, built in 1842, was converted into a diocesan 'Holy Name House', the residence of a small group of nuns of the Community of the Mission Sisters of the Holy Name of Jesus. The vicar and his family moved into a newly built house nearby.

The first incumbent of St John's, who was in office from 1838 to 1851, was Frederick Myers, who married Marshall's sister, Susan Harriet, in 1842. Ecclesiastical duties apart, he left his mark on both his own parish and the town in general.

He founded St John's School in 1840 and St John's Library in 1849, a solid and somewhat sombre symbol of Victorian earnestness and concern. Here on Saturday mornings he ran his Provident Club, handing out religious tracts and talking to parishioners. Here on Saturday evenings he met his Sunday School teachers for reading and discussion and preparation for their duties on the following day. Here on Wednesday evenings improving lectures were given; on Mondays in the winter months a social gathering enjoyed exhibitions and music.

Although the programme of activities was dictated by Myers and controlled by his strong paternal hand, it must be seen as innovative and well-intentioned, a forerunner of the numerous clubs and societies and meetings that proliferated a few years later and came to be taken for granted as part of both church and secular life in the town.

Myers' eldest son, Frederick William Henry, is more widely known than his father. Poet and essayist, he was deeply interested in life after death and was a founder member of the Society for Psychical Research, inaugurated in 1882.

In November 1849, the Rev. Thomas Dundas Harford-Battersby was appointed curate to Frederick Myers. When Myers died on 20 July 1851, he was offered and accepted the living. For thirty years, he devoted himself wholeheartedly to his parish and his people, organising everything from prayer meetings to an old folks' dinner on New Year's Day, from lectures to a United Christian League for all the churches in Keswick with open air services three times a week. To the library, he added the lecture hall, which still bears his name, establishing it as the new home of the Mechanics Institute which had existed elsewhere in the town for some years.

He was an official in the Literary and Scientific Society and strongly supported the call for a pure water supply recommended in Rawlinson's 1852 report. Along with Dr Lietch, John Fisher Crosthwaite and others, he formed a small company to supply water from Skiddaw which lasted for twenty years until the Local Board assumed responsibility.

He was a reserved man whose interests were mainly centred on matters spiritual; his self-conscious preoccupation with his religious duties inhibited his social life but his influence on the parish and the town was profound, particularly in the foundation of the Convention, a unique annual gathering that still exists and flourishes.

The roots of nonconformity in Keswick reach back to 1653. This was the year that Quakerism arrived in Cumbria with the visit of George Fox to the county and William Dewsbury 'declared Truth at Portingskell' to four receivers, one of whom was Hugh Tickell.

Fox's *Journal* records a visit to Derwentwater in 1653 and the conversion of 'many hundreds'. Fox was in Northumberland at the time and 'Derwentwater' patently refers to the river Derwent in that county. The only mention of Keswick in the *Journal* is in 1663 when Fox was on his way from Pardshaw Crag near Cockermouth to Thomas Laythes' house at Dalehead by Thirlmere.

The small group of Friends at Portinscale declared their testimonies in public and suffered the customary punishment of 'ye Spoiling of their goods and Imprisonment of their bodys'. Hugh Tickell was twice committed to Carlisle jail but in 1685 ('it pleased ye Lord to bestow worldly riches on him') he bought a building and an orchard in Keswick and conveyed it to the Friends as a Meeting House.

It stood on a bend of the river Greta at High Hill near the junction with Crosthwaite Road. Tickell's original building was replaced by a new Meeting House in 1715, a centre of worship for local Friends, small though numbers were. In 1740, for example, there were only six Quaker families in Crosthwaite parish.

There was certainly no Meeting in Keswick in 1807. On 3 December of that year, Southey wrote to Charles Wynn: 'My views of religion approach very nearly to Quakerism... Were there a meeting in Keswick, I should silently take a seat in it.'

Parson and White's *Directory* of 1829 records: 'The Keswick National School where about forty girls are taught reading, writing and plain needle work, was established in 1820, in the deserted Quaker's (sic) chapel.' The school moved to new premises in 1833 and the old Meeting House appears to have stood empty for some years – in 1847 it was described as 'a mean and deserted building'. At some time, it was converted into three cottages and later into a single dwelling – today's 'Quaker Cottage', whose name preserves the historical associations.

Presumably the few Friends there were during these years met at one another's houses but occasional public meetings were arranged. On 28 September 1880, Mr W. Pollard from Manchester, 'a minister of the Society of Friends' addressed a gathering for worship in the Oddfellows' Hall; a Quaker report of 1896 mentions an 'allowed meeting' at Keswick.

In the early 1900s, the Friends, still small in number, continued to meet in private houses – a cottage on Ambleside Road, Portland House in Ratcliffe Place. In 1920-21, Henry Wilson of Dowthwaite on Chestnut Hill bought the premises in Church Street which served as a centre of worship and fellowship for a small but vigorous band of faithful Quakers for well over seventy years. A generous legacy from Doris Liversidge in 1987 provided ample funds to build a new Meeting House off Tithebarn Street in 1994.

The origins of the Congregational Church in Keswick are obscure, although there are reasons for believing its roots were Presbyterian. The minutes of the Cockermouth Congregational Church, founded in 1651, record that on 29 April 1657 the two sister churches met at Thornthwaite Chapel and the two pastors, Larkham and Cave, preached. Congregationalism was patently active in the Keswick area: Larkham was the Cockermouth pastor and James Cave, who in 1653 was appointed to be 'itinerant preacher at the chapelries in the parish of Crosthwaite', was described as 'the pastor of the other Society, Keswick'.

The 1662 Act of Uniformity, which outlawed any form of religious worship other than Anglican, forced the Congregationalists to meet in secret. In May 1668, the two churches, Cockermouth and Keswick, with the pastor of the latter in charge, met at John Bell's house at Embleton and in September 1672 a midnight gathering at Tallantire was attended by 'one of the broken people at Keswick' – the enigmatic adjective carries undertones of persecution.

The Toleration Act of 1689 restored freedom of worship and presumably the Keswick Congregationalists practised their religion unhampered. In his will of June 1715, John Allason of Burns near Keswick left £5 to be invested, the profits to be paid 'to the Dissenting Minister of Keswick'. A little later, Ann Waterson, one of the Allason family, bequeathed to four trustees 'that house in Keswick now fitted for a meeting house' and £200 to be invested on behalf of the 'Minister, Pastor or Teacher of the Congregation of Protestants or Presbyterians at Keswick Meeting House now fitted for that purpose'.

The exact location of this Meeting House is unknown but it is possible that it stood behind the site of the present chapel in Lake Road, which was built in 1803 with funds from an anonymous donor whose ancestors had lived in the town.

Congregational Church,
KESWICK.

FLORAL BAZAAR,
Sept. 14th & 15th, 1898.

CATALOGUE
OF THE
Grand Exhibition
OF
FINE + ARTS,
CONSISTING OF
Portraits, Models, Curios, & Ancient Relics, &c.

MANY of the EXHIBITS are FOR SALE, the Prices of which may be obtained on application to the attendant.
Visitors are earnestly requested not to deface or injure the Exhibits by touching them.

Admission (by Catalogue) 3d. each.

Visitors are requested not to communicate to their friends the nature of this exhibition, but to prevail upon them to visit the collection and form their own unbiassed opinion of its merits.

No Pass-out Checks will be given.

No Money returned, but visitors who have had too much **may pay again** on leaving the Exhibition.

The Congregational Church organises a Grand Exhibition and Bazaar

The Rev. Thomas Gritton came to the church in 1819, a young, vigorous and zealous pastor who initiated evening meetings in some of the neighbouring villages and began a Sunday School in 1820, some thirteen years before Crosthwaite's. It was not unknown for him to take services at Bootle in south-west Cumbria, a three-day commitment which involved walking over Sty Head on Friday and returning on Monday.

When he died in 1828, a period of decline set in: the church building was neglected, pastors stayed for only short periods and at times there was no pastor at all. The arrival of the Rev. T Davison in 1851 and the Rev. W. Colville in 1854 heralded a revival in both chapel and Sunday School. New premises were opened on 28 December 1859, to be followed in 1867 by a Sunday School across the road. In 1933 this building, too small for the growing number of children, was replaced by the present school alongside the chapel.

The strongest manifestation in Keswick of the nonconformist movement that swept through the country in the 1700s and 1800s was Methodism, both Wesleyan and Primitive. John Wesley came to Cumberland on a number of occasions – twenty-six visits to Whitehaven between 1749 and 1788 – and though he passed through Keswick there is no record of his ever having preached in the town.

It is possible that a small group was active as early as 1763 when a society of nineteen Methodists was established in Cockermouth. In the early 1800s, Robert Gates, a Penrith saddler and preacher, held Bible classes and services, traditionally in a cottage opposite the Crosthwaite Parish Room in Main Street.

The first Methodist chapel was built in 1814 in Temple Court or Temple Yard, later Chapel Yard, just above the King's Arms and opposite the Moot Hall. Here the Wesleyans worshipped under their first full-time minister, the Rev. Edmund Warters, who was appointed in 1836. It is believed that a few Primitive Methodists were active in the town about this time; by 1850 they were meeting in a room over a stable in Heads Lane.

In 1863, the Wesleyan Methodists launched an appeal for funds to build a bigger and more salubriously sited chapel: the Chapel Yard premises were too small, too difficult for strangers to find, too dilapidated, and too near the smell and noise of an adjacent candle manufactory.

The Methodist Church in Southey Street

The new chapel in Southey Street, with seating for 200, was opened on 18 October 1863, a wet and miserable day that failed to dampen either the enthusiasm or the satisfaction of the members.

In 1869, the Primitive Methodists built their chapel in Tithebarn Street, a substantial structure enlarged some thirty years later by the addition of a Sunday School.

Southey Street chapel was further extended in 1909; nearby Carlton House, bought in 1923, still serves as two flats and a home for the chapel caretaker. In the same year, Sir John Randles, a prominent and dedicated Wesleyan Methodist, bought and presented 'The Birches' in Crosthwaite Road as a minister's house – it had been rented since 1907 by the chapel trustees.

Rawlinson's 1852 report identified a chapel in High Street. Built in 1851, it was called 'Bethesda Free Chapel' and initially used by the Baptists. On 9 June 1861, the well-known evangelist, Dr C. Haddon Spurgeon preached here but by the late 1870s the building was used as an art school. At this time, a small group of Brethren met in a room over a stable in Grandy Nook, today's Station Street. Looking for more suitable premises, three members negotiated the hire of Bethesda for an annual rent of one shilling.

The chapel reopened for worship on 29 June 1884. On 3 October 1900, it was registered for the solemnization of marriages. Eventually the property was bought outright and is held under trust deed. The present building can seat over 150 and today's congregation has neither distinctive name nor allegiance to any particular denomination.

The Salvation Army was active in Keswick in the 1880s, possibly inspired by a holiday visit in September 1880 of General Booth, the founder of the Army. The faithful were not always received with the same fervour that characterised their religion. On 22 July 1884, there was an open air meeting in the Upper Market Square; the Promenade String Band was playing beside the Moot Hall; the Keswick Drum and Fife Band was marching up and down Main Street. The Salvationists' trumpets and tambourines stationed themselves outside the Queen's Hotel. The cacophony of conflicting noises was further augmented by a crowd of local people yelling and cheering; some of the rougher element threw stones and sods at the Salvationists.

In March 1885 a detachment of the Army Singing Brigade, twelve men and twelve women, marched through the Streets and gave a well-attended performance in the Oddfellows' Hall. Among the speakers who confessed their sins and their rescue by the Army were 'the one-eyed prophetess, the saved infidel, the Scotch lassie, and the Welsh drunkard'.

The Army maintained a tenuous presence until recent times but the once familiar uniform is now a rare sight in the town. Today the 'Citadel' in Heads Road, formerly the Salvationists' headquarters, is a drop-in social centre for older Keswickians.

Roman Catholicism in Keswick had no public facilities for worship until the 1920s. In 1926, Father Stephen Dawes, priest at St Joseph's in Cockermouth, bought a plot of land at High Hill. He commissioned an architect and undertook the responsibility of building the church, dedicated to Our Lady of the Lakes and St Charles. It was officially opened on 1 July 1928 by Thomas Wulstan Pearson, Bishop of the Diocese of Lancaster.

A modest building of Threlkeld granite, planned in Italian style, it seated about 120. Father Stephen Whiteside carried through the completion of the church and in 1972, under the guiding hand of Monsignor Wilfred Buxton, a presbytery was added.

For many people all over the world, the name 'Keswick' is associated with an organisation whose roots lie deep in the evangelical movement of the nineteenth century. In 1859, Canon Battersby of St John's and a few friends set up an 'Evangelical Union for the Diocese of Carlisle', inspired by an earnest wish that Christians of differing denominations should work and worship together.

In August 1874, Battersby attended a conference in Oxford on 'The Promotion of Scriptural Holiness' and came away deeply and permanently affected. He met a fellow Cumbrian, Robert Wilson of Broughton Grange near Cockermouth. A business man, with lucrative interests in coal and railways, he was a Quaker by faith, but superintended the Baptist Sunday School in the village and regularly attended the parish church – a true ecumenical Christian.

Our Lady of the Lakes and St Charles

Both Battersby and Wilson were impressed by the chairman and moving spirit of the Oxford conference, Robert Pearsall Smith, an American preacher. In March 1875, Battersby wrote to Wilson suggesting a series of meetings in Keswick at the end of June, with Pearsall Smith as the main speaker.

Wilson was keenly in favour and plans were made. A tent was erected at the bottom of the vicarage garden, with room for up to 600 people who were invited to attend three days of 'union meetings for the promotion of practical holiness'.

Just four days before the convention was due to open, Battersby received a telegram announcing that Smith was ill and was returning to America. Shaken but undaunted, he managed to engage substitute speakers and with the help of John Postlethwaite, who was to act as registrar for the next thirty years, made all the arrangements to cope with the expected hundreds. Those three days in the last week of June 1875, packed tight with meetings, services and prayers, were successful, in spite of a daily downpour of Lakeland rain: the Keswick Convention was born.

Its early years were overshadowed by its associations with Pearsall Smith. Some evangelists regarded his teachings as heretical and his reputation was further blackened by an unsupported accusation of adultery, that most heinous of crimes in Victorian eyes. It took many years before the truth was known. Smith had helped a young woman who was passing through an emotional crisis and she had spread a lurid and false version of the relationship. The slanders and rumours made Smith ill and he retreated to America, his ministry in ruins. Opponents and critics of the Keswick Convention were only too willing to condemn its origins as tainted and unreliable, but Battersby and Wilson, strong in faith and persistent in purpose, were undeterred: the Convention continued and prospered. Battersby presided every year until his death on 23 July 1883, the first day of that year's Convention; Wilson acted as Chairman until 1900, five years before his death.

From the beginning of the Convention, the problem of accommodating the ever-increasing number of worshippers exercised the organisers. In 1882, Battersby and Wilson bought a plot of land in Eskin Street and a tent with a capacity of about 600. In 1885 it was replaced by a 2,250 seater and twelve years later a second tent was erected in Skiddaw Street. By 1926 seating capacity had risen to nearly 6,000 and microphones and loudspeakers were in place. In 1954, with Billy Graham's Harringay crusade stimulating even wider interest, the Eskin Street tent was enlarged and a wooden annexe was added to the Skiddaw Street 'canvas cathedral': closed circuit television meant that nearly 7,000 people could see and listen simultaneously. In 1975, centenary year, Billy Graham himself addressed a large open-air rally in Crow Park.

Recent developments include the selling off of the Eskin Street site, including Convention Lodge, the office and administration headquarters since 1892, and the building in 1987 of a permanent block of offices and other accommodation in Skiddaw Street, with facilities for hooking on a 4,000-seater tent.

As numbers increased over the years, so did the need for a properly constituted, business-like administration to replace the benevolent but wholly inadequate despotism of Wilson and a handful of trustees. The Mission Council, set up in 1896, provided a structured body to handle the finances and organisation of the Convention. From 1900, when Wilson resigned, the management was rationalised, with the Trustees in full executive control. During a century of activity, the administrative organisation has been adapted, revised and modernised. In 1919, the Convention Council of trustees and speakers, assisted by several sub-committees, took over executive responsibilities. Today, the Trustees (never fewer than five and never more than ten) and appointed members make up a Council of up to fifteen. A Speakers' Committee is responsible for the programme; a Business Committee looks after property and the day-to-day running of the Convention; a permanent secretariat handles the nuts and bolts of administration – among its duties in 1989, for example, was the despatch of some 7,000 letters excluding circulars.

From its early days, the Convention was closely linked with missionary work abroad. By 1887, special meetings were held for missionaries and year after year men and women were inspired to offer their services in foreign fields. A fund was created to help those who were willing to take the message to faraway places: the first to receive a grant was Amy Carmichael, Robert Wilson's adopted daughter. She served in Japan, India and Ceylon, the pioneer of a steady stream of Keswick Missionaries who spread the good news to all parts of the world.

At home, the popularity of the Keswick gatherings sparked off local conventions in various parts of the country – Glasgow in 1882, Belfast in 1887, for example. The movement spread abroad and today's network of over 120 conventions stretches worldwide. Modern technology has helped to spread the Keswick message of 'All One in Christ Jesus': landline relays to congregations far removed from the tent, tapes and videos sent to all corners of the globe.

Personal testimonies of change and conversion abound. One of the most significant was in 1908, when an American arrived in Keswick, depressed and in spiritual turmoil. He went to a service in an unspecified 'stone built chapel' – actually Tithebarn Street Primitive Methodist. There, in a small congregation of only seventeen, he listened to a woman preacher whose message 'produced in me a vibrant feeling, as though a strong current of life had suddenly been poured into me and afterwards a dazed sense of a great spiritual shaking-up'. The American was Frank Buchman: that 'vibrant feeling' led directly to the founding of the Oxford Group, later Moral Rearmament.

The Convention continues as an annual event in Keswick life. Special trains no longer transport the faithful: today's headache is how to accommodate the hundreds of cars. Hotels, boarding houses and private homes are still packed to bursting and temporary bookstalls dotted along the streets near the tent draw crowds of browsers and buyers.

The annual Keswick Convention - the town's busiest week

A full daily programme, once described as 'spiritual gourmandising', caters for the ever-present enthusiasm which is so characteristic of the Convention. Its interdenominational emphasis attracts pilgrims of all persuasions, including many young people: it is significant that both the Inter-Universities Christian Union and the Student Christian Movement owed their beginnings to Keswick-inspired leaders.

Traditionally, Convention Week is wet ('when the tents go up, the rain comes down') and wind and storm have, on a number of occasions, played havoc with the tents. Worshippers are underterred: it would need much more than inclement weather and a collapsed tent to dampen their ardour.

The relationship between the town and the Convention is, on the whole, friendly; the economic benefits outweigh the inevitable overcrowding and the introduction of a second 'Holiday Week' some years ago was welcomed for the extra business it generated. There have been occasions when smooth relationships were strained: in 1926, for example, a confidential memo from the chairman, John Holden, claimed 'the rapacity of landladies and, in very many cases, the unsatisfactoriness of the accommodation and services provided was, this year, more evident than ever. Many and bitter were the complaints received'.

One feature of the Convention has remained firm and unshaken: its central faith. New ideas, radical opinions, the rejection of traditional Christianity have produced conflict and challenge but failed to undermine the fundamental principles that continue to pull in the crowds – a robust witness to the claim that the Convention has 'maintained a Christian gold-standard of sterling value in an age of depreciation'.

Hardwicke Drummond Rawnsley

15

School Days

The early history of education in Keswick is, not surprisingly, closely linked with Crosthwaite Church: the town's first school stands only a few yards from the main entrance gate to the church.

Over the centuries, it has been known by a variety of names, from Crosthwaite Old School and Crosthwaite Boys' Elementary Endowed School to Crosthwaite High School and Crosthwaite Free Grammar School. The date of its foundation is unknown, though it could be as early as the 1360s when Thomas de Eskhead was vicar of the parish. This learned cleric, it is said, was sent by the Vatican to arbitrate in the quarrel between Furness and Fountains Abbeys over their adjoining lands in Borrowdale. It is not unreasonable to suppose that he may have set up some form of small school but there is no firm evidence to support what must remain pure conjecture.

The first reliable, though vague, documentary reference testifying to the school's ancient foundation is found in 'Three Solemn Decrees' relating to the church and the 'very aged and much esteemed Free Grammar School'. These valuable documents are dated 1571, 1616 and 1637. The 1571 Decree refers several times to 'the Common and Free School at Crosthwaite' in terms which hint that it had been in existence for some time. In the second, thirteen 'good and lawful men' swore on oath 'that there hath been a Grammar School within the Parish of Crosthwaite in the said County, time whereof the memory of Man knoweth not the contrary' – yet another indication of an early date.

For several centuries until the 1870s, the management of the school was in the hands of the 'Eighteen Sworn Men'. These trustees may have been the descendants of a similar body appointed by the Abbot of Furness in the twelfth century with the right to nominate the vicar and to collect the tithes.

The Sworn Men were certainly in existence in 1571: the Decree of that date ordered that annually on Ascension Day they and the churchwardens for the year were to be elected. The choice was in the hands of a motley group which included the vicar, Sir George Radcliffe, five bailiffs, the forester of Derwent Fells, and 'the Sealer and Receiver of the Queen's Majesty's Portion of the Mines'. Refusal to serve either as a Sworn Man or a churchwarden incurred a fine of forty shillings 'to the use of the Parish and increase of the Stock of the School'.

With the vicar as overseer and auditor, the Sworn Men assumed financial responsibility for the school. They were charged with collecting twopence from every firehouse in the parish to augment the salary of the schoolmaster and the parish clerk – a local hearth-tax which operated nearly a century before the national hearth-tax of 1662.

World War Two: boys of Crosthwaite School dig for victory

The core of the school stock in 1571 was nearly £150, a sum donated over the years by parishioners and available for the Sworn Men to use as profitably as possible. To maintain a ready supply of cash, the Sworn Men appointed 'Taskers' to extract from the parishioners 'a reasonable sum, towards the maintenance of the said School, Schoolstock and other necessary Occasions of the said Parish'.

The responsibility of selecting, appointing and dismissing the schoolmaster and of drawing up the rules for running the school lay with the Eighteen Sworn Men. The success of the administration and of the teaching of the master may be assumed from a statement in the 1616 Decree that 'they have bred and brought forth many good scholars within the said Parish'.

It is easy to see that the vicar might resent the powers of the Sworn Men. The school was on his doorstep and it would be highly desirable to have a master he could control and possibly employ as an unpaid curate. Trouble – and, in a sense, a test case – arose in 1614. The Sworn Men dismissed Thomas Garth 'for divers gross offences and negligence'. He refused to go and was supported by Giles Robinson, the vicar of Crosthwaite from 1602 to 1623, and his brother, Henry Robinson, Bishop of the diocese from 1598 to 1616.

Exercising his powers as an Ecclesiastical Commissioner and a Justice of the Peace, the Bishop committed thirteen of the Sworn Men to prison, accusing them of disobeying his order that Thomas Garth should remain the master and of failing to administer the school funds properly.

An Inquisition on 16 February 1616 examined the case and decided that the Eighteen Sworn Men alone had the power to appoint and dismiss the schoolmaster and to act as 'sole and only Governors of the said School and School-stock'. Thomas Garth's dismissal was confirmed.

A further instruction that no master should be employed as a curate or compelled to undertake any parish office which would cause him to neglect his educational commitments shows an admirable concern for the welfare of the pupils and a strong hint that Thomas Garth had been employed by the vicar for parochial duties.

By 1691, the school stock had grown to £224: investment in land and property (including Knott Farm at Crosthwaite), rents and bequests like that of £100 from Edward Grisedale, a London tailor, in 1687, continued to swell the coffers.

Arthur Young, whose *Six Months' Tour through the North of England* was published in 1770, refers to the ancient custom of 'cockpenny'. At Shrovetide every year, the pupils were allowed cockfighting, a privilege for which they paid the master. The principle, apart from augmenting the master's income, was, according to Young, that 'learning effeminated and softened the mind too much and therefore these cruel sports were permitted to harden their feelings and encourage a martial spirit and ferocity of temper'. The custom was discontinued at some date before 1820 when a report by the Charity Commissioners stated that 'the cockfight and the payments of the cock-penny were both abolished when the rent of the land increased so as to afford a sufficient remuneration to the Master without such payment'.

In 1801, a curious incident occurred. The master at the time was the Rev. William Parsable, curate of Newlands – an appointment that suggests the provisions of the ancient decrees had been relaxed. Mr Parsable had a reputation of being ill-tempered and 'Peppery Billy', as he was known, seldom hesitated to punish his pupils, often with extreme severity. Complaints were made to the Sworn Men but to no avail: 'ivverybody was as flayte (frightened) on him as were t'scholars' – everybody except William Slack.

This gentleman, who lived at Monk Hall, had a nephew at Crosthwaite School. One day the boy was flogged and William, roused to anger, marched to the school and had a battle of words with Parsable. It ended with Slack seizing the master and running him out of the school, much to the delight and amusement of the pupils. The fight, it seemed, was continued outside the school.

Slack was taken to court for breach of the peace and tried in Lancaster. He lost his case and was heavily fined: the only compensation was a hero's welcome on his return to Keswick. The story is traditional and may well have been distorted with telling, but the essentials have the ring of truth.

There was more trouble in 1832. The Rev. J W Whiteside, curate under the Rev. James Lynn, was a violent opponent of strong drink. He tried to revive an old law which gave the parson the power to arrest anyone found in a public house during church service time. His attempts to trap the tipplers appear to have failed but in a subsequent sermon he severely condemned the ungodly and drunken people of Keswick. This tirade roused much anger and resentment, not only against Mr Whiteside but also against the master of Crosthwaite School, who was a friend and supporter of the curate and allowed his premises to be used for Sunday School.

The Eighteen Sworn Men met on 1 September 1832 and passed several resolutions. The master and his assistant usher were to be dismissed; the Sunday School was to be discontinued immediately. To assist the finances of the school, a public subscription and a levy of one farthing on every pupil were proposed.

Twelve years later, anxious to give Crosthwaite children the advantages of new educational ideas, the Sworn Men issued a circular in November 1844 headed 'Rules and

Regulations of the Free Grammar School'. It announced that under the management of Mr Burn the Madras or Monitorial System was to be adopted. This method of instruction used the older pupils to help in teaching the younger; prayers began and ended each day; strict punctuality and personal cleanliness were as important as learning.

Children were admitted to the school from the age of six and were expected to provide their own books and slates. The only other obligation was a charge of sixpence a year for heating. The range of subjects was impressive: the basics – reading, writing and 'cyphering' – were buttressed by mathematics, geography, English grammar, Latin and Greek.

It is impossible to know how successful the school was or how many pupils did in fact wrestle with calculus or the ablative case. A report by one of Her Majesty's Inspectors in 1855, when the one-armed Mr Peter Harrison was master, stated that 'the school seems to be improving', though there were 'great deficiencies in respect of order and method'.

By the late 1860s, the total of the school's endowments, charities, investments and stock had risen to £4,000, which produced an annual income of £120. In 1864, a government grant of £60 was withdrawn and pupil teachers' salaries were no longer funded. Five years later, a Schools Inquiry Commission made a number of proposals, among them that all pupils should pay a quarterly fee and that all girls should be transferred to the National School at High Hill which had opened in 1833.

The school at High Hill - a local landmark for well over a century and a half

Although this suggestion would have helped overcrowding – there were 160 pupils, 97 of them under ten years of age – the idea of charging for tuition would have destroyed the centuries-old principle of the Free Grammar School.

The Eighteen Sworn Men took up the challenge and rejected both proposals. The school was enlarged, the playground extended, and a teacher was appointed to train the girls in sewing and knitting.

The 1870 Education Act and further legislation in 1874 brought a fundamental change in the government of the school. The Eighteen Sworn Men, after perhaps 500 years, were abolished and their place taken by a board of governors – a shift of responsibility which did little to increase the efficiency and achievements of the school. In 1878, with an upper class of twenty-four and a lower school of 126, only three boys were learning Latin and four boys and two girls French. An inspector's report brought no comfort: the proficiency of the pupils was of 'a rather low level' and grammar in the higher classes 'displayed gross ignorance'.

Educational reform was in the air. In 1880, the year that school attendance up to the age of ten was made compulsory and the upper department at Crosthwaite School was recognised as a failure, the governors put forward several propositions. The two most important were that the girls should attend the National School at High Hill, as had been suggested in 1869, and that half of Crosthwaite's income should be set aside for a new school for higher education for boys to replace the senior class at Crosthwaite.

Some parents welcomed the concept of a separate building for older pupils; others were angry at the idea, foreseeing the payment of fees to fund it. The proposal persisted and was considerably strengthened by an event in June 1882 which was to shape the educational future of Keswick.

The managers of Crosthwaite School received a letter from Henry and Thomas Hewetson, Keswick's benefactors extraordinary, offering some twenty-five acres of land stretching from Keswick Bridge to Crosthwaite Church and including High Hill Farm. This gift was to supplement the existing endowments and help to implement the scheme for a new high school. It was conditional on three principles: girls should be admitted 'on an equality in all respects with boys'; girls should be eligible for scholarships; and part of the income should be used to provide a pension for Mr Peter Harrison on his retirement from the mastership of Crosthwaite School.

Henry Hewetson, feeling strongly that Britain needed well-trained 'middle-class youth' insisted that the gift was a stepping-stone 'to a first class Public school'. In 1884, the brothers bought Williamson's Close or Saw Pit Field near Greta Bridge as a possible site for the new school and offered it to the managers.

Progress was temporarily halted in 1888 with the death of Mrs Arthur Dover. When her husband died in 1873, he left £500 to be paid to the trustees of Crosthwaite School when his wife died. Her will added a further £300 but Mrs Dover was strongly opposed to using Crosthwaite School endowments for building the new school. Feelings ran high: legal opinion supported the view that the Dover bequests should go to Crosthwaite School; contrary opinion pointed out that when Mr Dover died in 1873 there was no scheme for a new high school.

Canon Rawnsley interviewed the Charity Commissioners; the local MP, Mr J W Lowther, was approached; a threat was made to raise the whole problem in the House of Commons. An expensive law suit to settle the matter was out of the question but suddenly a solution appeared.

In May 1895, Henry Hewetson died. Among his many liberal bequests was £200 a year for the projected new school and a further gift on the death of the last member of his family. This amounted to £33,000 ... the way to the new school was clear.

Crosthwaite School, meanwhile, was struggling under considerable difficulties. Absenteeism was rife; standards were low; staff were often poorly qualified. Children were kept off school to run errands, to help on the farm or assist with catering for visitors; bad weather all too often provided an excuse for non-attendance. Many parents showed little interest in the welfare of their children and the school itself was cold and uninviting – on 23 January 1879 the log book records 'scholars had no writing on account of ink being frozen in inkwells'. Successive inspectors' reports were almost universally critical and depressing.

It was into this sad state of apathy and inefficiency that a new headmaster, Henry Swinburn, was plunged in 1891. A new era began. He was a fully trained teacher and stayed at Crosthwaite for the next thirty-five years, a highly regarded and active member of the community.

Within a year, the quality of education at Crosthwaite had improved. Swinburn's discipline was severe, his expectations were high, and before long he established Crosthwaite's reputation as a well-equipped school with, it was claimed, the best attainments in the county. The standards he set and the innovations he pioneered – gardening, woodwork, local studies, for example – were maintained by his successors: Alfred Grave (1927-1933); William Slee (1933-1966), who was headmaster when Crosthwaite became a primary school in 1951 with the transfer of its senior pupils to a new secondary modern school at Lairthwaite; and Brian Wilkinson (1966-1974), who was responsible in 1968 for a school swimming pool and in 1974 had to face the unenviable task of closing the school in the reorganisation of primary education in Keswick.

Fortunately, the town's other primary schools have neither the lengthy nor the complicated history of Crosthwaite. Early efforts to provide some form of basic education were often linked with private initiative or Sunday Schools. As far back as 1781, the Rev. John Wilson, rector of Uldale, advertised his educational wares in Keswick, when he offered a range of subjects taught 'carefully and correctly', particularly for intending clergymen. Board and lodging were available in his house.

In 1789, Mrs M Barker was promoting her school for young ladies, with fees at £14.14.0. a year; directories of 1829 and 1847 list six or seven 'academies'. Miss Brindle had a girls' school at Greta Hall from 1872 to 1887.

It is difficult to assess either the popularity or the efficiency of this proliferation of privately organised educational opportunities. Their provision was plainly for the few: the majority of children relied on the interest and efforts of the churches.

The first Sunday School in Keswick was established in September 1818, mainly through the efforts of Joseph Mayson and the Rev. Thomas Gritton, pastor of the Congregational Church. Within three weeks, over 100 children were learning to read religious tracts; subscribers, William Wilberforce among them, donated money for books and twelve men and fifteen women gave their services to teaching the increasing numbers of pupils – 116 girls and 104 boys by the end of the first year.

In July 1833, Crosthwaite National School at High Hill was opened, financed by James Stanger, supervised by the Rev. J W Whiteside and designed primarily as a Sunday School – probably as a direct result of the decision in 1832 of the Eighteen Sworn Men to discontinue the use of Crosthwaite as a Sunday School.

As many as 350 children are said to have attended the National School on Sundays and during the week sixty girls paid their twopences to be taught reading and writing, sewing and knitting. The staff in the 1860s consisted of a mistress, a pupil teacher and a monitor – hardly adequate for up to seventy pupils – and it is not surprising that inspectors' reports were a dismal catalogue of failures and short-comings. Attendance was irregular and almost any excuse seems to have kept the girls away from school: a circus in town, a cattle fair, a temperance demonstration, 'a grand gala on the ice'. On the other hand, the introduction of cookery lessons in 1885 appears to have been very successful.

A separate building for infants was added in August 1889; a report of 1891 indicates that both schools were in good order and were maintaining a reasonable standard of attainment. By 1904, there was accommodation for 160 juniors and eight-one infants – an allowance of eight square feet per child. Improvements to the structure continued and by 1929, with 190 places available, it was removed from the Board of Education's list of public elementary schools with defective premises.

Coping with evacuees from Newcastle-upon-Tyne and South Shields in 1939 brought considerable problems of both overcrowding and the satisfactory provision of an adequate timetable. From 1952, operating as an infants' school for the five to eight range of pupils, its numbers fluctuated wildly – sixty-seven in 1977, twenty-eight in 1981 – and possible closure was threatened. By 1989, primary education was once again under review and by 1992 plans had been approved for a new purpose-built school for all children of primary school age in the town.

The story of St John's schools, like that of Crosthwaite Girls' and Infants', is closely linked with Sunday Schools and the benevolence of a local philanthropist. Having provided the finance for St John's Church, the Marshall family funded a Sunday School in 1840 which, on weekdays, served as an infants' school and later as both infants' and girls'. By 1855, there were 108 children in five classes under the headmistress, Miss Buxton, and two untrained assistants.

In February 1873, the Rev. Harford Battersby laid the foundation stone of a new infants' school. By 1904, numbers of pupils in the two schools had grown considerably with 304 on roll. Overcrowded rooms meant formidable problems of teaching and discipline: the buildings were extended and classes were taught in the Battersby Hall and the Library across the road. At one stage, the nursery group was located in the nearby Hollies, home of the local R A F A Club, and St John's could boast that it was the only primary school in the country with its own bar!

In 1849, concerned with the lack of a boys' school in his parish, the Rev. F Myers decided to build one, provided his curate, the Rev. Harford Battersby, could find a suitable headmaster. Mr R D Marshall gave a plot of land at Brigham; Battersby found his schoolmaster and the school was built. A plaque on an inside wall commemorated the foundation of a school where boys 'should be trained herein to habits of piety and Christian virtue, as well as instructed in such branches of knowledge and industrial art as might fit them to become useful members of society'.

Brigham was fortunate in having as its first headmaster Edward Highton, Battersby's choice. The two men had worked together in Gosport, where Battersby had been a curate and Highton had been in charge of the Preparatory National School for neglected children in 'that terribly vicious and irreligious seaport'. Later he took the post of master on the convict training ship 'Hebe'.

In January 1851, he accepted Battersby's offer and moved to Keswick. His first, temporary school at the Forge was for a mere nineteen pupils: three months later he transferred to the new school with fifty-eight boys. He stayed for the next thirty years, during which time the roll increased to nearly 200. He took an active part in local affairs: church organist and choirmaster (in thirty years, he never missed a service, Sundays or weekdays), founder member of the Temperance Reformation Society, secretary of the Mechanics' Institute and the Oddfellows' Masonic Lodge, a member of the Local Board – a prime example of Victorian devotion to duty. He was succeeded at Brigham by his son, Thomas Edward, who held the post for twenty-seven years – a remarkable family record. He is commemorated by a plaque on the outside wall of the school and a stained glass window in St John's Church, unveiled and dedicated by the Bishop of Carlisle on 25 March 1909.

A new classroom was added in 1888 and in 1895 an infants' department was opened. A gift of £1,330 from Miss Emma Langton and anonymous donations from friends provided the capital for the building on land given by Mr R D Marshall.

The main problem in the early 1900s was the familiar one of overcrowding. Up to 220 children were on the register, including some thirty girls, and teaching three or four large classes in one room was hardy conducive to successful education. The transfer of the senior girls to St John's in 1908 eased the congestion only slightly and in 1927 the Junior Girls' and Infants' departments were closed and the pupils switched to St John's, leaving Brigham once more for boys only.

In 1951, when Lairthwaite was opened for the over elevens, Brigham was a five-class school with 124 on roll: it joined the other primary schools to feed either Keswick School, the long established grammar school, or the new secondary modern at Lairthwaite.

By 1969, more reforms were being discussed. The total number of pupils in Keswick between the ages of three and eleven was 513: Crosthwaite 132, Crosthwaite Infants' 71, Brigham 117, St John's Infants' 107, St John's Girls' 86. It was finally decided to keep only Brigham, Crosthwaite Infants' and St John's Infants' open as First Schools and build a new school for the eight to elevens near the Windebrowe housing estate.

Trinity School opened in 1974 for about 200 pupils from the three feeder schools. In 1989 yet another reorganisation was planned, with the proposed closure of the three First Schools and the building of new premises for nursery and infant pupils. In July 1993, Crosthwaite, St John's and Brigham closed and in September the new St Kentigern's Church of England (Voluntary Aided) Infant and Nursery School for pupils from three to seven-year-old opened on a site adjoining Trinity School with 140 children aged from four to seven and fifty-two aged from three to four. This reorganisation means that all children up to the age of eleven are now accommodated in two adjacent schools, which are up-to-date in equipment and facilities, easier to administer, and promise more efficient liaison and continuity.

The redundant premises have been earmarked for diverse development. Crosthwaite has been bought by the Roman Catholic church, its neighbour across the road, for use as a meeting room, aptly named 'The St Herbert Social Centre'. St John's is to be converted into residential accommodation but at the time of writing plans for Brigham are unresolved.

To trace the development of secondary education in Keswick, it is necessary to go back to the proposals of the 1890s for a new High School and Henry Hewetson's generous financial support.

On 6 October 1897, Lord Muncaster, the Lord Lieutenant of Cumberland, laid the foundation stone of the new school. A year later, on 10 September 1898, it was officially opened by the Bishop of Hereford on Saw Pit Field, just as the Hewetsons had wished. Keswick School, as it was called from 1905, was something of a pioneer in co-education. The first headmaster, the Rev. Cecil Grant, was an enthusiast for this type of education, particularly after a visit to America where he had seen it in operation. The experiment of a mixed secondary school for boys and girls at Bakewell in Derbyshire had raised a number of objections. The boys, it was claimed, would become effeminate, the girls rough and uncouth; Cupid would oust classics; corporal punishment could hardly be administered to the girls.

Keswick School - the Rawnsley Hall with School House behind

Such quaint reservations had little effect on Keswick School and a mere two years after its foundation a comment in the Crosthwaite Parish Magazine stated: 'It is interesting to note that already the Keswick School is being quoted as a pioneer in the field of dual education'.

The original building, designed to accommodate not fewer than eighty day pupils and not more than twenty boarders, consisted of a large hall divided by a moveable screen, with three small classrooms at one end and a staff-room, sixth-form room and another classroom at the other. The first pupils – thirty boys and twenty girls – arrived on 28 September 1898.

Two years later, Canon Rawnsley and Robert Slack of Derwent Hill at Portinscale bought Greta Hall and rented it to the headmaster as a girls' boarding house. The school and its future were very dear to Rawnsley's heart: he was Chairman of the Governors and from Cumberland's Director of Education at the time earned the tribute of being described as 'a pioneer of secondary education and the real founder of the Keswick High School'. He maintained a close link with the school until his death, acknowledged as both a practical adviser and an inspiration.

A pupil who went as a boarder in 1901 at the age of ten remembered living at Leaming House on the Heads, a small boarding house for girls under the supervision of the French master, M. le Maistre, and his wife. She later moved to Elm Grove opposite the school and later still to Greta Hall. She recalled being punished for using the front stairs at Greta, which were out of bounds: for this minor misdemeanour, she was sent to bed with bread and water for supper.

All seemed set for a bright and successful future, but by 1904, only six years after the foundation of the school, a major crisis erupted. Mr R D Marshall, an alderman of Cumberland County Council, moved a resolution that the grant of £100 to the school be withdrawn. He condemned the management of the school and argued that the manner in which it was being conducted was contrary to the intentions of the Hewetsons, the original benefactors – it was not 'of that commercial character which was suitable for the sons of tradesmen'.

The governors vigorously refuted the criticisms, supporting their case by four reports which had appeared between 1900 and 1903, all commending the achievements and general tone of the school. The Oxford Board for Local Examinations, for example, reported that 'the proficiency of the scholars is of a high order of merit...the excellence of the classics and French is exceptional'.

In the face of so formidable a barrage of flattering comments and high praise, Mr Marshall's strictures crumbled, though they may in part have been responsible for a formal statement in 1906 of the Instruments of Government of the school, regulations which remained in force for the next twenty years. These included a pledge that the number of boarders would not exceed that of day pupils. The headmaster was not allowed to undertake any other office or employment, ecclesiastical duties included; his salary was £120 a year, supplemented by a capitation allowance of between £1 and £3 per pupil. The minimum age of admission was seven, which left the way open for a kindergarten or preparatory department.

Cecil Grant always cherished the idea of having his own school and chapel. On holiday, one of the staff, M. le Maistre, discovered St George's School, Harpenden standing empty. This was the opportunity Grant had been waiting for. In 1906, he resigned from his Keswick headship and moved south, taking several of his staff and some pupils with him.

A strong link between the two schools was forged and maintained for many years, an association kept alive and active by exchange visits and sporting contests. On 4 October 1914, Canon Rawnsley dedicated St George's new chapel and the paten and chalice which were made at Keswick School of Industrial Arts. Dormitories and common rooms at St

George's were given Cumbrian names – Skiddaw and Greta, Cat Bells and Borrowdale.

The two schools shared the same motto and the same hymn. One cannot help feeling that St George's pupils might be a little baffled by 'Levavi oculos' (I will lift up my eyes) on their school badge and a hymn ('Assurgit Skiddaw stabilis' – Skiddaw rises firm and steadfast) that refers to a mountain 300 miles away.

Cecil Grant was succeeded by Mr Hudson. In 1920, the Governors bought Greta Hall, the first of several boarding houses which later included Greta Grove, Bristowe Hill and Bridge House. The following year, Hudson retired and his post was taken by Mr H W Howe, a scholarly, vigorous and far-seeing headmaster, who had been a member of staff at St George's. One of his first tasks was to raise funds for much needed extensions. In 1926, the Hewetson Building was opened, with seven classrooms and a small kindergarten unit. Woodwork, art and music rooms were also built at the same time, most of the total cost of £9,000 coming from local subscriptions.

By now, the age range for pupils was from eight to eighteen. Prospective entrants, facing an entrance examination, had to be able to read: 'a love of and proper care for books', declared the 1927 prospectus, 'is held to be one of the chief aims of education'. Tuition fees were £11 a year, boarding fees £70, and music £1 for ten lessons.

Discipline was reinforced by strict rules. Preparation, for both boarders and day pupils who lived within a convenient distance, was compulsory from six o'clock to seven-thirty every evening, an imposition that involved pupils working an eight-hour day. Those who travelled by train had to walk from the station to the school through Fitz Park, never through the town. A midday meal was supplied to day pupils at a cost of one shilling and 'under no circumstance must pupils lunch at a cafe or hotel'.

Some idea of the standard of excellence pursued by the school and the range of cultural activities it encouraged is evident from the programme of the twenty eighth Speech Day on 25 July 1927. Prizes apart, a school orchestra played and the girls' choir sang; three members of the sixth form presented a scene from Sophocles' *Antigone*, first in English and then in Greek.

By 1936, numbers had grown to over 250 and more accommodation was needed. The old block was demolished and rebuilt as the Rawnsley Hall, with cloakrooms, science laboratories and classrooms. Mr Chuter Ede, making his first public appearance as Secretary to the Board of Education, officially opened the new building on 24 May 1940.

Boarders continued to form a substantial part of the pupil population, coming from remoter areas of Cumberland where grammar school facilities were not available, from overseas (particularly children whose fathers were in the Forces), and from parents who wanted boarding education for their children in a small grammar school where fees were reasonably priced.

Towards the end of the war, plans were in the air for the building of a secondary modern school to meet the provisions of the 1944 Education Act. Mr Howe welcomed the proposal, seeing it as the first step towards a single, integrated school for the over-elevens, with no selection, no entrance examination, no sense of failure, no 'us and them' attitude. In his thinking, he was nearly forty years ahead of what eventually happened.

One pressing problem was that of status. Should Keswick School continue as a voluntary aided establishment, as Mr Howe and his governors wanted, or should it become a controlled county school, as the Ministry of Education preferred? The dispute sparked off Mr Howe's decision to resign and lingered on until 1952 when the school was granted its aided status. This allowed it to retain certain privileges and duties – the upkeep of buildings, the appointment of staff, the fixing of holidays – while the local authority assumed responsibility for most matters financial.

Lairthwaite School

The new secondary modern school, built with the old mansion of Lairthwaite as its core, was ready for occupation by September 1951 and officially opened a year later. It had high aims for its pupils: 'In this vigorous school community, they will be led on to develop to the full their abilities and interests and to live richly in co-operation with their fellows'.

In the evenings, Lairthwaite continued the concept of a vigorous community by taking on the role of a further education centre. Its popularity may be judged by the statistics of a typical year, 1974-75, when 1,162 students (or 25% of the population of Keswick) enrolled in over sixty classes.

Lairthwaite was one of the very few secondary modern schools in the country with boarding facilities, so that when rumours of amalgamation between the two secondary schools were rife – an amalgamation, it must be said, which was not received with universal approval in the town – there was at least one important feature to ease the unification.

Various schemes were suggested to effect a union of the two schools into one comprehensive and finally Keswick School governors bought Lairthwaite (as a voluntary aided school, they had to raise only 15%, about £100,000, of the purchase price) and in 1980 the two schools merged into a single eleven to eighteen comprehensive on a split site. The voluntary aided status, with its small measure of independence, was retained by the new school.

Once the merger was complete, with a roll of 860 pupils, 200 of them boarders, and a sixth form of 140, it quickly became obvious that more money was needed. An appeal was launched for £100,000, a target reached in three years. But in the economic climate of the 1980s, with increasing costs and falling numbers, problems persisted. By 1985, the total number of boarders had dropped to 160; financial losses amounted to over £20,000; boarding fees rocketed to just under £2,000 a year.

The merger was decisively tested only two years after its initiation by a thorough inspection. Keswick was chosen as one of five schools in England and Wales for a full survey of how secondary schools were responding to falling rolls. A satisfactory report revealed that academic standards had been maintained, and there were no major disciplinary problems and that boarders were well cared for. It was clear that, in spite of misgivings in some quarters, progress towards a fully integrated and mature comprehensive school was well in hand.

Links with Rawnsley continued. A new Rawnsley Craft, Design and Technology Centre on the Lairthwaite site was opened in 1986, the funding appropriately provided from the sale of the School of Industrial Arts.

By 1989, it had become increasingly obvious that the difficulties of running a split site school had to be resolved. There was only one solution: the closure of either the Keswick School site or Lairthwaite site, with an expansion of buildings and facilities into a single complex. The governors faced an unenviable decision but, after much debate, consultation and heart-searching, agreed that at some future date, as yet unspecified, the Lairthwaite site should be adopted.

One special period that brought its own educational problems was the Second World War, when Keswick accepted evacuees from Newcastle and South Shields. Local schools were filled to capacity as limited space was shared. Keswick School had to cope with 300 girls from Newcastle High School; St John's expanded from 96 in 1939 to 165 in 1940; St John's Infants' from 77 to 128; Brigham from 81 to 133, with a Roman Catholic school using the premises in the afternoons.

Roedean, the well-known public school for girls, moved from Brighton to the Keswick Hotel, with the Millfield Hotel as the junior department. Classes were held in Southey Street Methodist Church, the station waiting rooms, the hotel garages. The 'swanky rodents' made full use of the fells, the frozen lake and the security of peaceful surroundings. Former pupils have expressed their affection for Keswick in 1940 in spite of their privations and inconveniences – happy memories which even make light of sour porridge, a green soup with yellow lumps in it, and barley pudding looking like 'a grey slimy wadge covered with a thin jam sauce'.

Graham Sutton

16

Comedy and Climbing

Modern Keswick is patently geared to tourism. Traditional occupations, apart from pencil making, have disappeared and the town's economy is firmly and deeply rooted in catering for the needs of visitors.

A survey conducted in the town in 1976 during the months of June to September by two researchers from the University College of North Wales gives some indication of the volume and importance of the tourist trade. The 1,612 interviews produced results and projections which were inevitably approximate but the basic trends were clear.

The most popular kind of accommodation was bed and breakfast (67,470) and guest house (48,626) with hotels (35,104) and camping (15,228) well behind. Caravans – touring, own static and rented static – accounted for 12,770; inns, 8,368; furnished lets, 6,753; friends and relatives, 4,446; second homes, 1,425; farmhouse, 1,155 – a grand total of 201,363, to which must be added 1,239,011 day trippers, giving a final figure of 1,440,374 and an estimated expenditure of £13,013,925. In 1994, nearly twenty years later, these statistics need considerable upgrading in certain categories to give a true picture.

While bed and breakfast accommodation, boarding houses and self-catering have expanded – Keswick claims to have the highest number of bed and breakfast facilities per head of population in the country – hotels have shrunk or been converted into shops. The Royal Oak, the Skiddaw and the Lake hotels have trimmed their accommodation in favour of retail outlets; some have disappeared altogether. The King's Head is remembered only in the name of King's Head Yard; the Woolpack has been converted to a sports-wear shop; the Black Lion and the Crown were demolished in 1990 to make way for flats – Hewetson Court – and shops.

Old names have disappeared. Many years ago, the Oddfellows' Arms was known as the Rose and Crown; the Shoulder of Mutton became the Central Hotel, now lost for ever as part of the Old Friar's sweet shop. The Bank Tavern was once the Waggon and Horses; the George and Dragon has shed its dragon, the Queen's Head its head.

Hotels and inns apart, other places in the town have been rechristened, the prosaic often replacing the unusual. Frying Pan Alley in Derwent Street is now St George's Square; Pear Tree Lane opposite the foot of Stanger Street (did it ever have its pear tree?) used to be known as Chitty Puss Lane. Dixon Gate, linking the Royal Oak corner with Lake Road, is still locally known as Paraffin Alley; the old name of the Market Place, Summer Birks Brow, has long since been forgotten.

The yards off the Market Square and Main Street, so typical of a medieval burgage layout, have been mauled and destroyed out of all recognition, though here and there truncated remains give some idea of their original look. Once they bustled with life, with cottages unhygenically crowded into any available space and cheek-by-jowl with pig styes and cow byres, stables and workshops which ranged from joiners and plumbers to smiths and cycle repairers.

Some yards housed larger premises: Mr Bakewell's printing works on Main Street between Bank Street and Stanger Street; the old Police Station in Police Court Yard opposite Derwent Close flats; the Assembly Room in the King's Arms Yard, the first home of the Derwent Club and for over seventy years from 1907 to 1981 the printing works of G W McKane and the *Keswick Reminder*; the Oddfellows' Hall, that most patronised of assembly halls, transformed into a walk-around drapery emporium in the 1920s by Mr Harold Clough.

An ever-growing population, fuelled by the attractions of Keswick for retired people, produced a boom in housing stock. Following the expansion in Leonard's Field in the late 1800s, the town spread in all directions, mainly in the eastern sector. The council housing estates of the Heads, Windebrowe Avenue, Latrigg Close and Millfield Gardens were joined by smaller private ventures at Briar Rigg, Brundholme Gardens and Brow Ridding. On the outskirts, Borrowdale Road, Chestnut Hill, Springs Road and Eleventrees provided sites for modest development. Within the town itself, practically any vacant space qualified for in-filling by either shops or flats, fortunately on a small scale. The old mill buildings on the bank of the Greta were transformed into holiday accommodation; the Convention tent site in Eskin Street provided yet another location for modern flats; the compact shopping precincts of Herries Thwaite and Packhorse Court were kept to suitable proportions.

Keswick's 'Garden City' with Greta Hall in the background

Greta Hamlet, tucked away at the top of Stanger Street, merits special comment. Conceived in the mould of the 'Garden City' movement responsible for Welwyn and Letchworth, an estate of twenty-five houses was built in 1910-11 at a cost of nearly £7,000. Tenants were urged to take shares in the venture, officially named Derwentwater Tenants Ltd, and to be actively involved in the administration of the estate.

The site was popular as an elevated, healthy situation, doubly welcome to the rehoused inhabitants of the crowded town yards. Great emphasis was laid on cleanliness and neatness; gardens were kept trim and tidy. The spirit of pride and co-operative effort has continued through the past eighty years and there is no shortage of prospective tenants when property becomes vacant.

Although Keswick is not as badly affected by the second home syndrome as some other places in the Lake District, it does have an ageing population. Out of 4,777 people in 1981, 1,477 or over 30% were sixty years old or more. For the work force, opportunities have been narrowed to three main areas: tourism, service occupations and the pencil factory. Attempts to create work in the neighbourhood have ranged from complete failure to continuing success: a silica brick works at Wythop in the mid 1930s collapsed almost before it began; the long-established quarries at Honister and Threlkeld no longer operate; the Forestry Commission at Whinlatter and Skiddaw still provides employment.

Entertainment has also kept pace with changing tastes: there are no temperance rallies or Young Men's Improvement Classes today but slide shows and guided walks, discos rather than formal dances. The Agricultural Show continues to be well supported, the display of animals and produce swollen by an ever-increasing number of stalls – a mini Royal Smithfield cum Petticoat Lane. Crowds of over 10,000 are drawn by the promise of spectacular entertainment such as sky diving, acrobatic aeroplanes or parachute jumping.

Dramatic performances have been given in the town for at least 200 years. At the time of the regattas in the 1780s, travelling players performed for the entertainment of 'the Ladies, Gentlemen and Nobility of Keswick and its Vicinity'. Budworth, who came to Keswick in 1792, attended a performance of *The Merchant of Venice* in an unroofed building, with the sky visible through the ceiling boards and the unplastered walls decorated with cast-off scenery. 'The house was as full as it could possibly cram,' wrote Budworth, although there were only twenty-four people in the pit. The second night, the audience dwindled to four and the show was cancelled.

Some years later, in 1803, Charlotte Deans, a travelling actress born in Wigton, arrived in Keswick with her itinerant company on the first of several visits. A private performance at Derwent Bank in 1813 for Lord Sunderlin and his guests appears to have been well received and enjoyed by some fifty adults and twenty children.

On one of the visits, Charlotte's company played Coleridge's *Remorse* in 'a newly created theatre, better than any that had been in the town before'. Mr Deans, 'having sacrificed to Bacchus too liberally', was not in top form; breaks and pauses in his delivery were all too frequent but 'notwithstanding he was pronounced excellent'. On another occasion, the company was in Keswick for the summer, the forerunners of the seasonal performances by the Century Theatre players in the 1970s and 1980s.

Visiting companies and groups of local amateurs continued to provide entertainment for both residents and visitors. On 7 October 1842, for example, Mr Thorne's company rounded off its season with 'The Battle of Waterloo', an extravaganza of 'Marches, Counter-Marches, Evolutions, Choruses and Terrific Combats'. In 1863, a group of comedians performed in the Oddfellows' Hall; a thirty-strong comic opèra group used the Hall in 1884 and advertisements in plenty indicate that over the years this was the usual venue for theatrical and other shows.

From 1895, the 'Queen of the Lakes Pavilion' in Station Road provided the equivalent of a theatre, with a seating capacity of over 1,000 and a stage capable of accommodating 250. Crowds were drawn by a range of productions, from the Sadlers Wells Opera presentation of *La Traviata* to farces by the local Garrick Club and an annual pantomime. Whatever the reasons for its closure and demolition in 1988, many Keswickians deplored the loss of a building that would have made a much-needed public hall or a permanent theatre for the 1990s and beyond.

Vandalised - but the show goes on

In recent times, the Century Theatre has provided a summer season of plays of high quality. The Blue Box, as it is known, began life as a mobile theatre, a curious but efficient set of four huge trailers which could be towed to practically any venue and linked together to make an auditorium, stage, dressing rooms and foyer – a complete theatre with seating for over 200.

Its first tour was with a production of *Othello* in 1952. The Blue Box remained on the road, crisis never far away; the imaginative enterprise of its staff, persistently fuelled by enthusiastic audience reaction and the loyalty and camaraderie of the players themselves, was adequate to tackle any problems and frustrations.

In June 1961, the Century arrived in Keswick for the summer season – fourteen weeks and seven different plays, including *Twelfth Night*, *She Stoops to Conquer* and the world premiere of Henry Livings' *Big Soft Nellie*. The success of this first season encouraged a return the following year and Keswick has had its summer theatre ever since. The sites of the Blue Box have included the Town Cass; the local rubbish dump near the lake which now houses a caravan park; the car park behind the Skiddaw Hotel; the piece of land where the library now stands; the old bus station, now the premises of Caterite; and finally the Lakeside Car Park where it remains, an eyesore by any standards, prime amenity though it is.

There have been problems: planners, not surprisingly, have always felt that the unsightly clutter of decaying metal boxes on so sensitive a site was 'detrimental to the visual amenities of the area'. Heavy rain turns the theatre into a drum: the roof has often failed to be completely waterproof and it is not unknown for performances to be temporarily suspended in particularly strong storms.

One of the worst setbacks occurred on the night of 25 July 1981, when 1,000 or so members of scooter clubs from all over the country gathered in the Lakeside Car Park. Trouble began after the public houses had closed. Police, in riot gear and armed with protective shields, managed to keep a disorderly crowd contained within the confines of the car park. Had the defensive line been breached, the town centre would without doubt have suffered considerable damage.

Thwarted, the rioters turned to the undefended Century Theatre. A caravan was burned to the ground; the box office, foyer, bar and gallery were wrecked; windows were smashed and the nearby Tea Gardens were also damaged. Sunday morning revealed a depressing scene of destruction but local supporters of the theatre turned out in force and, in the true tradition of show business, the theatre was ready for a performance on the Monday night.

The idea of a permanent theatre for the town has been around for many years but in the 1980s, backed by 'The Friends of the Century Theatre', the scheme was pursued with more vigour and purpose by a small group of enthusiasts. Two sites were considered suitable: the Lakeside Car Park and the disused station. Preference emerged for the former and planning permission was requested. It was refused; local authorities were very reluctant to offer funding; the Friends' appeal for donations, backed by such eminent names as Lord Olivier, J.B. Priestley, and Chris Bonington, failed to attract enough hard cash. Economic stringency nationwide drastically reduced promised grants: plans for a swimming pool were also in the pipe line and it was felt that Keswick's finances could not stand two major fundings.

After five years of committed effort by the few and apathy by the many, the Friends disbanded in August 1984, after having raised some £6,000. A new group, Cumbria Theatre Trust, took up the cause: a planning application, refused by the Planning Board, was granted on appeal. All that was needed was money, but neither Cumbria County Council nor Allerdale District Council was willing to promise the local funding which was essential for widening the appeal to national and international contributors.

By the end of 1989, it was apparent that plans for the lakeside building were in ruins. The Theatre Trust announced that 'if there is to be a theatre in the county, it almost certainly cannot be at the lakeside site by Derwentwater and our efforts must be directed elsewhere'. South Lakeland District Council immediately expressed an interest but later decided not to take up the option. A revived initiative centred on Keswick once again: new plans were accepted on appeal and at the time of writing it looks as though there is a good chance that current efforts will be successful.

For many visitors to Keswick, the main source of leisure activity is not a night at the theatre or even a modest guided walk, but a day on the fells. Numbers of walkers and climbers have increased dramatically, bringing their peculiar problems – erosion of footpaths, vandalism, interference with farming, and accidents.

It was an accident in April 1946 that prompted the formation of the Keswick Mountain Rescue Team. Wilfrid Noyce, later to join John Hunt's successful team on Everest, and Claude Elliott, headmaster of Eton, were climbing on Shark's Fin on Great Gable's Tophet Bastion when a gust of wind blew Noyce off a hold and he broke his leg. In appalling weather and in the dark, with only an exhausted torch for illumination, a small scratch party, fortunately of experienced climbers, rescued Noyce. It took three and a half hours to inch an awkward stretcher up 120 feet of vertical rock.

One of the rescuers, Colonel Horace ('Rusty') Westmorland, realised how near the incident had come to disaster. The official responsibility for dealing with mountain accidents was vested in the police, who were neither trained nor equipped to cope effectively with climbing mishaps. Rusty decided that the only answer was a Rescue Team. An appeal for volunteers resulted in over thirty local climbers offering their services and the Team was in business.

Keswick Mountain Rescue Team - early days, with Rusty Westmorland on the left

It has been in business ever since, still voluntary and coping with an average of forty call-outs a year. The simple and inadequate stretcher and ropes of the 1940s have been replaced by modern and sophisticated equipment. Radio and reliable land-rovers, RAF helicopters and trained search dogs are an integral part of an efficient service which, for many years, was led by George Fisher, proprietor of a well-known mountaineering equipment shop in Lake Road.

For Rusty Westmorland there was the satisfaction of seeing the development of a community service that has saved many lives. A Penrith man, he emigrated to Canada in 1911 and worked as a climbing surveyor in the Rockies. At the outbreak of war in 1914, he joined the Canadian Army; after thirty-two years, he was invalided out and returned to his native Cumbria to live at Threlkeld. A series of operations for cancer and a forecast that he had months rather than years to live did nothing to curb his activities: he made no concessions to age or ill health. He continued to climb and ski: he made his sixtieth ascent of Pillar Rock in 1951, celebrated his seventieth birthday by climbing Eagle's Nest (a VS route on Great Gable) and his ninetieth with a walk up Skiddaw.

He was awarded an OBE in 1965 for services to mountain rescue – a fitting tribute to both the man and his team. Rusty died in 1984 at the age of ninety eight.

Accidents and rescues apart, Keswick's position in the Lake District has meant that it has been a Mecca for rock climbers ever since Haskett Smith climbed Napes Needle in 1886 and effectively launched rock climbing as a sport. Many of the pioneering cragsmen found Keswick a convenient base for the fells and rocks. Locally, one of the best known and most highly respected was John Wilson Robinson. Born at Lorton in 1853, he worked on the family farm and later in Keswick as a land agent. His death in 1907 robbed Lake District climbing of a key figure, thoroughly dependable on rock and a popular companion on the fells. He is commemorated by Robinson's Cairn at the end of the High Level route to Pillar Rock, a crag he had climbed 100 times.

Central to the early development of rock climbing were two Keswick men, George and Ashley Abraham. Professional photographers, they left a priceless heritage of pictures of rock climbs and rock climbers and countless scenic views. Their contribution to the climbing scene was, however, much more than recording their own exploits and those of others on film.

'The Keswick Brothers', as they were known, put up an impressive list of first ascents and George could boast a climbing career spanning fifty years – a patient, precise cragsman who never had an accident. He and Ashley were founder members of the prestigious Fell and Rock Climbing Club in 1907, with Ashley as President and George as Honorary Member.

The brothers were often the target of objectors. The Abraham photographs and picture postcards, books and lectures, it was felt, brought damaging publicity and professionalism into a sport hitherto reserved for gentlemen and academics. The criticism lingered, epitomised perhaps in the fact that George was over eighty before he was elected a member of the Alpine Club.

The large Abraham shop in Lake Road, which had its own lecture room, the Victoria Hall, and a scale model of the Lake District, was built in 1887. When it closed as a photographic shop in 1967, it was taken over by George Fisher, himself a notable local climber, who ran it as a successful mountaineering equipment shop until 1989.

The Fisher twins, George and Richard, climbed from the age of fourteen, learning their techniques on Castlehead with the aid of a cart-rope. Surprisingly, Keswick has produced few top class climbers. After the Abraham era, local men such as Ralph Mayson and Dunbar Usher kept the spirit of the early tigers alive and the core of Rusty Westmorland's Rescue Team was made up of keen and competent climbers such as the Fisher brothers, Jim Barber, Des Oliver, Mike Nixon and others.

Star of the group was Paul Ross. Small in stature but extremely agile and determined, he tackled routes that demanded a high degree of skill and gymnastic flexibility. He often climbed solo, believing that climbing was something to be enjoyed, not endured: he treated the whole climbing game with mischievous irreverence.

He worked as a forester and an Outward Bound School instructor before tuberculosis of the spine landed him in Blencathra Sanatorium in 1962. After a year or so's inactivity, he bounded back with typical dynamic enthusiasm, opened the Lamp Lighter cafe in Lake Road and got himself back on the crags. In 1969 he emigrated to America and achieved considerable success as the proprietor of a climbers' shop, the organiser of a climbing school, and a breeder of Jack Russell terriers, before returning to Keswick in 1988.

Ray McHaffie moved to Keswick in 1965 after a somewhat stormy upbringing in Carlisle. He was introduced to the fells and was immediately hooked. His first experience of rock climbing was typically off-beat: he shinned up Kern Knotts Crack and down the Chimney with a hobnailed boot on one foot and a slipper on the other – he had cut his foot on a broken bottle. Without any formal training, he has emerged as a climber of ability and drive, with over 200 new routes to his credit. He is still capable of unorthodox responses to a challenge: on three occasions he has climbed Little Chamonix on Shepherd's Crag in roller skates and wearing boxing gloves.

On a more sedate level, Ray has spent a number of years acting as a guide to walkers and climbers and more recently has led a team of National Trust employees repairing fell paths. Their restoration of the badly eroded track up Sty Head from Stockley Bridge earned a medal of honour in 1990 from Europa Nostra, the federation of associations formed to protect Europe's natural and cultural heritage. Eight of these medals were awarded throughout the Continent: that for the Sty Head scheme was one of only two in Britain.

As a mountain guide, Ray McHaffie was part of a tradition that goes back to the last century when the principal hotels often provided knowledgeable mentors for their guests who wished to venture on the fells.

The first professional guide was probably Josef Gaspard from the Dauphine, who was hired by the season at Ritson Whiting's Wastwater Hotel in the early 1900s. In 1925, J.E.B. (Jerry) Wright, widely known as 'The Keswick Guide', founded the Lakeland Mountain Guides, with Seatoller House as headquarters. His self-advertisement and promotion were frowned on by the purists and his charges were reckoned to be high enough to make 'rock climbing a sport for plutocrats, instead of what it essentially is, the most democratic of all recreations', as the Fell and Rock *Journal* of 1927 pithily observed. A measure of his competence may be taken from his ascent of Napes Needle in sixty-five seconds, a remarkable achievement condemned by his detractors as a cheap publicity stunt.

Stanley Watson, operating in Borrowdale, lacked the brashness of Jerry Wright and advertised the services of his climbing school at Newton Place (opposite the Borrowdale Hotel) in rather more restrained terms. His expertise and knowledge not only put many aspiring climbers and walkers firmly and safely on the crags and fells: he was also often called out to help those in trouble or to lecture on the sport.

Acknowledging that guiding and climbing were a young man's province, he retired after a successful career and turned his energies to handicrafts. His Borrowdale workshop was a magnet for tourists in search of high-class trays and bowls in metal and wood.

Men like Stanley Watson were the forerunners of today's trained and officially certificated climbing instructors and the more humble leaders of guided walks. Every day in the season, groups of visitors leave the Moot Hall for a fell walk under the friendly guidance of local experts, who currently include a writer of mountaineering books and an ex-President of the British Mountaineering Council.

Millican Dalton, Professor of Adventure

One of the best known guides in the early part of this century was Millican Dalton, a mild eccentric who was a familiar figure in Keswick between the wars. Born in 1867 at Nenthead in remote eastern Cumbria, he went to the Friends' School at Wigton before moving south to Epping. He abandoned an orthodox career in insurance and eventually settled in Borrowdale as a self-styled 'Professor of Adventure'. His homes ranged from the Holiday Fellowship Guest House in Newlands, where he was secretary for a season or two, to a tent at High Lodore and a more permanent base in a cave on Castle Crag.

This spacious accommodation had two 'rooms', running water (through a crack in the roof), bracken for bedding and a plentiful supply of wood for a fire. Carved into the rock near the entrance was the injunction 'Don't!! Waste Words. Jump to Conclusions'.

Vegetarian and teetotaller, Millican Dalton baked his own bread and lived sparingly, though his healthy life-style was somewhat undermined by an addiction to strong coffee and Woodbine cigarettes. He was a patient and proficient guide, always erring towards safety and caution, never asking for a fee but grateful for any small donation towards his minimal living expenses.

Politically, he had leftist leanings and was a great admirer of Bernard Shaw. A committed pacifist, he apparently wrote several letters to Winston Churchill in an effort to stop World War II but Downing Street took no notice of the pleas from a cave in faraway Borrowdale.

This unambitious, courteous and contented man died in 1947, 'respected by all who knew him, a man of simple pleasures and tastes, conducive to a mind at peace with the world', as his friend, Ralph Mayson, wrote.

No account of mountaineering and outdoor activities in Keswick could ignore a bold and highly successful experiment in this field for disabled people.

In 1974, a group of local people formed the Calvert Trust to provide adventure holidays for the disabled. Two farmhouses were made available by Mr and Mrs John Spedding of Mirehouse and suitably converted for accommodation and recreation: Little Crosthwaite, about five miles from Keswick on the Carlisle road, and Old Windebrowe, the house where William and Dorothy Wordsworth stayed in 1794 at the invitation of their friend, William Calvert – hence the name of the Trust.

The Centre was officially opened by the Duke of Buccleuch on 15 April 1978 and the first group of physically and mentally handicapped people moved in to enjoy challenges and opportunities normally denied to them. Indoors, a swimming pool, a sports centre, a riding school and a spacious barn for social gatherings are available. Outdoors, pursuits range from sailing and rock climbing to bird watching and the study of geology.

The sense of achievement in facing and accomplishing a challenge fuels the whole enterprise. For those who thought that paddling a canoe, pitching a tent or scaling a crag was not for them, the feeling of exhilaration and euphoria must mark a high point, and in some cases a turning point, in their restricted lives – the blind man who climbed Skiddaw, the horse riders who swop wheel chair for saddle, the legless playing a vigorous game of table tennis.

Disability, the Calvert Trust proves time and time again, is not inability.

Reaching for the heights

17

Literary Lions

Keswick's literary tradition, firmly established by Coleridge and Southey, and their visitors, has continued to the present day, though the town can claim only one indigenous writer of note.

Eliza Lynn was born at Crosthwaite Vicarage on 10 February 1822, the youngest of twelve children. A few months later, her mother died and within a year, Charlotte, the eldest girl, was also dead. Asked by the Bishop of Carlisle, his father-in-law, what he intended to do with his large family, Parson Lynn replied: 'I shall sit in my study, my lord, smoke my pipe and commit them to Providence.'

He appears to have done just that. There were servants at the vicarage but life was simple and for young Eliza even harsh. She was plagued and bullied by her older brothers and sisters, a scapegoat for their mischief and often falsely blamed and unjustly punished. 'Our house in those days,' she wrote, 'was like nothing so much as a farmyard full of cockerels and pullets for ever spurring and pecking at one another.'

Inevitably, she grew up something of a rebel, wilful and resentful, sensitive to kindness and affection. She found solace in books and taught herself half-a-dozen languages. She became disillusioned with Christianity, particularly as it was practised in the strict regime of Crosthwaite Vicarage, her widening and deepening studies adding to her disenchantment.

She began to write and the acceptance of a poem by *Ainsworth's Miscellany* helped to nurture her decision to seek a career as a writer. Her father was furious. The very idea of a bishop's grand-daughter writing for money was inconceivable and women were not encouraged to write at all: Eliza was a contemporary of the Brontes and George Eliot, who managed to appear in print only by masquerading as men.

Parson Lynn ordered the 'obstinate young puppy' never to mention such ridiculous rubbish again. 'If you go to London as you propose,' he thundered, 'you go without my consent and the curse of God rests on disobedient children to the end of their lives.'

Eliza found an unexpected ally in the family solicitor who persuaded Lynn to change his mind. She moved to London and eventually emerged as a famous and prolific novelist and journalist. She was the first woman on the staff of a national newspaper to be paid a regular salary; she was a friend of such eminent men as Dickens, Henry James, Swinburne and Rider Haggard.

Her marriage in March 1858 to William Linton, artist and engraver, was a failure. For some years, the two lived at Brantwood on the shore of Coniston Water, the house that Linton sold to John Ruskin in 1871. Eventually, in 1865, Eliza and her husband parted, but they were never divorced. 'We separated on incompatibility,' Eliza wrote to her step-daughter. 'Tastes, temper, and mode of life were all contrary one to the other.'

Independent and industrious, she argued strongly for women's rights but, at the same time, this emancipated careerist supported the role of the female as domestic anchor. The strong-minded and determined woman who had escaped from the rigid bonds of a conventional upbringing had neither time nor admiration for 'the shrieking sisterhood' who demanded that women should take a full and active part in political and occupational life.

Even so, her contemporaries recognised her merits and abilities, though she cannot be reckoned as either a major or an outstanding novelist. Rider Haggard found her 'a most honourable and upright lady, very kind-hearted, though at times she could be bitter with her pen, rather contradictory in her views...one of very ablest and keenest intellects of her time'. Swinburne was equally complimentary: 'she was not only one of the most brilliant and gifted, but one of the kindest and most generous of women...I never knew any one more nobly upright and unselfish and loyal and true'.

She never lost touch with Keswick and on occasion returned to her birthplace. She admitted to Canon Rawnsley that it was only the climate that prevented her from going back to Keswick 'to live and die at the foot of the dear old mountains which seemed ours, exclusively ours'. She died on 14 July 1898; on 30 September 1898, her ashes were buried in Crosthwaite churchyard at the foot of her father's grave. Little known and unhonoured in her native town, her name lives on in the Lynn Linton Prize for English awarded annually at Keswick School.

While Eliza was growing up at Crosthwaite Vicarage, a mile or two away at St John's in the Vale John Richardson was beginning to learn his father's trade as mason and waller – and absorbing the local language and stories which were to inspire his homely dialect verses and tales.

He was born in 1817 at Stone House, now Piper House, a cottage tucked into the western flank of Naddle Fell. In his twenty-five years as a stone-mason, he built or repaired a number of farms and houses in the district, including St John's in the Vale vicarage and Derwentwater Place opposite St John's Church in Keswick.

Exchanging his hammer and trowel for book and pen, he took charge of the village school for some thirty years and in 1871 published *Cummerland Talk*, a mixture of tales and poems in dialect, many of them based on his own experiences, local characters and the fell country he loved. He died on 30 April 1886 and is buried in the churchyard of St John's in the Vale, a few yards from the school where he taught for so many years.

Eliza Lynn and John Richardson apart, it was the literary visitors and incoming residents who helped to make the name of Keswick so well known in the world of letters.

John Ruskin's first visit to Keswick in 1824 is commemorated by a memorial monolith at Friars' Crag, erected in October 1900. It reminds us that 'the first thing which I remember as an event in life was being taken by my nurse to the brow of Friars' Crag on Derwentwater'. That first view of and from Friars' Crag made a deep impression on the five-year-old boy and years later he described the incident as 'the creation of the world for me'.

After a brief stay in Keswick in 1826 en route for Perth, the Ruskins returned in 1830 for a three week Lake District tour. Young John recorded his experiences in *Iteriad*, a poem of 2,310 lines in verse which varies from doggerel to the highly competent for a boy who was only eleven years old.

He packed a full programme into the week the family spent at the Royal Oak from 23 June to 1 July. A return visit to Friars' Crag was marred by the sight of some of the local women doing their washing in the lake and hanging clothes on the bushes and trees fringing the shore. His frank reactions to the display in Crosthwaite's Museum were far from complimentary: he found everything, including the proprietor, 'full of dust, full of dirt, full of age, full of grease'.

Crosthwaite Church, too, was far from clean but the boy found some compensation in seeing Southey with his black and grey hair, his flashing blue eyes, his nose 'rather hooked like an eagle's and sharp at the end'.

A trip to Buttermere inspired several purple passages but a meal of 'taties and mouldy veal pie' at the Fish Inn and a storm of relentless rain, thunder and lightning dampened his ardour.

He was back in Keswick in 1837 and 1838. His unfortunate marriage to Effie Gray in 1848 began with a week's honeymoon at the Royal Oak. The newly-weds climbed Skiddaw and Causey Pike and Ruskin confessed that his main motive for staying in Keswick was the presence and teaching of the Rev. Frederick Myers, vicar of St John's. There cannot be many men who have selected the place for their honeymoon by the qualities of the local parson.

It was another nineteen years before Ruskin visited Keswick again, by which time – 1867 – he was a nationally revered and distinguished public figure. His affection for the Lakes was undiminished: four years later, he bought Brantwood on the shore of Coniston Water where he was to live for the next thirty years, a private and sheltered haven from the demands of his professional commitments and, in his final years, a retreat for a mind that gradually sank further and further into dementia.

At his funeral in 1900, the coffin was covered with a pall made by the Keswick Linen Industry that he had helped to found. Plain, unbleached linen, lined with silk, it was embroidered with roses, Ruskin's motto 'Unto this Last' and the initials J R.

Thousands of tourists who have never heard of Ruskin echo his views on two prominent local viewpoints. The popular panorama from Ashness Bridge he assessed as 'the best piece of composition...of all landscape I ever saw'; the scene of Derwentwater and Borrowdale from Friars' Crag he claimed was one of the three or four finest in Europe. Canon Rawnsley records that Ruskin once told a neighbour of his that when he first saw Keswick, it was a place almost too beautiful to live in. I wonder what he would say today?

Not long after young Ruskin had been sizing up Southey's nose in Crosthwaite Church, Alfred Lord Tennyson came to stay at Mirehouse on Bassenthwaite Lake, the home of his friend, James Spedding, 'the wisest man I ever knew', Tennyson called him. Spedding devoted his life to editing a massive collection of Bacon's works and an equally meaty biography – justice for Bacon, certainly, but a formidable mountain of words for all but committed Baconians.

It has been claimed that Tennyson's well-known poem, 'Morte d'Arthur', was inspired, at least in part, by this 1835 visit to Mirehouse: Excalibur, Arthur's sword, drawn into the depths of Bassenthwaite by an arm 'clothed in white samite, mystic, wonderful'; the dusky barge carrying Arthur's body down the lake; the old church of St Bega the site of the 'broken chancel with a broken cross'.

The links are tenuous, particularly as the first draft of the poem was in manuscript in 1833. Perhaps the final version has fine detail suggested by the Mirehouse visit but the identification of specific locations in a work of the imagination is unwarranted.

Other literary personalities who were welcome at Mirehouse included Edward Fitzgerald, translator of the *Rubaiyat of Omar Khayyam*, and Thomas Carlyle, the Southeys and the Wordsworths, Matthew Arnold and John Stuart Mill. The elegant seventeenth century mansion is open to the public at certain times, its portraits and manuscripts, artifacts and memorabilia a reminder of the Spedding family's involvement in important national and international affairs.

One of the letters on display, written by Southey and dated 27 March 1811, reports 'some mischief having been committed upon my out-houses during Monday night' and urges the need 'for taking measures for putting some check to outrages which almost every night are committed in this town of Keswick'. Problems of law and order were obviously as acute two hundred years ago as they are today.

Speddings have lived at Mirehouse since 1802

The celebrities associated with Mirehouse are well-known in the catalogue of names in our literary heritage. Among the forgotten writers who have lived in Keswick, William Smith deserves a mention.

Born in Hammersmith in 1808, he abandoned his profession of barrister in favour of studying metaphysics and writing. He moved to the newly-built Derwentwater Place opposite St John's Church in 1856, partly to be near his friend, Dr Lietch of Portinscale. Here, he not only finished *Thorndale*, his best known book, but also met his future wife, Lucy Cumming, herself a fellow poet and author. They married in 1861 and three years later settled at Newton Place opposite the Borrowdale Hotel, a devoted couple whose shared spiritual and intellectual experiences were enshrined in books and articles rarely read today. Smith died in Brighton in 1872; Lucy lived for another ten years, visiting Borrowdale and Patterdale where she and William had walked and talked.

Between 1885 and 1907, Beatrix Potter spent a number of holidays at Lingholm and Fawe Park: the two houses, their gardens and the surrounding landscape provided material for several of her books and the illustrations which are so essential a feature of the stories.

Much of The *Tale of Benjamin Bunny* is set in Fawe Park garden; *The Tale of Peter Rabbit* draws on Lingholm for scenes in the vegetable garden, with its distinctive wicket gate, but, as Beatrix wrote later, 'it would be vain to look for it there, as a firm of landscape gardeners did away with it and laid it out anew with paved walks.' Owl Island in *The Tale of Squirrel Nutkin* is St Herbert's Island, the destination of a convoy of squirrels who cross the lake on rafts using their tails as sails.

On her walks from Lingholm, Beatrix met the young Lucie Carr, daughter of the vicar of Newlands. She wrote *The Tale of Mrs Tiggy Winkle* for her, the story of a washer-woman hedgehog who lived in the back of Catbells. Many of the illustrations are easily recognisable – the Goldscope valley, Skelghyll Farm, Littletown.

The Fairy Caravan, longer and larger than the usual mini-sized Potter book, follows the adventures of a travelling circus. One illustration shows Messrs Rattan and Scratch selling their Hair Elixir in Keswick Market Square; others show Skiddaw and Walla Crag. An episode, based on a true incident at Thirlspot and transferred to Falcon Crag overlooking Derwentwater, tells of a sheep, Belle Lingcropper, trapped for thirty days on a narrow ledge before a shepherd rescues her.

On her 1903 visit to Lingholm, Beatrix bought a small sketchbook which she filled with sketches of local scenes. Published in 1984, the facsimile is a collector's item of considerable interest.

From 1881 to 1897, Beatrix kept a journal, a coded confession which includes only one of her Keswick holidays, that of 1885. She visited Carlisle and braved the discomforts of the Buttermere Round. Keswick itself was 'a terrible place for drink', with women as well as men jailed for drunkenness and the peace of Derwentwater shattered by shouting and raucous singing.

The Lodore Hotel, she tells us, had a bad reputation as the resort of Keswick roughs on weekend binges. Casualties, some fatal, were common as boats pursued their erratic course back to Keswick. The victims received scant sympathy from Beatrix: a triple drowning earned the pithy comment of 'they belonged to the lowest set in the town and will not be missed'.

In later years, when she was settled in Sawrey, her visits to Keswick were usually connected with sheep, selling them at the Fair, exhibiting or judging them at the Show. She was highly regarded by her fellow farmers as a sheep breeder and expert on sheep diseases. In 1930, the year in which she won the silver challenge cup for the best Herdwick ewe in the Lake District, she was elected the first woman president of the Herdwick Sheep Breeders' Association – a singular honour in a heavily male-dominated organisation.

Hall Caine, or to give him his full title, Sir Thomas Henry Hall Caine, was born of Manx and Cumbrian parents in 1853. A popular novelist, he lived for a time at the Hawthorns in Keswick and at least two of his books, *The Shadow of a Crime* and *Son of Hagar*, use a Cumbrian background.

He came to Keswick, he once said, 'because I want to study human nature... Here every one and everything are known to me.' Both he and his wife were exceptionally energetic and industrious, he with his pen, she with her cheese and butter-making from the milk of the cow she kept.

In 1881, Caine and his friend, Dante Gabriel Rossetti, stayed at Fisher Place at Legburthwaite. Here Rossetti hoped to recover his failing health, to write and paint, and perhaps rid himself of his dependency on chloral. Weak though he was, he managed to climb the 1,000 feet of Great Howe opposite Fisher Place but a month's holiday did little for him. His health continued to deteriorate; his ability to work and walk declined; his addiction to drugs remained unconquered. He returned to London without having seen Greta Hall, Shelley Cottage or Borrowdale and died a few months later in April 1882.

Two of Hall Caine's novels have a special place in British publishing. In 1890, William Heinemann published his first book – Caine's *The Bondman*. It was a tremendous success and put the new firm on the road to becoming the most prestigious publisher of fiction in the twentieth century. In 1894, Heinemann issued The *Manxman*, a one-volume novel: it broke the mould of the traditional three-decker, which had been the established style of novels published in the nineteenth century.

Caine was a much-admired writer in his day but few people read his novels now. Hugh Walpole, however, has continued to attract readers, particularly of his Cumbrian titles.

Born in New Zealand in 1884, he spent an unhappy childhood at boarding schools in England. A shy, sensitive boy, suffering among other trials from undiagnosed short sight, he was buffeted and battered by the rough and tumble life of a public school: memories of beatings and bullying lasted a lifetime.

He first visited the Lakes on holiday for eight successive years during the 1890s, when the family stayed at Sower Myre Farm near Gosforth in West Cumbria. 'My love for Cumberland, my trust and faith in Cumberland,' he confessed, 'had their birth in those years.'

It was some considerable time later that he bought a house in Cumberland. 1 November 1923 was a red letter day. A stray remark from the proprietor of the Keswick Hotel led him to Brackenburn at Manesty above Derwentwater. Here was a home, a place where he could put down roots. Over the years, he altered and extended the house and transformed the garage across the lawn into a library, writing room and art gallery.

He settled at Brackenburn with his secretary-chauffeur, Harold Cheevers, and Mrs Cheevers. Jack and Edith Elliot moved in as resident caretakers and Walpole, with typical zeal, was soon involved in the life of Keswick – buying books from Mr Chaplin, silver from Mr Telford and showing an active interest in everything from Toc H to St John's Library, from cricket to drama productions, from Keswick and Borrowdale Schools to local charitable causes.

He loved the peace and remoteness of Brackenburn but he was restless, much in demand, anxious not to miss anything. In the seventeen years he owned his 'little paradise on Catbells', the longest period he spent there was five weeks. Usually it was a few days, a couple of weeks, and he was off to London, America, or wherever the call of success demanded, lecturing to huge audiences, meeting the famous, dining with royalty.

The first of his Cumbrian novels was published in 1929. A friendship with J B Priestley produced *Farthing Hall*, a novel in letters written alternately by the two men. The setting is Keswick and Borrowdale; the plot is somewhat melodramatic and punctuated by sinister revelations and robust incidents. Walpole's name ensured wide sales and Priestley, free from financial worries, was able to settle down and write *The Good Companions*.

Hugh Walpole and J B Priestley at Brackenburn

In 1936, Walpole's *A Prayer for my Son* appeared, with a background of Keswick and Blencathra. By this date, he was well into the series of Cumbrian novels that was to boost his popularity even further and bring many thousands of visitors to Keswick – the Herries saga.

He began the first volume of this long family chronicle on Christmas Eve 1927. *Rogue Herries* spearheaded an ambitious and complex narrative which was not only the story of a family through several generations but also a blend of romance and history on a much broader canvas. It was an attempt to explore 'the spirit of England, which, as I see it, gets its strength and its ardour from the struggle in its character between common sense and fantasy...Prose and Poetry, Fact and Fancy'.

Rogue Herries (1930) was followed by *Judith Paris* (1931), *The Fortress* (1932) and *Vanessa* (1933). Four more volumes were in the pipeline, with yet another six to take the story to 1950. *The Bright Pavilions*, the fifth, was published in 1940; *Katherine Christian* was unfinished when Walpole died in the following year.

In the early days of the Second World War, the Cheevers' home in London was bombed while Walpole was staying with them. He retreated to Brackenburn and on 17 May 1941 took part in Keswick's War Weapons effort. Unwonted exertion put him to bed and a week later he lapsed into a coma – he had been a diabetic since 1925. He died on 1 June from a coronary thrombosis and is buried at St John's church: his grave on a terrace near the west door – a privileged location – looks towards Brackenburn and Borrowdale.

Keswick has every reason to remember Walpole with affection and gratitude. He was always ready to support worthy causes with generous donations and was much in demand at a wide variety of functions. A corner of Fitz Park Museum is devoted to the man and his work, with letters from the famous, manuscripts of his books, pictures, and an Epstein bust.

His facility with words and the fluency of his language (he seldom revised) undoubtedly produced novels urgently in need of pruning and polishing. Some readers find the Herries books too long and diffuse; others revel in their detail and comprehensive sweep. Whatever their faults, they create an historical and imaginative picture of Keswick and district in the eighteenth and nineteenth centuries which is rich, vibrant and inspired by genuine affection: the fair in Keswick when Rogue Herries sold his mistress; the fireworks display when Judith met George Paris; Grange, where Mrs Wilson was drowned as a witch, and Rosthwaite, where Rogue lived and Judith was born; Watendlath, home of George and Judith; High Ireby, Walter Herries' mansion; lonely Skiddaw House where Uhland and John Herries fought and died.

Though there is little resemblance to Walpole in personality or literary output, Graham Sutton also chose the family saga as his medium for five local novels about the Flemings.

Born at Scotby near Carlisle and educated at St Bees, Sutton taught in London for a time, broadcasting and writing anything from drama criticism to study books for foreign students, detective stories to radio plays. In 1953, he moved to Scalebeck, immediately rechristened 'Dancing Beck', an old schoolroom and house at the western end of the Applethwaite and Millbeck terrace. He was home.

The books of the Fleming saga have not received the attention they deserve. Thoroughly researched and their details sustained by a confident historical perspective, they are fuelled by plenty of action and a native's insight into the Cumbrian character. They are buoyant with a rich sense of local colour and local life, firmly rooted in the author's extensive knowledge of sheep farming and mining, railway building and the theatre, rock climbing and quarrying.

The Fleming novels span the centuries from the 1590s to the 1870s. Topographically, the setting is Cumbria (and beyond), with Keswick and district claiming a good share: the ambush on Sty Head in *Shepherd's Warning* (1946); the smuggling of wad for sale in Keswick in *Smoke across the Fell* (1947); Mr Nixon's coffee-house in the town where Ewan Fleming meets Kemble, 'the most famous actor in England', in *North Star* (1949); Stockley Beck, where John Fleming and Red Nugent fight bare-fisted in *Fleming of Honister* (1953); the exciting escape across the back of Skiddaw and the tense scene in a Skiddaw gill that provides the climax to *The Rowan Tree* (1955).

This versatile and skilful writer died in 1959. His tombstone at Scotby carries the simple inscription: 'He loved Cumbria and his fellow men' – a tribute nowhere more apparent than in the Fleming novels.

In recent times, Keswick has retained its literary associations. Edmund Casson, a master at Keswick School in its early days, wrote a good deal of poetry and several plays, locally inspired. George Abraham's dozen or so books on mountaineering, now expensive rarities, introduced readers to an increasingly popular sporting activity. In 1900, he published O G Jones's *Rock Climbing in the English Lake District*, arguably the pioneer classic that initiated the publication of books about mountaineering in Britain.

George Abraham's daughter, Enid Wilson, delighted readers of the Guardian for thirty years with her polished contributions to its 'Country Diary'. Historical novelist, Robert Neill, and children's author, Lorna Hill, migrated to Keswick; Bob Langley, writer of adventure thrillers, forsook the bustling world of television to settle here. Alan Hankinson has put the story of rock climbing under the microscope and written perceptively about the Abrahams in *Camera on the Crags* (1975), about Peter Crosthwaite and Joseph Pocklington in *The Regatta Men* (1988) and Coleridge in *Coleridge Walks the Fells* (1991). Jane Gillespie maintains a steady flow of novels, some with local settings, which combine sharp observation of both the modern and the historical domestic scene with a subtle appreciation of psychological motive and conflict.

From her remote cottage near Keswick, Molly Lefebure has produced some of the best books on Cumbria in recent years – informative and deeply researched explorations of places and people, history and mystery, along with academic studies of Coleridge and his family. Anyone looking for a reliable and readable introduction to Cumbria could do no better than plump for her *The English Lake District* (1964), *Cumberland Heritage* (1970) and *Cumbrian Discovery* (1977).

Though he cannot claim to be a Keswickian, Cumbria's most distinguished modern novelist, Melvyn Bragg, earns a place among the Keswick literati for his local novels, in particular *The Maid of Buttermere* (1987), a best-seller with much of its story set in Keswick.

Sir Percy Mirehouse Hope and Lady Hope

18

Worthies at Work

It would be unfair, and certainly unbalanced, to think of Keswick's well-known characters as only literary personalities: our worthies embrace a much wider field, from medicine to geology, mountaineering to conservation.

Dr William Brownrigg, 'a physician and philosopher eminently distinguished' as his memorial tablet in Crosthwaite Church describes him, was a member of a family long established in the Applethwaite and Millbeck area. He was born at Highclose Hall near Wigton in 1712 and studied medicine in London and Leyden in Holland, the latter internationally recognised as the unrivalled centre of medical training.

The learned doctor practised in Whitehaven where his interests and activities extended far beyond treating patients for coughs and colds. His research into fire damp or methane gas in the coal mines earned him a Fellowship of the Royal Society; his scientific investigations ranged from analysing mineral waters and the art of making common salt to the treatment of plague and the first-ever recorded introduction of platinum in Europe.

In 1760, he inherited Ormathwaite Hall at Applethwaite. He built a laboratory and continued his scientific work, though his substantial library was evidence of a much wider span of interest, from travel to poetry, history to Italian. In 1772, he entertained Dr Benjamin Franklin, the distinguished American scientist, and Sir John Pringle, president of the Royal Society. The three men took a boat out on Derwentwater and conducted an experiment to test the calming effects of pouring oil on troubled waters (no planning permission required!).

Brownrigg does, however, appear to have over-strained himself financially, particularly with the acquisition of Millbeck Hall and a lease on Skiddaw Forest. He was rescued from heavy debt by his niece's husband and continued his hectically busy life, writing an unpublished history of Cumberland, introducing agricultural improvements at Ormathwaite and acting as a magistrate for many years. His 'passion for the improvement and notoriety of Keswick' helped him to persuade Thomas West to write the popular guidebook to the Lakes which, it was claimed, 'sent shoals of visitors to the neighbourhood of Keswick'.

He died on 6 January 1800 aged eighty-eight, universally admired and respected, a deeply religious man possessed 'of every qualification necessary to form a chemical philosopher, a dogmatic physician and an elegant scholar'. Had he been prepared to slim down his multifarious activities, he might well have become one of the most eminent of eighteenth century scientists.

A fellow scientist, working in a very different field, is commemorated by a plaque in King's Head Yard opposite the Moot Hall. By a flight of steps a wall tablet reads: 'Here lived Jonathan Otley 1766-1856, geologist and clockmaker. A humble student of nature and science who laboured for his fellows'.

Otley was born at Nook House or Scroggs near Loughrigg Tarn between Grasmere and Skelwith Bridge. He followed his father's profession as a basket-maker and from an early age showed a flair for mending clocks and watches. In 1791 he crossed Dunmail Raise and spent the next sixty-five years in Keswick. He earned his bread and butter by repairing clocks but he won his place in the annals of Keswick by his knowledge and practical experience as guide, geologist and meteorologist: among his correspondents were the Astronomer Royal, Dr John Dalton (the so-called father of the atomic theory), Professor John Phillips, Professor Adam Sedgwick and officials of the Ordnance Survey.

Trudging over the fells, Otley kept careful notes of rock formations, weather, soil, wind and wild life; he answered queries of all kinds from correspondents, varying from the origin of place-names to information about the last eagle in Borrowdale, and sent geological specimens to all who asked for them.

In 1817 he drew a map of the district. Five years later, he included it in his guidebook, which has become a classic of its kind. *A Concise Description of the English Lakes, the Mountains in their Vicinity, and the roads by which they may be visited: with remarks on the Mineralogy and Geology of the District* (1822) was based on first-hand acquaintance with the fells. It was one of the earliest reliable guides, factual and disciplined, avoiding romantic exaggeration, a pioneer achievement of considerable importance firmly rooted in personal experience, local knowledge and scientific observation.

In 1831, Professor Adam Sedgwick pointed out to the members of the august Geological Society of London that it was Otley who first recognised the three distinct groups of rocks of the Lakeland fells. Jonathan called them Clayslate, Greenstone and Greywacke: today we know them by their more familiar names of Skiddaw Slate, Borrowdale Volcanic and Coniston Limestone. Equally important was his recognition of the distinction between bedding and cleavage in highly contorted strata such as Skiddaw Slate – a fundamental principle for geological study.

For many years, Otley kept careful records of rainfall in Keswick, an indisputable reminder that nineteenth century weather was as unpredictable as it is today. He logged the rise and fall of the water level of Derwentwater. In the dry summer of 1826, he cut a notch in the rock of Friars' Crag to mark the low water level: it can still be identified, the forerunner of a series of markers – slate slabs inscribed with the date and the initials of the donor, who is usually the chairman of the council, or some other leading citizen. A recent visitor, puzzled by these stone slabs, asked a guided walks leader why people were buried in the lake!

Otley must have felt a great sense of sadness when, at the age of eighty seven, he found the steps to his room too steep. He moved into a cottage in St John's Street; his books, his botanical and geological specimens, his watchmaker's tools and instruments – 336 lots in all – came under the auctioneer's hammer, leaving him after expenses a mere £20.

Soon after an emotional and final meeting with his old friend, Adam Sedgwick, he died on 7 December 1856. Some of his relics are on show in Fitz Park Museum – a modest tribute to a Keswickian who has aptly been called the Father of Lakeland Geology.

While Otley was busy mending clocks and tapping rocks, Robley Dunglinson (1798-1869) was laying the foundation of a career in medicine by working as an assistant to Dr John Edmundson. He left Keswick to train in Edinburgh, Paris and London and in 1823 he was appointed Professor of Medicine at the University of Virginia. He became personal physician to several American presidents, including Thomas Jefferson and, as a key figure in medical education, earned the tribute of being described as 'the most able and popular teacher of physiology of his day in America'.

A man of exceptional industry, this accomplished and versatile Keswickian wrote widely on topics as varied as seventeenth century fashions in England, ancient canals, early German poetry and Lake District legends, apart from a stream of medical books.

He died in Philadelphia in 1869, almost forgotten in his birthplace but honoured in America for his prolific writings and pioneering influence on medicine. In 1986, his grave was restored and marked by the erection of a suitable headstone, a tribute from Thomas Jefferson University, where he had been Professor and Dean for thirty-two years.

Samuel Ladyman (1813-1885) earns his rosette for his good works. Something of a Jack-of-all-trades – joiner, ironmonger, pencil-maker, butcher – he provided at his own expense seats and drinking fountains at appropriate viewpoints in and around the town. He financed road repairs and gave money and food to the poor.

In 1885, he published *Thoughts and Recollections of Keswick and its inhabitants during sixty years*, an eccentric booklet which, among other information, lists over 250 householders who lived in the town about 1825. Ladyman remembered the removal of the old shambles from the Moot Hall and the days when there were twenty-two woollen manufacturers in the town. His grandfather was the architect and builder of Joseph Pocklington's house on Derwent Island, though he does not appear to have been the most efficient of designers: when the house was nearly finished, it was discovered that he had forgotten the staircase.

Ladyman mentions several local characters – Anthony Gibson, parish clerk for half a century; Neddy Birkett, guide and boatman; James Little who for fifty years crossed Helvellyn for his weekly provisions – but, oddly enough, omits any reference to one of Keswick's best-known eccentrics, George Smith (c.1825-1876), also known as the Skiddaw Hermit or the Dodd Man.

He came to Keswick from near Aberdeen and built himself a 'nest' on Skiddaw Dodd, a basket-shaped concoction of interlaced branches, bracken, moss and grass. Barefoot and hatless, he wore only a shirt and trousers rolled to the knee, his odd appearance emphasised by his long, flowing hair and bushy beard.

His visits to Keswick were frequently designed to satisfy his inordinate devotion to whisky. He raised cash for his tipple by painting and sketching portraits and dabbling in phrenology; for the price of a drink, he would declaim at length from Burns and Shakespeare. At times, he preached to the sheep near his nest and it is not surprising that his strange behaviour sparked off ridicule and insults from some Keswickians, while others, children in particular, were afraid of him.

Eventually he left Keswick and lived in other parts of the Lake District, though no community seemed to want him for long. Listening to a travelling preacher at Bowness, he was converted, giving up drinking and claiming to see visions. He died in an Aberdeen asylum in 1876, devoted to his Bible to the last.

During the latter half of the nineteenth century, when modern Keswick was emerging as a major tourist centre, a handful of local men were at the heart of most that was happening in the town. Whether it was the Board of Health or school governors, the Rifle Volunteers or the Mechanics Institute, the Literary and Scientific Society or the soup kitchens, familiar names appear time and time again – Mumberson, Fitzpatrick, Spedding, and, above all, Crosthwaite, Jenkinson, Ward and Rawnsley.

There were Crosthwaites in the district from the thirteenth century and in 1780 Peter Crosthwaite opened his famous museum. His grandson, John Fisher Crosthwaite (1819-1897), was postmaster from 1846 to 1888, an office of expanding services and responsibilities which he coupled with the duties of agent for the Keswick branch of the Cumberland Union Bank. He was the first sworn-in volunteer of the Skiddaw Greys in 1860 and for twenty years was in command of the unit as Captain. His association with

Crosthwaite Church spanned a lifetime and included sixty years as a chorister. His connexion with the Sunday School lasted even longer – from 1833 to 1897 – as scholar, teacher and superintendent.

His keen interest in the history of Keswick earned him a Fellowship of the Society of Antiquaries in 1882 and his published papers are a valuable source of information on topics as varied as ancient families of the district and rainfall, mining and parish registers, old Borrowdale and the Derwentwaters.

He refused to commit himself to active participation in local government, preferring to channel his energies elsewhere for the benefit of the community: Fitz Park, a public water supply, the hospital. As his obituarist succinctly commented, 'every movement of a philanthropic character found him a liberal and cheerful giver'. Few men have contributed more to the life and welfare of Keswick.

Henry Irwin Jenkinson (c.1840-1891) arrived in Keswick around 1865. As we have already seen, he was the driving force behind the creation of Fitz Park, the footpath battles of the 1880s, and the annual dinner for the old people of the town. He reintroduced a sports meeting and regatta in 1878 and organised what today we would call guided walks. He was a guidebook writer of distinction, his handbooks covering areas as far apart as the Isle of Man and the Isle of Wight, Wales and the Roman Wall. His Lake District volume – reliable, comprehensive, practical – was, like Otley's, built on intimate, first-hand knowledge of the fells.

He died at Brentwood in Essex on 28 August 1891, a man, suggested one contemporary, 'who may be said to have sacrificed his life to the good of his fellow townsmen and others'. It is sad to record that those fellow townsmen, who owed so much to Jenkinson, were inordinately slow in contributing to his memorial – the main gates into Fitz Park.

James Clifton Ward (1843-1880), born in Clapham and trained as a professional geologist, came to Keswick in 1868 to investigate the district for the Geological Survey. In 1877, he resigned from his scientific work and at Christmas 1878 he was ordained. After a short spell as curate of St John's, he transferred to the living of Rydal and curate at Ambleside but, after a brief illness, he died on 15 April 1880.

Never a robust man, he tended to overwork, both as a geologist and a clergyman. He was responsible for the formation of the Cumberland Association for the Advancement of Literature and Science and served as secretary, treasurer and editor of its *Transactions*. Along with Canon Battersby and Dr Knight, it was Ward who took the first steps to establish what became the Fitz Park Museum and to lay the foundation of its excellent rocks and minerals collection. He was a popular lecturer and much in demand as a leader of walks, field days and excursions. He was sadly missed, 'a martyr in the truest sense of the word', suggested one appreciation, 'to over-incessant activities for the good of his kind, which have tended to exhaust the nervous energy of a physical frame originally none too strong'.

Infinitely more robust, Canon Rawnsley, vicar of Crosthwaite from 1883 to 1917, was a man of boundless energy, a man who identified abuses and attacked them with exceptional vigour, a man whose range of involvement was unbelievably far-reaching and comprehensive. We have already noted his successful opposition to the Braithwaite-Honister railway, his fight to keep footpaths open, his founding of the Keswick School of Industrial Art and, above all else, his vital role in the formation of the National Trust. But there was more, much more...

Hardwicke Drummond Rawnsley (1851-1920) was born at Shiplake vicarage near Henley-on-Thames and educated at Uppingham School and Balliol College, Oxford. At school, he showed a marked ability as an athlete; his interest in the world of nature was encouraged, widened and deepened; his facility as a versifier developed. His years as a pupil of Edward Thring imbued him with the ideas and ideals of that great headmaster: chivalrous unselfishness, sincerity and service, absolute devotion to truth, sympathy for the less fortunate, strict Christian principles.

After Oxford, he took holy orders and in 1878 accepted the living of Wray on Windermere for five years before moving to Crosthwaite, an appointment described by a bishop of Carlisle as 'as near Heaven as anything in this world can be'.

He plunged into the life of the town with energetic enthusiasm, using his Parish Magazine as a miniature newspaper. He inaugurated the annual May Day celebration and procession, the Bird and Tree Day, the Cumberland Nature Club and gave his strong support to Newton Rigg Farm School, the Mary Hewetson Hospital, the Blencathra Sanatorium – to mention only a few of his formidable catalogue of local good causes. For six years, from 1889 to 1895, he represented Keswick on Cumberland County Council, tackling his extra duties with typical commitment and championing a range of good causes, from tuberculosis in cattle and pollution in rivers to footpath repairs and signposting.

A number of curious enthusiasms persisted throughout Rawnsley's life: writing commemorative sonnets whenever the occasion arose, campaigning against vulgar post-cards, erecting monuments, building bonfires. Many of the memorial stones and plaques for which he was responsible still remain: the Gough memorial on Helvellyn, the Brothers' Parting Stone on Grisedale Hause, the Ruskin monolith at Friars' Crag, the Wordsworth fountain in Harris Park at Cockermouth. It was his suggestion that some form of permanent memorial to the Lake poets should be erected, preferably a reading room and museum for both students and the general public. He preferred Keswick as its location but in 1890 Dove Cottage was bought and handed over to trustees, one of whom was Rawnsley. His dream of Keswick as the Mecca of literary pilgrims disappeared in favour of Grasmere.

Perhaps it was appropriate that 'the most active volcano in Europe', as one of his parishioners once called him, should be devoted to bonfires, both locally and nationally. Skiddaw was the favoured site for blazes to celebrate the 300th anniversary of the defeat of the Spanish Armada, the golden and diamond jubilees of Queen Victoria in 1887 and 1897, King Edward VII's coronation in 1902 and George V's in 1911. Rawnsley's final big blaze was at the end of the First World War, when he was living at Grasmere: as general secretary to the national organising committee, he was responsible for distributing some 6,000 flares and 34,000 rockets from surplus war stores. He received letters addressed to 'Cannon, Rawnsley and Co.' – patently a pyrotechnic firm in Grasmere! – and requests for guns, tanks and even airships.

A passionate opponent of strong drink, he carried the temperance banner on every possible occasion; his 'Knights of St Kentigern' comprised reformed drunkards who had taken the pledge. His campaign for healthier eating was sparked off by the failure of young Cumbrians to qualify for entry into the Metropolitan Police Force because they had bad teeth.

Moral as well as physical health concerned him. He attacked the salacious and pernicious in books and films, posters and comic postcards: Keswick station quickly removed its 'What the Butler Saw' peep-shows. It was his drive and initiative primarily that was behind the foundation of Keswick School: successive headmasters continued to foster the ideals and practical aims that Rawnsley identified as the solid foundation of the school's ethos. He was a regular visitor to the other schools in the town, advising and encouraging – he helped to create a garden at Crosthwaite School, complete with beehive and barometer, which may have been the first of its kind in the country.

In 1907, Portinscale Bridge was condemned as unsafe by the highway authority. Rawnsley plunged into a seven-year fight to save this ancient, picturesque bridge, recommending 'grouting' (the forced injection of cement) as a successful method of preserving the structure. He roused such strong opposition locally and nationally that the bridge was grouted in 1913 and the engineer pronounced it 'only vulnerable to dynamite'. It stood firm for the next forty years until a heavy flood in December 1954 damaged it beyond repair. A temporary Callander Hamilton steel bridge was erected and remained in use until the present footbridge was built.

Portinscale Bridge about 1905

During the 1914-18 war, he channelled his energies into helping the struggle against an evil enemy, speaking at recruitment meetings, encouraging the welcome and housing of Belgian refugees, and raising funds to provide an ambulance.

A restless, over-filled life was made even more hectic by extensive foreign travel and the continual flood of articles, verses and books that flowed from his pen. Inevitably, the strains took their toll: in 1917 he was so ill that he was unable to attend either his wife's funeral or her memorial service.

He resigned his Crosthwaite living, moved to Allan Bank at Grasmere and in June 1918 married an old friend, Eleanor Simpson. He was far from idle in his retirement but on 28 May 1920 he died. A stone plaque in a wall a couple of hundred yards from Friars' Crag commemorates a man 'who, greatly loving the fair things of nature and of art, set all his love to the service of God and man'.

How, it may legitimately be asked, could one man do so much? And, from a myriad of activities, what has he left to posterity? His successes (and some failures) affected many parts of the Lake District but his prime achievement was without doubt his part in the founding of the National Trust. The conservation movement he nurtured with so much fervour and devotion is as vital as ever, as tourist pressure and the quick-profit incursions of insensitive entrepreneurs mount. Rawnsley, thou should'st be living at this hour; Keswick hath need of thee...

Not far from Rawnsley's vicarage is Bristowe Hill, a superbly sited house which is now part of Keswick School as a residence for boarders. For many years, it was home to one of Keswick's most liberal benefactors and philanthropists, Sir John Randles (1857-1945). Son of a Wesleyan minister, he was a lifelong Methodist who gave generous and unremitting support to local congregations.

For forty years, he played a leading role in the industrial and political life of West Cumberland. It would be no exaggeration to describe him as the man who put the county's iron and steel industry on the map, fusing a number of diverse enterprises – iron and steel companies, mines, blast furnaces – into a highly successful combine, with himself as chairman. His political career was crowned by a stint of ten years in parliament as the member for Cockermouth.

In 1922, he retired to his Keswick home, taking a particular interest in the local hospital and contributing generously to its development: the Lady Randles operating theatre, officially opened on 2 June 1932, was said to be the finest in the north of England in its day. He was a staunch supporter of the National Trust and donated Castlehead, Cockshot Wood and Crow Park to the nation.

One of his contemporaries was Arthur William Wakefield (1876-1949), a local doctor who served in the South African War and the First World War and worked with the Grenfell Medical Mission for six years in Newfoundland and Labrador.

A pioneer in fell running, he set up a record in 1905: 23,500 feet of ascent and descent in twenty hours and seven minutes. It stood for fifteen years, when Eustace Thomas (with Wakefield's help) reduced it by nearly an hour. In June 1932, Bob Graham of Keswick ran up forty-two peaks in twenty-three hours and thirty-nine minutes – a total height of some 33,000 feet. This record has long since been broken but still continues to inspire challenges by superbly fit fell runners. Those who are successful are eligible for membership of the exclusive Bob Graham Club.

Wakefield began climbing with the Abraham brothers in the 1890s and in 1922 he was selected for the Everest expedition, an unsuccessful attempt overshadowed by the death of seven porters. Wakefield does not appear to have been much of an asset to the team. Charles Bruce, the leader, described him as 'a complete passenger...dear old thing for all that' – not the most complimentary remark about a man of forty-six.

Two years later, Wakefield and his American wife settled in Keswick, he working as a general practitioner, she an active member of many local organisations. Plenty of cycling, including his professional calls, and almost daily swims in Derwentwater kept him fit until his death in 1949.

Modern Keswick owes a great debt to Percy Mirehouse Hope (1888-1972). PM, as he was often called, was the son of a local bank manager. Trained as an architect, he turned down a War Office appointment after a distinguished military career in the First World War, in favour of returning to Keswick.

He was closely associated with many housing and business projects; he founded the Lake District Hotels company which, for many years, owned the Royal Oak, the Queen's and the George. An original member of the British Hotels and Restaurants Association, he served the organisation for over fifty years, for eleven of which he was chairman.

His record of public offices in Keswick and Cumbria was long and impressive; member of the Urban District Council from the 1920s, County Councillor from 1946, Lake District Planning Board, police committee, a magistrate from 1934. At one time, he reckoned, he was spending up to three days a week on his public duties.

Throughout his life, he was keenly interested in sport, first as a participant and later as supporter. He played rugby and cricket for the county; he was master of the Blencathra Foxhounds for over thirty years. Most organisations in the town, from Rotary Club to St John's Church, Conservative Club to school governing bodies, found a willing and effective ally in PM.

He was knighted in 1954. He lived unpretentiously in Brundholme Terrace for most of his life, a familiar, portly figure, an institution almost, remembered with affection and gratitude – not least for his gift of Hope Park and Lady Hope's Garden, strategically situated on the way to the Lake and a popular attraction for visitors.

19

Walkaround

Since the end of the Second World War, the story of Keswick, broadly speaking, is one of reaction to expanding tourism. The construction of the M6 brought ten million or so people within a three-hour drive of the Lake District and the upgrading of the A66 from Penrith to Workington produced a marked increase of visitors to Keswick.

The proposal to build a major highway through the National Park sparked off a fierce battle. The industrialists and most inhabitants of West Cumbria saw the A66 as an economic lifeline; conservationists condemned it as an insensitive and unnecessary gash through prime landscape and suggested a viable alternative by Sebergham which, although it was four miles longer, avoided the Park.

The Greta Gorge flyover takes shape

A seven-week public enquiry resulted in a controversial decision in December, 1972, by the Secretary of State for the Environment in favour of the route through the National Park – 'a permanent monument to insensitivity towards superb scenery' commented the Countryside Commission.

Two features in particular were denounced. Along Bassenthwaite Lake, the shore was sacrificed to an engineered embankment and over Greta Gorge a huge viaduct towers over the Forge where four centuries ago the German miners processed their copper.

Any hopes that the A66 by-pass of Keswick would solve the traffic problem of the town were ill-founded. Heavy lorries no longer negotiate narrow streets and awkward corners but ease of access has brought many more car-borne tourists with the attendant headache of parking. If the national estimates of cars are even remotely accurate – twenty-four million in Britain in 1990 and up to a 140% increase by 2025 – they predict a dire future for Keswick, with roads choked by lines of stationary metal boxes and the National Park transformed into a National Car Park.

On the other hand, tourism remains the life-blood of Keswick. A survey in 1977 taken during the months of June to September revealed a total of nearly two and a quarter million visitor days and an associated expenditure of over £13 million.

The resident population has remained stable: 4867 in 1951, 4836 in 1991. Nearly one third of the residents are over sixty years of age (double the national average), a statistic which underlines the popularity of Keswick for retired people and the resulting housing problems: special provision for the aged, inflated prices, the exodus of young people unable to compete as first-time buyers, lack of acceptable building sites.

The 1980s and early 1990s were years of controversy, with several major disputes in progress. Attempts to turn the Market Place into a traffic-free zone were opposed by tradesmen and hoteliers who feared loss of business and pleaded lack of rear access for delivery vehicles. Something of a compromise was reached in November 1984 when it was agreed that traffic should be excluded from the area on Saturdays, the day of the traditional market. The Keswick Local Plan proposes full pedestrianisation, at least from June to October; this would remove a number of parking spaces and business proprietors may well raise strong objections to a blanket restriction of traffic covering the main tourist season.

The pattern of shopping facilities has changed with the growing demands of increased tourism. Long established local firms have disappeared: Birkett's (shoes), Cartmel's (butchers), Metcalf's (grocers), Graham's (grocers), Fink's (greengrocers), Telford's (jewellers), Aston's (china), Banks and Mayson's (ironmongers), Bargett's (outfitters), Allinson's (grocers) – to name only a few. Basic provision apart, the emphasis has moved to shops for visitors: gifts, mountaineering equipment, knitwear, for example, combined with a huge increase in the number of establishments providing food, from fish and chip shops and take-aways to up-market restaurants and four-star hotels. On the other hand, once thriving hotels such as the Royal Oak and the Skiddaw have converted parts of their premises into retail outlets; areas of old Keswick have been cleared to make way for shopping complexes at Herries Thwaite and Packhorse Court.

The 1980s saw the battle of the bus station. With bus services declining, it was no longer required: several entrepreneurs, including a local businessman, applied for planning permission to build a supermarket on the site. The wheeling and dealing included a summer season when the bus station was packed with broken-down buses, effectively blocking vital parking space for visiting coaches – a petty action which roused the anger and disgust of both the business community and the residents.

Eventually local enterprise won the day and in 1990 the Lakes supermarket was opened, sympathetically designed and incorporating parking space for cars, buses and coaches.

Even more dramatic is the long-running saga of the leisure pool and restaurant on the old station site and the nearby timeshare complex. It is a story that goes back at least a century. An article in the *English Lakes Visitor and Keswick Guardian* of July 1878 suggested among other improvements (including the demolition of the Moot Hall!) the provision of a swimming pool. Such an amenity, claimed the anonymous writer, 'ought to be amongst our local institutions: indeed, in a land like ours there is not the slightest excuse why one should not at once be erected for the good of the entire community'.

100 years later, Keswick was still without its pool, though several abortive attempts had been made to find a site and raise funds. When the CKP railway finally closed in 1972, a number of proposals were in the air for developing this 'festering waste' as a Civic Trust report of 1977 called the derelict station site.

Agreement between British Rail and the Lake District Special Planning Board paved the way for development. The Board insisted that any schemes should be 'appropriate to the interests of the town as a whole', complementing the character of Fitz Park and preserving the principal station buildings.

By 1982, a definite plan had emerged. Allerdale District Council would buy the site and the adjacent Archery Field. This field would house eighty timeshare units whose revenue would provide the funds for building a leisure pool and profits for both the Council and the developer. The station itself, with ample parking, was to be converted into a restaurant, platform bistro and administrative offices, conveniently situated for both pool users and timeshare owners.

The plan was received locally with mixed feelings: some people preferred a simple tank pool, with no expensive frills; others welcomed the more elaborate leisure pool, with its water flume, plastic landscaping and wave-making machine – and a constant eighty degrees temperature to provide a tropical holiday atmosphere all the year round whatever the state of the weather outside. A well-attended public meeting in May 1986, held in a 'now or never' atmosphere, enthusiastically endorsed the proposals. All seemed set to turn a dream into reality.

The key financial factor was the sale of the timeshare units to provide capital and this is where the whole project went sadly, tragically wrong. Of the original seventy-six apartments planned, only twenty or so were built. Of these a mere one third were sold, in spite of their high standard of comfort and facilities: revenue plummeted and the profit for the year 1987-88 was a pathetic £562. The District Council was faced with paying off a loan of six million pounds plus interest. Economies at the pool and hard-sell at the timeshare failed to solve the dilemma: the operations manager admitted that 'we have got a disaster on our hands'.

By 1990, after much discussion in private meetings, Allerdale Council was no nearer a solution. Liquidation loomed; rescue schemes roused considerable public opposition. A senior official was dismissed as, again in secret, a thorough investigation was initiated. At the time of writing, the general public, and Allerdale ratepayers in particular, frustrated and ill-informed, continue to speculate on what is really happening, relying mainly on newspaper reports rather than on frank and open official statements.

To round off this story of Keswick, to tie up loose ends and to link together some of the material of this book with the scene as it is today calls for a leisurely guided stroll through the town.

The obvious starting place is the Moot Hall in the Market Square. It no longer sports the white coat it had for many years; its conversion back to natural stone some years ago was not universally welcomed. The ground floor information centre is a magnet for tourists and upstairs two rooms accommodate a variety of public activities, from coffee mornings to art exhibitions, sales to lectures – all maintaining the tradition of a meeting hall which, over the centuries, has been home to council deliberations, court proceedings, a butter and fruit market, and a museum.

There appear to have been several rebuildings of this distinctive landmark. A letter in 1571 from Richard Dudley to Sir William Cecil refers to 'an old court house situate in the midst of Keswick' to be used as a storehouse for copper after its ruins had been repaired. An incident in 1657 suggests a rebuilding in the late 1650s: William Munkhouse was drowned when his boat, it is said, overloaded with stones from the dilapidated Radcliffe home on Lord's Island, sank near Friars' Crag.

A lease dated August 1664 refers to 'one certaine house situate being and standing in the middle of the said Towne of Keswicke...belonging to the said Sir Francis Radcliffe commonly known by the name of Courthouse or Moot hall'.

Jonathan Otley gives the date of the last rebuilding as 1812, a year when he was living only a stone's throw away from the Moot Hall.

Two interesting features are the one-handed clock and the bell. The latter has an enigmatic inscription 'H D 1001 R O' The type of bell, insist the experts, makes the date completely wrong: 1001 is almost certainly intended to be 1601. 'R O' probably stands for 'Robert Oldfield', a peripatetic bell-founder of the early 1600s, but 'H D' remains unexplained.

No traces remain today of the fountain that used to stand in the Square: it was removed a century ago after many complaints about the mud and standing water that surrounded the drinking-trough. Gone, too, has the ring where bulls were tied to be baited by dogs, a barbaric spectacle that appears to have drawn large crowds. It was claimed that prime beef came only from baited animals: however true that may have been, the practice was prohibited by an act of parliament in 1835.

The Upper Market Square sets out its stalls

The open-air market held every Saturday in the shadow of the Moot Hall maintains a tradition that goes back to the charter of 1276. Two centuries ago, cereals were the major item on sale. A public announcement dated 30 March 1787 states: 'The Inhabitants of Keswick and the Country round have come to a unanimous Resolution to make Keswick a Perpetual CORN MARKET, for all kinds of Grain'. Wheat and barley were exposed for sale in the lower Market Place, then known as Summer Birks Brow; the upper area was reserved for oats, rye, peas and beans.

For many years, hiring fairs were held in the Market Square: farm servants and labourers paraded for selection and engagement by prospective employers. Whit Saturday and the Saturday before St Martin's Day (11 November) were reserved for Hiring Days when 'those who wish to engage as Servants are desired to appear upon Summer Birch Brow, with Green Branches in their hands, at Ten o'clock of the Forenoon on each Day'.

By the late 1870s, the custom was dying out; good servants, it was reported, 'can now find situations without exhibiting themselves like so many white slaves'.

Across the road from the Moot Hall and next to Lloyd's Bank is Packhorse Yard, one of a number of yards on both sides of the Square. These enclosed areas, with narrow access from the town centre, are the remains of the medieval burgage plots, discussed earlier. They have been subjected to drastic alterations over the years: Packhorse Yard has become Packhorse Court – shops, flats, and an arcade linked with Station Street, giving no hint of its former character as a bustling, noisy centre for packhorses and their drivers, with stabling for the animals and an inn for the men.

The town shambles were here. Older residents remember a forge, a joiner's shop and a byre for cows kept by the proprietors of the Central Hotel, a hostelry recently incorporated in 'Ye Olde Friars' sweet shop, itself once a popular 150-seater cafe.

The Packhorse Court development has also taken in New Street, once a convenient right-of-way from the Market Square to Back Lane or Standish Street, now the site of the aptly-named 'Cars of the Stars' Motor Museum. Old photographs show New Street with half-a-dozen well-kept cottages, each with its colourful window box of flowers. The occupier of one of them, it is said, used to bake bread rolls for Lowther Castle near Penrith.

The next building, traditionally the home of Sir John Bankes, and currently a clothing shop, gives no hint of its former importance. Long neglected, its upper room had the remnants of panelling and a moulded plaster ceiling, a reminder of what must have been a splendid example of a seventeenth century room. It was finally destroyed in the 1980s; parts of the ceiling, one with the date 1602 inscribed, are on display in the Fitz Park Museum and a section of the panelling, expertly cleaned and restored, may be seen in Young's antiques' shop on request.

Through the arch alongside this antiques' shop is the flight of steps to Jonathan Otley's workshop, commemorated by a memorial plaque. The name of this yard, King's Head Yard, recalls an inn that once occupied the premises of Young's furniture shop. Cottages have long since been demolished or converted as part of development projects. This has been the fate of a succession of yards that we pass before reaching the Post Office. A map of 1852 shows them as the Queen's Head Yard, the Golden Lion Yard (with its good example of an original wall), Banks' Yard, Wren's Yard, Powley's Yard, the Wool Pack Yard, and Richardson's Yard. Cottages and workshops have disappeared; ancient burgage fronts have been replaced by shop windows; the Bell Close car park has sliced off large sections of the rear sections of the yards.

The Post Office was built in 1890 on the site of Sir John Bankes' Poorhouse. In his will dated 1642 (two years before he died), he left £200 for the building and to raise 'a stock of Wool, Flax, Hemp, Thread, Iron and other necessary wear and stuff to set the poor on work who were born in the Parish of Crosthwaite'.

Inmates of the Workhouse were to include children whose parents were unable to maintain them, orphans and widows, the ageing poor and indigent paupers. Profits from the sale of cloth and linen made by the inmates were to be directed to helping the halt and lame, the blind and the incapacitated, and to organising apprenticeships.

It would appear that Sir John's insistence on gainful employment was ignored and what had been intended as a workhouse declined into a comparatively comfortable parish poorhouse. Its popularity grew so much that 'the Great House', as it was called, had at times up to eighty inmates, among them whole families.

The Poor Law Amendment Act of 1834 put a stop to such intensive use. The Great House was nearly destroyed: the influence of Southey with the Charity Commissioners ensured its continuance but the number of residents was reduced to eighteen poor and aged persons. The 1862 enquiry by the Charity Commissioners into Keswick's sixteen local charities, one of which was Bankes', ordered that the poorhouse should be closed and the funds used to provide relief for selected impoverished Keswickians who would, as a result, manage to struggle along in their own homes rather than spend their declining years in the workhouse at Cockermouth – an early example of today's 'Care in the Community'.

The Bankes Charity funded other projects: the provision of food and fuel for the needy, grants for nursing and educational facilities, support for the Moral Welfare Society and Crosthwaite Provident Society – not quite what Sir John had intended but certainly fulfilling the spirit of his generous endowments.

The Post Office opened for business in 1891. Behind it are the Police Station and Court rooms, modest premises built in the 1890s. The road dividing the Post Office and the building opposite is Bank Street, named after the Cumberland Union Bank built in 1864. Currently the Town Council offices, it also housed the Post Office until 1891.

Our walk continues past the Wild Strawberry cafe, for many years the premises of Thomas Bakewell, the principal printer in Keswick, to the next street. This is Stanger Street, named after a well-known local family of philanthropists. It is worth a diversion to climb the hill to look at the 'Garden City' of Greta Hamlet at the top of Stanger Street.

Back on Main Street, our walk takes us past Hewetson Court, developed in 1991 on the site of two old inns, the Crown and the Black Lion.

A little further on, just before reaching Keswick School, is Crosthwaite Parish Room. Officially opened in November, 1879, it is a memorial to the Rev. George Gonville Goodwin. After a short spell as curate at Crosthwaite Church, he succeeded Canon Henry Gipps to the living in 1878, appointed by his father, Bishop Harvey Goodwin of Carlisle. His incumbency lasted only two months: it appears that he caught a fatal disease while visiting a parishioner in Portinscale.

He had cherished the idea of a parish room for meetings, classes and services for the old and infirm who were unable to go to church. It was suggested that such a building would be a fitting memorial and Keswick responded quickly and generously to the appeal for funds.

To fulfil the dual function of meeting-room and chapel, a simple altar and sanctuary were positioned behind a moveable screen. In its 100 years or so, it has served the parish – and the town – in the spirit intended by its founders: a room for religious services but also a conveniently situated building for a multitude of activities, from educational classes to coffee mornings, tea parties to slide shows, lectures to annual general meetings.

Immediately beyond the Parish Room, we pass Keswick School, with Greta Hall perched on the hill behind. At some time in the future, when the single-site secondary school is sited at Lairthwaite, the fate of these premises – a prime location within easy reach of the centre of the town and including a literary shrine of international importance – will have to be decided.

Just before crossing Greta Bridge, turn along Southey Lane, now Carding Mill Lane, for a visit to the Pencil Museum. The factory itself is not open to the public.

A few yards before the building on the corner of Crosthwaite Road – once Crosthwaite C of E Infants' School and now the St Herbert Social Centre – look for the remains of one of Samuel Ladyman's drinking fountains in the wall. Over the wall there are the restored 'retting' steps where flax, used by the Ruskin Linen Industry cottages across the road, was soaked in the Greta.

Crosthwaite Road, which heads off to the right towards the hospital and Bristowe Hill, has three buildings to note: the old school, built in 1833; Quaker Cottage behind it, recalling the early Quaker meeting house there; and the Catholic Church opposite.

Cross the road to the church and continue along the main road to the end of the houses on your right. Turn over the small Crossings Bridge and immediately left. The straight road leads to Crosthwaite Church and what was once Crosthwaite Old School, with the buildings of Keswick School, Lairthwaite site, on the hill to your right.

A visit to Crosthwaite Church is an essential feature of any walk round Keswick: allow plenty of time to savour a rewarding experience before retracing your steps back to Crossings Bridge.

Cross the road. The field on your right is the venue for Keswick's annual agricultural show on August Bank Holiday Monday.

On the return walk, there is little to note until two cottages opposite the St Herbert Social Centre. A plaque on the first depicting joiners at work is the traditional site of the Joiners' Arms; next to it was the Toll House, active in the days of the Turnpike Trusts and strategically positioned to trap all travellers to and from Cockermouth and the west and Carlisle and the north.

A little further along is a row of cottages, one called Porch Cottage, the other Ruskin Cottage. From 1894, for nearly thirty years, these were the home of the Ruskin Linen Industry, the small but thriving venture presided over by the formidable Miss Maria Twelves.

Immediately beyond the cottages is Ravensfield, a purpose-built home for old people opened in 1970. The building next to it, now the Primavera Restaurant, was the Keswick School of Industrial Art for nearly a century until it closed in 1984.

Pause on Greta Bridge and look down stream. On your left is the Youth Club, once a woollen mill and in the late 1800s a pencil mill owned by Ann Banks, widow of Joseph Banks, the principal pencil manufacturer in the town at the time.

The route into the town centre continues past the Labour Club and Bridge House (part of Keswick School) to Tithebarn Street, which, sadly, long ago lost all traces of the old tithebarn.

Our route continues towards the Market Square, passing more hidden yards, and the site of Peter Crosthwaite's museum, now the Herries Thwaite Shopping Centre. A commemorative stone plaque set in the pavement near the entrance records its former name and function.

The area from Herries Thwaite to the Moot Hall has been subjected to considerable change. The old police station, along with Atkinson's and Gatey's Courts, was demolished to widen Derwent Close and build flats. The cottages of Police Court Yard, refurbished and modernised, are still occupied. Extensions and alterations to shops and hotels and the creation of the Central Car Park have transformed the area behind the lower Market Square.

Just beyond the King's Arms Hotel is yet another yard, variously known as Temple's Court or Chapel Yard, an insalubrious, malodorous site for the Wesleyan chapel in the early nineteenth century. The Oddfellows' Arms Yard, apart from housing stables, a slaughterhouse and a smithy, boasted its own bowling green and assembly room. Woolworth's occupies the site of Storm's Cafe, once a popular rendezvous owned by a local farming and catering firm which also ran the Lakeside Tea Gardens.

A fine display of Christmas poultry

Rathbone's, between Woolworths and the Midland Bank, was earlier the fish shop owned by Mr Percy Todd, whose imaginative and lavish displays were one of the sights of Keswick, rivalled only by those of nearby Hudson's. Poplar Street, one of the few remaining yards still providing accommodation, once had more cottages, storage buildings and workshops.

Round the corner, behind the Dog and Gun in Lake Road, is Wickham's Court, well worth looking at as a fine example of renovation which has preserved the atmosphere of the old yard and provided modern amenities for the inhabitants of the nine cottages.

A little further along Lake Road, past the Congregational Church, is a large shop trading under the name of George Fisher, an emporium which enjoys a national reputation as a mountaineering equipment shop. From 1887 to 1967, this was Abraham's, one of the most famous photographic shops in Britain and possibly the oldest family photographic business in the country.

The road to the right between George Fisher's and the garage leads to Hope Park, the Blue Box Theatre and Derwentwater. At the turn of the century, on the left behind Mayson's, there was a rock and Alpine garden owned by Thomas Hayes, founding father of the firm which runs the large garden centre at Ambleside. Mr Hayes came to Keswick in 1890; his garden boasted the rarest ferns in Britain and plants from all over the world – edelweiss from Switzerland, dwarf juniper from Japan, barberry from India. His eye for beauty and his technical expertise shaped many gardens, from the Marine Drive at Southport and the Memorial Park at Coventry to the Japanese Garden at Lowther Castle and Derwent Hill at Portinscale.

He was active in local church affairs and a member of the Urban District Council for twenty years. He died in 1927, the year in which the business moved to Ambleside: he was indeed a man who 'passed through the waste places of the world and touched them to greater beauty'.

From George Fisher's shop, our route continues along Borrowdale Road to a group of cottages known as 'The Plosh'. Almost opposite the end cottage is a rising footpath that leads to St John's Church and the panoramic view from its terrace. At the end of the path, where it joins St John's Street, pause for a moment. Opposite on the right is Derwentwater Place and the Chaucer House Hotel, the site of the building where William and Elizabeth Smith met. Opposite on the left is the Battersby Hall; the building immediately on your left is the former St John's First School.

Turn left along St John's Street and after a few yards left again along High Street to see Bethesda Chapel and The Hollies, for many years the R A F A Club. Turn right along The Seams (formerly Union Street or Sim's Street) to Derwent Street (once Harriman Field) and right again to join St John's Street, noting en route the tiny St George's Square (formerly Spedding's Yard or Frying Pan Square).

As you join St John's Street, with the Alhambra Cinema on your immediate right, glance across the road at a small shop called 'Open all Hours': its facade is decorated with a striking collection of vintage advertisements.

'Open All Hours' with its nostalgic exhibition of old advertisements

Turn left and walk towards the George Hotel, past the large building across the road which was for many years the home of the Co-op. The George claims to be the oldest inn in Keswick, dating back to at least 1613 and until the accession of George I called the George and Dragon. Opposite the George is the Derwent Club, built in the 1730s by Edward Stephenson as 'Governor's House'.

Turn right along Station Street, once known as Grandy Nook. Cross the road to the canopied entrance of the Packhorse Court development of 1990 and a much reduced Royal Oak Hotel. This once central meeting place for locals and a popular holiday venue for visitors, including royalty, has a long history. Among its attractions was the large dining-room with stained glass windows depicting notable literary personalities of the Lake District which, fortunately, have not been destroyed in its recent conversion to the 'Beatrix Potter's Lake District' exhibition.

Continue along Station Street and cross the end of Victoria Street to Station Road. 100 yards or so along Station Road, stand on the bridge over the Greta and look downstream. Immediately on your left is the block of Riverside Lodge flats which replaced the Queen of the Lakes Pavilion in 1989, itself the successor of an old tannery. Next to it is the Youth Hostel, once the Park Hotel. Beyond the hostel are more flats, converted from the old pencil and corn mills on the river bank.

Walk along Station Road, with Fitz Park on either side, to the Museum and Art Gallery. A little further on is the ill-fated leisure pool and short-lived platform restaurant, a nostalgic mecca for railway enthusiasts who at least have the imposing Keswick Hotel as a reminder of days of steam and a bustling station.

Cross the road from John Fisher Crosthwaite's memorial gate to that of Henry Irwin Jenkinson and look at the bust of Sir John Bankes hidden under a tree a few yards inside the Park on your left.

Walk back up Station Road towards the town, noting the memorial plaques and a drinking fountain in the wall on your left. At the end of the road is the War Memorial, honouring the dead of two World Wars. On the back of the Memorial a copper tablet lists the names of employees of the CKP railway who were killed in the 1914-18 War.

Cross the road into Station Street and return to the Market Square. One building merits a special mention. A few yards along the street is the office of the *Keswick Reminder*. This unique newspaper – there is, apparently, no other in the country with the word 'Reminder' in its title – is the key to the town's activities: it is jokingly said that if it isn't in the *Reminder*, it hasn't happened.

It has progressed from a modest free advertising handout to a substantial local newspaper, eagerly awaited each week and conscientiously read in practically every house in Keswick and district – and by Keswickians in exile in Britain and abroad. Founded in 1897 by George Watson McKane, it has remained in the family. Its four owner-editors have respected the founder's principle that no court cases are reported and that scandal is rigorously avoided.

'As long as the *Keswick Reminder* flourishes,' Chris Brasher once wrote in the *Observer*, 'there will be one corner of these islands that is forever England.' That compliment would seem to be an appropriate finale with which to end this story of Keswick...

Had they any idea in 1879 of what would happen to their town?

Bibliography

I was once told, on good authority, that there are at least 50,000 books which have some association with the Lake District and Cumbria. Quite how the figure was calculated, I don't know but, whatever the total, many of this mountain of titles will have references to Keswick and its history.

This bibliography is necessarily selective. It excludes, with a few exceptions, modern guide books, picture books, books of walks and fiction.

Any works by the following authors are recommended for background information: W G Collingwood, W Heaton Cooper, J F Crosthwaite, A H Griffin, Molly Lefebure, Jessica Lofthouse, Norman Nicholson, W T Palmer, H D Rawnsley, William Rollinson, A Wainwright.

A Bibliographies, indexes, catalogues

BICKNELL, P and WOOF, R. *The Discovery of the Lake District 1750-1810: a context for Wordsworth.* Trustees of Dove Cottage, 1982.

BICKNELL, P and WOOF, R. *The Lake District Discovered 1810-1850: the artists, the tourists and Wordsworth.* Trustees of Dove Cottage, 1983.

CROUCHER, T. *Cumbria: index 1951-1992, Vols. 1-41.* Dalesman, 1992.

ELSBY, W. *Guide to Local History: Keswick.* Cumbria County Library, nd.

HINDS, J P. *Bibliotheca Jacksoniana.* Titus Wilson, 1909.

HODGSON, H W. *A Bibliography of the History and Topography of Cumberland and Westmorland.* Joint Archives Committee for Cumberland, Westmorland and Carlisle, 1968.

NEATE, J. *The Lake District: a reader's guide.* Chaplins of Keswick, 1987.

PARRY, D. *Newsplan: Report of the Newsplan project in the Northern Region.* British Library, 1989. (Contains full listing of all N Region (inc. Cumbria) local newspapers to 1989, with known extant copies and locations).

RAYMOND, S. *Cumberland and Westmorland: a genealogical bibliography.* Federation of Family History Societies, 1993.

THOMASON, D and WOOF, R. *Derwentwater: the Vale of Elysium: an eighteenth century story.* Trustees of Dove Cottage, 1986.

B Transactions, Journals

CUMBERLAND AND WESTMORLAND ASSOCIATION FOR THE ADVANCEMENT OF LITERATURE AND SCIENCE. *Transactions 1875-1892.*

CUMBERLAND AND WESTMORLAND ANTIQUARIAN AND ARCHAEOLOGICAL SOCIETY. *Transactions 1874-1900 (Old Series), 1900 – (New Series).*

FELL AND ROCK CLIMBING CLUB OF THE ENGLISH LAKE DISTRICT. *Journal 1907 –*

Journals of local societies, eg Lakeland Dialect Society, Cumbria Geological Society, Cumbria Family History Society, Cumbria Railways Association, Cumbria Branch of the Wesley Historical Society, etc.

C Newspapers

Carlisle Journal 1798-1968

Cumberland News 1910 –

Cumberland and Westmorland Herald (variously named) 1860 –

Cumberland Pacquet 1774-1915

Derwentwater Record 1854-1857

English Lakes Visitor and Keswick Guardian 1877-1910

Keswick Advertiser 1952-1956

Keswick Reminder 1896 –

Penrith Observer 1860-1968

Skiddaw Spring and Lake District Herald 1859-1860

West Cumberland Times and Star (variously named) 1874 –

BARNES, F and HOBBS, J L. *Handlist of Newspapers published in Cumberland, Westmorland and North Lancashire.* C W A A S, 1951.

D General Background

APPLEBY, A B. *Famine in Tudor and Stuart England.* Liverpool U P, 1978.

BAILEY, J and CULLEY, G. *General View of the Agriculture of the County of Cumberland.* 1794.

BARRINGER, J C. *Lakeland Landscape: a geographical approach.* Dalesman, 1970.

BOUCH, C M L and JONES, G P. *The Lake Counties 1500-1830: a social and economic history.* Manchester U P, 1961.

BOUCH, C M L. *Prelates and People of the Lake Counties.* Titus Wilson, 1948.

BRUNSKILL, R W. *Vernacular architecture of the Lake Counties.* Faber, 1974.

CARRUTHERS, F J. *Around the Lakeland Hills.* Hale, 1976.

CARRUTHERS, F J. *Lore of the Lake Country.* Hale, 1975.

CARRUTHERS, F J. *People called Cumbri.* Hale, 1970.

COLLINGWOOD, W G. *The Lake Counties.* Warne, 1932.

COLLINGWOOD, W G. *Lake District History.* Titus Wilson, 1925.

DENTON, J. *An Accompt of the most considerable estates and families in the County of Cumberland* (ed R S Ferguson). C W A A S, 1887.

DENYER, S. *Traditional Buildings and Life in the Lake District.* Gollancz, 1991.

EYRE, K. *Famous Lakeland Homes.* Dalesman, 1975.

HERVEY, G A K. and BARNES, J A G. *Natural History of the Lake District.* Warne, 1970

HODGE, E W. *Enjoying the Lakes: from post-chaise to National Park.* Oliver & Boyd, 1957.

HUGHES, E. *North Country Life in the eighteenth century: Volume two - Cumberland and Westmorland 1700-1830.* O U P, 1965.

HUTCHINSON, W. *The history of the County of Cumberland* (two volumes). Jollie, 1794.
KELLY, S F. *Victorian Lakeland Photographers*. Swan Hill, 1991.
LEFEBURE, M. *Cumbrian Discovery*. Gollancz, 1977.
LEFEBURE, M. *Cumberland Heritage*. Gollancz, 1970.
LEFEBURE, M. *The English Lake District*. Batsford, 1964.
LELAND, J. *The Itinerary of John Leland in or about the years 1535-1543: Part IX* (ed. L T Smith). Centaur, 1964.
LEWIS, S. *A Topographical Dictionary of England*. 1831.
LINDOP, G. *A Literary Guide to the Lake District*. Chatto, 1993.
LONSDALE, H. *Worthies of Cumberland* (six volumes). Routledge, 1867-75.
MANNIX and WHELLAN. *History, Gazetteer and Directory of Cumberland*. 1847. Michael Moon, 1974.
MARSHALL, J D and WALTON, J K. *The Lake Counties from 1830 to the mid-twentieth century*. Manchester U P, 1981.
MEE, A. *The Lake Counties: Cumberland and Westmorland*. Hodder, 1937.
MILLWARD, R. and ROBINSON, A. *The Lake District*. Eyre & Spottiswood, 1970.
MURDOCH, J et al. *The Lake District: a sort of National property*. Countryside Commission/Victoria & Albert Museum, 1986.
MURDOCH, J. (ed). *The Discovery of the Lake District*. Victoria & Albert Museum, 1984.
NICOLSON, J and BURN, R. *The History and Antiquities of the counties of Westmorland and Cumberland*. 1777. E P Publishing, 1977.
NICHOLSON, N. *The Lake District: an anthology*. Hale, 1977.
NICHOLSON, N. *Portrait of the Lakes*. Hale, 1963.
NICOLSON, W. *Miscellany Accounts of the Diocese of Carlisle* (ed. R S Ferguson). Bell/Thurnam, 1877.
PARSON and WHITE. *Directory of Cumberland and Westmorland*. 1829. Michael Moon, 1976.
PEARSALL, W H and PENNINGTON, W. *The Lake District*. Collins New Naturalist, 1973.
PEVSNER, N. *The Buildings of England: Cumberland and Westmorland*. Penguin, 1967.
RICE, H A L. *Lake Country Towns*. Hale, 1974.
ROLLINSON, W. *A History of Cumberland and Westmorland*. Phillimore, 1978.
ROLLINSON, W. *A History of Man in the Lake District*. Dent, 1967.
ROLLINSON, W (ed). *The Lake District: landscape heritage*. David & Charles, 1989.
ROLLINSON, W. *Life and Tradition in the Lake District*. Dent, 1974.
SMITH, K. *Early Prints of the Lake District*. Hendon, 1973.
SUTTON, G. *Fell Days*. Museum Press, 1948.
VALENTINE, H and A W. *Tales of a Tent (1913)*. Michael Moon, 1977.
WILLIAMS, L A. *Road Transport in Cumbria in the Nineteenth Century*. Allen & Unwin, 1975.
WILSON, J. *Victoria History of the County of Cumberland* (two volumes). Constable, 1905.
WINCHESTER, A J L. *Landscape and Society in Medieval Cumbria*. Donald, 1987.
YOUNG, A. *A six month Tour through the North of England*. 1770.

E General Background - Keswick

BARBER, S. *Beneath Helvellyn's Shade: notes and sketches in the Valley of Wythburn*. Elliot Stock, 1892.
BATTERICK, E. *A Lakeland Summer*. Cicerone, 1979.
BIRKETT, G. *The Islands of Lake Derwentwater*. nd.
BRIERLEY, H. *Parish Registers: Crosthwaite* (1562-1812 - four volumes). C W A A S, 1929-31.
BROATCH, J. *Old Keswick*. 1911.

BROATCH, M. *Keswick and Derwentwater*. nd.
BURGESS, J. *A History of Keswick*. 1989.
COLLINGWOOD, W G. *Thirteenth Century Keswick*. C W A A S, 1920.
CUMBRIA MAGAZINE. *Keswick: a practical guide for visitors*. Dalesman, 1976.
CUMBRIA MAGAZINE. *Keswick and Northern Lakeland*. Dalesman, 1963.
DENWOOD, E R. *The Derwent Valleys and John Peel Country*. 1952.
DEWDNEY, J C and WARDHAUGH, K G. *The Newlands Valley*. Geography Department, University of Durham, 1960.
DIXON, J. *Borrowdale in Olden Times as gathered from the Conversation of the late Sarah Yewdale, Queen of Borrowdale*. Bailey, 1869.
HALL, J H V. *Threlkeld, Cumbria: glimpses of Village History*. 1977.
HARRIS, R. *Watendlath* (Woodbrooke Essay 19). Heffer, 1928.
HARRISON, P. *Keswick and its Neighbourhood: a Handbook for the use of Visitors*. Garnett, 1852.
HEYWOOD, A. *A Guide to Keswick and its Vicinity*. 1903.
IMRIE, D. *Lakeland Gamekeeper*. Batchworth, 1949.
LAKE DISTRICT NATIONAL PARK AUTHORITY. *Keswick Local Plan*. 1989.
LEAROYD, W H A. *Around Keswick*. St Catherine's Press, 1947.
MARSH, J. *Keswick and the Central Lakes in Old Photographs*. Sutton, 1993.
MARTINEAU, H. *Keswick and its Environs*. Garnett, nd.
MILLWARD, R and ROBINSON, A. *Borrowdale and West Cumberland*. Macmillan, 1972.
PATTINSON, J M. *Conserving the Character of Keswick*. Lake District Special Planning Board, 1992.
SMITH, R. *42 Peaks: the story of the Bob Graham Round*. nd.
SUTTON, S. *The Story of Borrowdale*. Borrowdale Women's Institute, 1960.
TAYLOR, W R. *Keswick R U F C. Centenary Year 1879-1979*. McKane, 1979.
TRINITY SCHOOL. *Welcome to Keswick*. Trinity School, 1988.
USHER, J. *Where to go and what to see about Keswick*. nd.
WATSON, J. *Lakeland Towns*. Cicerone, 1992.
WILSON, E J. *Enid J Wilson's Country Diary*. Hodder, 1988.
WILSON, E J. *A Lakeland Diary*. Fleece Press, 1985.
WILSON, T. *All about Keswick: a Guide to the Hills and Dales*. nd.
WILSON, T. *Let's Go for a Walk round about Keswick*. nd.
WINTER, H E. *A History of Keswick and District*. 1991.
WITHERS, P. *In a Cumberland Dale*. Grant Richards, 1914.

F Chapter by Chapter

Introduction

BOARDMAN, J. *Classic Landforms of the Lake District*. Geographical Association, 1988.
CUMBERLAND GEOLOGICAL SOCIETY. *The Lake District*. Unwin, 1982.
DAVIS, R V. *Geology of Cumbria: Lakeland's Rocks and Minerals Explained*. Dalesman, 1977.
DAVIS, R V. *Geology of Lakeland*. Dalesman, 1988.
DODDS, M. *Lakeland Rocks and Landscape: a Field Guide*. Ellenbank/Cumberland Geological Society, 1992.
HOLLINGWORTH, S E. *The Geology of the Lake District*. Benham/Geologists' Association, 1954.
MARR, J E. *Geology of the Lake District*. C U P, 1916; Chivers, 1968.
MITCHELL, G H. *The Geological History of the Lake District*. Yorkshire Geological Society, 1956.

MONKHOUSE, F J. *British Landscapes through Maps: the English Lake District.* Geographical Association, 1960.
MOSELEY, F. *Geology of the Lake District.* Geologists' Association, 1990.
MOSELEY, F. *The Geology of the Lake District.* Yorkshire Geological Society, 1978.
MOSELEY, F. *Geology and Scenery in the Lake District.* Macmillan, 1986.
MOSELEY, F. *The Volcanic Rocks of the Lake District.* Macmillan, 1983.
POSTLETHWAITE, J. *The Geology of the English Lake District.* Bakewell, 1897.
PROSSER, R. *Geology explained in the Lake District.* David & Charles, 1977.
SHACKLETON, E H. *Geological Excursions in Lakeland.* Dalesman, 1975.
SHACKLETON, E H. *Lakeland Geology: where to go; what to see.* Dalesman, 1966.
SHIPP, T. *The Lake District.* Cumberland Geological Society/Unwin Paperbacks, 1982.

CHAPTER 1 - STONES, SOLDIERS AND SAINTS

AILRED AND JOCELINUS. *Two Celtic Saints: the Lives of St Ninian and St Kentigern.* Llanerch, 1989.
BRADLEY, R and EDMONDS, M. *Interpreting the Axe Trade: Production and Exchange in Neolithic Britain.* C U P, 1993.
BURL, A. *Rings of Stone: the Prehistoric Stone Circles of Britain and Ireland.* Frances Lincoln, 1979.
BURL, A. *The Stone Circles of the British Isles.* Yale U P, 1976.
CLARE, T. *Archaeological Sites of the Lake District.* Moorland, 1981.
FELL, C. *Early Settlement in the Lake Counties.* Dalesman, 1972.
HARTLEY, B and FITTS, L. *The Brigantes.* Sutton, 1988.
HIGHAM, N. *The Carvetii.* Sutton, 1985.
HIGHAM, N. *The Northern Counties to AD 1000.* Longman, 1986.
JACKSON, K H. *The Sources for the Life of St Kentigern* (in CHADWICK, N K *Studies in the Early British Church.* C U P, 1958.)
MACDONALD, I. *Saint Mungo.* Floris Books, 1993.
NEWBY, G. *Henllywarc or the Druids' Temple near Keswick: a poem.* Longman, 1854.
RAWNSLEY, H D. *Five Addresses on the Lives and Work of St Kentigern and St Herbert.* Thurnam/Bell, 1888.
STREET, K. *Stone Circles in the North West.* St Martin's College, Lancaster, 1984.
THOM, A. *Megalithic Sites in Britain.* O U P, 1967.
WATERHOUSE, J. *The Stone Circles of Cumbria.* Phillimore, 1985.

CHAPTER 2 - SETTLING DOWN

ARMSTRONG, A H. et al. *Place Names of Cumberland* (three volumes). C U P, 1950.
ARNOLD, R. *Northern Lights: the story of Lord Derwentwater.* Constable, 1959.
ATKINSON, J C. (ed) *The Coucher Book of Furness Abbey.* Chetham Society, 1886.
BALDWIN, J R and WHYTE, I D. *The Scandinavians in Cumbria.* Scottish Society for Northern Studies, 1985.
BREARLEY, D. *Lake District Place Names.* Graham, 1974.
COLLINGWOOD, W G. *Scandinavian Britain.* 1908. Llanerch, 1993.
CROSTHWAITE, J F. *The Last of the Derwentwaters.* 1874.
DICKINSON, F. *The Castle on Devil's Water: the story of Dilston and the Tragic Earl of Derwentwater.* Spredden Press, 1969.
FERGUSON, R S. *The Northmen in Cumberland and Westmorland.* Longman, 1856.
GAMBLES, R. *Lake District Place Names.* Dalesman, 1980.

RAWLING, W. *Homage to the Herdwick.* Friends of Whitehaven Museum, 1986.
SEDGEFIELD, W J. *The Place Names of Cumberland and Westmorland.* Manchester U P, 1915.

CHAPTER 3 - ELIZABETHAN KLONDIKE

COLLINGWOOD, W G. *Elizabethan Keswick.* C W A A S, 1912. Michael Moon, 1987.
DONALD, M B. *Elizabethan Copper: the History of the Company of Mines Royal 1568-1605.* Pergamon, 1955. Michael Moon, 1989.
HAMMERSLEY, G. *Daniel Hechstetter the Younger: Memorabilia and Letters 1600-1639: Copper Works and Life in Cumbria.* Steiner Verlag, 1988.
PETROSKI, H. *The Pencil: a History.* Faber, 1990.
THOMSON, R. *Making Pencils.* Franklin Watts, 1986.
ROBINSON, T. *An Essay towards a Natural History of Westmorland and Cumberland.* 1709.

CHAPTER 4 - PICKING A LIVING

ADAMS, J. *Mines of the Lake District Fells.* Dalesman, 1988.
BENNETT, J. *A Guide to the Industrial Archaeology of Cumbria.* Association for Industrial Archaeology, 1993.
CAMERON, A D. *Slate from Honister.* Cumbria Amenity Trust Mining History Society, 1993.
CUMBRIA AMENITY TRUST MINING HISTORY SOCIETY. *Beneath the Lakeland Fells: Cumbria's Mining Heritage.* Red Earth, 1992.
DAVIES-SHIEL, M and MARSHALL, J D. *Industrial Archaeology of the Lake Counties.* David & Charles, 1969.
FRIENDS OF THE LAKE DISTRICT. *Slate Quarrying in the Lake District: a Cause for Concern?* Stephen Associates, 1988.
HINDLE, P. *Roads and Trackways of the Lake District.* Moorland, 1984.
MCFADZEAN, A. *Wythburn Mine and the Lead Mines of Helvellyn.* Red Earth, 1987.
MARSHALL, J D and DAVIES-SHIEL, M. *The Lake District at Work: Past and Present.* David & Charles, 1971.
POSTLETHWAITE, J. *Mines and Mining in the English Lake District.* Moxon, 1877. Michael Moon, 1975.
SHAW, W T. *Mining in the Lake District.* Dalesman, 1970.
TYLER, I. *Force Crag: the History of a Lakeland Mine.* Red Earth, 1990.
TYLER, I. *Honister Slate.* Blue Rock, 1994.

CHAPTER 5 - CURIOUS TRAVELLERS

BARBIER, C P. *William Gilpin: his Drawings, Teaching and Theory of the Picturesque.* O U P, 1963.
BICKNELL, P. *The Picturesque Scenery of the Lake District.* St Paul's Bibliographies, 1990.
BROWN, J. *A Description of the Lake at Keswick* (and the adjoining country) in Cumberland. 1767. (ed A F Wilson, 1985.)
BRITTON, J and BRAYLEY, E W. *A Topographical and Historical Description of the County of Cumberland.* 1803.
BUDWORTH, J. *A Fortnight's Ramble to the Lakes in Westmoreland, Lancashire and Cumberland, by a 'Rambler'.* Hookham & Carpenter, 1792. Preston Publications, 1990.
BURKETT, M E. *The Viewfinders.* Abbot Hall Art Gallery, 1980.
CLARKE, J. *A Survey of the Lakes of Cumberland, Westmorland and Lancashire.* 1787.
DALTON, J. *Descriptive Poem addressed to Two Ladies at their Return from viewing the Mines near Whitehaven.* 1755.

DEFOE, D. *A Tour through the Whole Island of Great Britain.* 1724-6.
DENHOLM, J. *A Tour to the Principal Scotch and English Lakes.* Chapman, 1804.
GELL, W. *A Tour in the Lakes made in 1797* (ed W Rollinson). Graham, 1968.
GILPIN, W. *Observations relative chiefly to Picturesque Beauty made in the year 1772 on several parts of England; particularly the Mountains and Lakes of Cumberland and Westmorland* (two volumes). Cadell & Davies, 1786. Richmond, 1973.
GRAY, T. *The Poems of Mr Gray; to which are prefixed Memoirs of his Life and Writings* (ed. W Mason). 1775.
HUSSEY, C. *The Picturesque: Studies in a point of view.* 1927.
HUTCHINSON, W. *An Excursion to the Lakes in Westmorland and Cumberland; with a Tour through part of the Northern Counties in the years 1773 and 1774.* 1776.
KETT, H. *A Tour to the Lakes of Cumberland and Westmorland in August, 1798.* 1800.
KITCHEN, T. *Traveller' Guide.* 1783.
KNIGHT, R P. *The Landscape.* 1794.
LYSONS, D and S. *Magna Britannia: being a concise Topographical Account of the several Counties of Great Britain* (Volume four -Cumberland). 1816.
NICHOLSON, N. *The Lakers: the First Tourists.* Hale, 1955.
PENNANT, T. *A Tour in Scotland and a Voyage to the Hebrides 1772.* 1774.
PRICE, U. *Essays on the Picturesque, as compared with the Sublime and the Beautiful.* 1794.
TEMPLEMAN, W D. *The Life and Work of William Gilpin.* 1937.
WARNER, R. *A Tour through the Northern Counties of England and the Borders of Scotland.* 1802.
WILBERFORCE, W. *Journey to the Lake District from Cambridge 1779.* (ed C E Wrangham). Oriel, 1983.
WILKINSON, T. *Tours to the British Mountains.* Taylor & Hessey, 1824.
YOUNG, A. *A Sixth Months Tour through the North of England.* (Volume three - Cumberland and Westmorland). 1770.

CHAPTER 6 - ROMANTIC REACTIONS

CROSTHWAITE, P. *A Series of Accurate Maps of the Principal Lakes of Cumberland, Westmorland and Lancashire first surveyed and planned between 1783 and 1794.* (ed W Rollinson). Graham, 1968.
HOUSMAN, J. *A Descriptive Tour and Guide to the Lakes, Caves, Mountains and other natural Curiosities in Cumberland, Westmoreland, Lancashire and a Part of the West Riding of Yorkshire.* 1800.
RADCLIFFE, A. *A Journey made in the Summer of 1794...to which are added Observations during a tour to the Lakes of Lancashire, Westmoreland and Cumberland.* 1795.
SYMONS, G J. *The Floating Island in Derwentwater, its History and Mystery.* Stanford, 1888.
WEST, T. *A Guide to the Lakes in Cumberland, Westmorland and Lancashire.* 1778. Woodstock, 1989. Includes Brown's description, Dalton's poem, and Gray's journal, listed here under Chapter 5.

CHAPTER 7 - KING POCKY'S ANTICS

BRAGG, M. *The Maid of Buttermere.* Hodder, 1987.
BROWN, A. *The Beauty of Buttermere or A Maid Betrayed.* Heinemann, 1979.
COMBE, W. *The Tour of Dr Syntax in search of the Picturesque.* 1812.
HANKINSON, A. *The Regatta Men.* Cicerone, 1988.
PLUMPTRE, J. *Britain: the Journals of a Tourist in the 1790s.* (ed I Ousby) Hutchinson, 1992.
PLUMPTRE, J. *The Lakers: a Comic Opera in Three Acts.* 1798. Woodstock, 1990.

Chapter 8 - Gentlemen and Guides

BURKETT, M and SLOSS, J D G. *William Green of Ambleside: a Lake District Artist 1760-1823.* Abbot Hall Art Gallery, 1984.
CROSTHWAITE, J F. *A Brief Memoir of Major General Sir John Woodford.* 1881.
GREEN, W. *The Tourist's New Guide.* Lough, 1819.
OTLEY, J. *A Concise Description of the English Lakes and adjacent Mountains.* 1823.
OWEN, F and BROWN, D B. *Collector of Genius: a Life of Sir George Beaumont.* Yale UP, 1988.
RIMMER, W G. *Marshalls of Leeds: Flax Spinners 1788-1886.* C U P, 1960.
SOUTHEY, R. *Letters from England: by Don Manuel Alvarez Espriella.* 1807.
WORDSWORTH, W. *A Description of the Lakes in the North of England.* 1820. (First published 1810 as introduction to Wilkinson, J. *Select Views in Cumberland, Westmorland and Lancashire).*

Chapter 9 - Gurus of Greta Hall

BERNHARDT-KABISCH, E. *Robert Southey.* Twayne, 1977.
BURTON, H. *Coleridge and the Wordsworths.* O U P, 1953.
BYATT, A S. *Wordsworth and Coleridge in their Time.* Nelson, 1970.
CORNWELL, J. *Coleridge: poet and revolutionary 1772-1804.* Allen Lane, 1973.
CURRY, K. *Southey.* Routledge, 1975.
GRANT, A. *A Preface to Coleridge.* Longman, 1972.
HANKINSON, A. *Coleridge walks the Fells.* Ellenbank, 1991.
HOLMES, R. *Coleridge: early Visions.* Hodder, 1989.
HOWE, H W. *Greta Hall.* 1943. ed R Woof, 1977.
HUDSON, R. *Coleridge among the Lakes and Mountains.* Folio Society, 1991.
LEFEBURE, M. *The Bondage of Love: a Life of Mrs Samuel Taylor Coleridge.* Gollancz, 1986.
LEFEBURE, M. *Samuel Taylor Coleridge: a Bondage of Opium.* Gollancz, 1974.
MADDEN, L. *Robert Southey: the Critical Heritage.* Routledge, 1972.
MARGOLIOUTH, H M. *Wordsworth and Coleridge 1795-1834.* O U P, 1953.
MUDGE, B K. *Sara Coleridge: a Victorian daughter - her Life and Essays.* Yale U P, 1989.
PURTON, V. *A Coleridge Chronology.* Macmillan, 1993.
SIMMONS, J. *Southey.* Collins, 1945.
(There is an extensive range of Wordsworth and Coleridge studies, including letters, diaries and journals).

Chapter 10 - Cause for Concern

RAWLINSON, R. *Report to the General Board of Health on a Preliminary Inquiry into the Sewerage, Drainage and Supply of Water, and the Sanitary Condition of the Inhabitants of the Town and Township of Keswick in the Parish of Crosthwaite and County of Cumberland.* 1852.

Chapter 11 - Engines and Coaches

ABRAHAM, G D. *Motor Ways in Lakeland.* Methuen, 1913.
BOWTELL, H D. *Rails through Lakeland.* Silver Link, 1989.
GRADON, W M. *A History of the Cockermouth, Keswick and Penrith Railway.* 1948.
HAMMOND, J M. *Cockermouth, Keswick and Penrith Railway - In Memoriam.* Round Tables of Keswick and Penrith, 1972.
JOY, D. *Railways of the Lake Counties.* Dalesman, 1973.

JOY, D. *A Regional History of the Railways of Great Britain: Volume 14 - The Lake Counties.* David & Charles, 1983.
MCGLOIN, P R. *The Impact of the Railway on the Development of Keswick as a Tourist Resort 1860-1914.* Unpublished MA thesis, University of Lancaster, 1977.
RAWNSLEY, H D. *A Coach Drive at the Lakes.* 1890 (Reprint from the Cornhill Magazine, October-December 1888).
ROBINSON, P W. *Railways of Cumbria.* Dalesman, 1980.
WHITE, S. *Lakeland Steam: a Celebration of the Cockermouth, Keswick and Penrith Railway 1861-1972.* Carel Press, 1985.
WILSON, W. *Coaching in Lakeland.* Garnett, 1885. Carel Press, 1983.

Chapter 12 - Call to Arms

ARMSTRONG, M. *Thirlmere across the Bridges to Chapel 1849-1852: from the Diary of the Reverend Basil R Lawson, curate of Wythburn.* Peel Wyke, 1989.
BATTRICK, E. *Guardian of the Lakes: a History of the National Trust in the Lake District from 1946.* Westmorland Gazette, 1987
FEDDEN, R. *The Continuing Purpose: a History of the National Trust, its Aims and Work.* Longman, 1968.
FEDDEN, R. *The National Trust, Past and Present.* Cape, 1974.
GAZE, J. *Figures in a Landscape: a History of the National Trust.* Barrie & Jenkins, 1988.
GREEVES, L and TRINICK, M. *The National Trust Guide.* National Trust, 1973.
HARWOOD, J J. *History and Description of the Thirlmere Water Scheme.* 1895.
MURPHY, G. *Founders of the National Trust.* Helm, 1987.
RYAN, P. *The National Trust.* Dent, 1969.
THOMPSON, B L. *The Lake District and the National Trust.* Titus Wilson, 1946.

Chapter 13 - Social Conscience

BENJAMIN, F A. *Derwent Club Centenary 1879-1978: a Century of Social History.* The Club, nd.
BENJAMIN, F A. *The Ruskin Linen Industry of Keswick.* Michael Moon, 1974.
BOTT, G. *The Mary Hewetson Cottage Hospital, Keswick: a Brief History 1892-1992.* McKane, 1992.
BOTT, G. *Sponsored Talk: Keswick Lecture Society 1869-1968.* The Society, 1971.
LAPWORTH, H. *Survey of Water Resources.* Cumberland County Council, 1945.
MAUND, T B. *Ribble.* Venture, 1993.
OGDEN, E. *British Bus Systems Number Two: Ribble.* Transport Publishing, 1983.
POSTLETHWAITE, H. *British Bus Systems Number One: Cumberland.* Transport Publishing, 1983.
PRICKETT, E. *Ruskin Lace and Linen Work.* Batsford, 1985.

Chapter 14 - Sermons in Stone

BATTERSBY, J. *Memoir of T D. Harford-Battersby, together with some account of the Keswick Convention.* Seeley, 1890.
BENJAMIN, F A and MATHEWS, O M. *A Facet of Life in Keswick 1757-1975: Methodism.* Keswick Southey Street Methodist Church Council, 1975.
BROWNRIGG, J W. *The Bells of St Kentigern's Church, Crosthwaite, Keswick 1775-1975.* nd.
BUTLER, D M. *Quaker Meeting Houses of the Lake Counties.* Friends Historical Society, 1978.
CAIGER, J. et al. *100 Years of the Keswick Convention.* Keswick Convention Council, 1975.

CLARK, J B. *Three Hundred Years: a History of the Congregational Church, Keswick.* nd.
ECCLES, F C. *The Parish Church of St Kentigern, Crosthwaite.* Thurnam, 1953.
GRIFFIN, E W. *Watchers of a Beacon: the Story of the Keswick and Cockermouth Methodist Circuit - a Centenary Souvenir 1854-1954.* nd.
HARFORD, C F. *The Keswick Convention: its Message, its Method and its Men.* Marshall, 1907.
LEWIS, W. *History of the Congregational Church, Cockermouth.* 1870.
MANDERS, H. *The History of the Church of Crosthwaite, Cumberland.* Nichols, 1853.
POLLOCK, J C. *The Keswick Story: the authorised History of the Keswick Convention.* Hodder, 1964.
SLOAN, W B. *These Sixty Years: the Story of the Keswick Convention.* Pickering & Inglis, 1934.
TRINITY CHURCH OF ENGLAND SCHOOL. *A Child's Guide to St John's, the Parish Church.* The School, nd.
WILSON, T. *History of Crosthwaite Parish Church.* nd.
WILSON, T. *The Windows of Crosthwaite Church.* 1954.

Chapter 15 - School Days

BROATCH, J. *Keswick School.* 1926.
CROSTHWAITE, J F. *The Ancient Free School of Crosthwaite.* Bakewell, 1887.
GRANT, C. *A School's Life: addresses by the Headmaster of Keswick School. Marshall, 1903.*
RAWNSLEY, H D. and MITCHELL-DAWSON, A. *An Open Letter on the Constitution and Work of Keswick High School.* Bakewell, 1904.
WILSON, T. *The History and Chronicles of Crosthwaite Old School.* 1949.

Chapter 16 - Comedy and Climbing

ABRAHAM, G D. *British Mountain Climbs.* Mills & Boon, 1909.
HANKINSON, A. *The Blue Box: the Story of the Century Theatre.* Melbecks Books, 1983.
HANKINSON, A. *Camera on the Crags: a Portfolio of the early Rock Climbing Photographs by the Abraham Brothers.* Heinemann, 1975. Silent Books, 1990.
HANKINSON, A. *A Century on the Crags: the Story of Rock Climbing in the Lake District.* Dent, 1988.
HANKINSON, A. *The First Tigers: the early History of Rock Climbing in the Lake District.* Dent, 1972.
JONES, O G. *Rock Climbing in the English Lake District.* Abraham, 1900. Morten, 1973.
JONES, T and MILBURN, G. *Cumbrian Rock: 100 years of Climbing in the Lake District.* Pic Publications, 1988.
MARSHALL, F. *A Travelling Actress in the North and Scotland: Memoirs of the Life of Mrs Charlotte Deans (1837).* Titus Wilson, 1984.
ROGERSON, F. *History and Records of Notable Fell Walks 1864-1972 within the Lake District.* 1973 (plus supplements).
SMITH, B. *Studmarks on the Summits: a History of Amateur Fell Racing 1861-1983.* S K G Publications, 1985.
WESTMORLAND, R. *Adventures in Climbing.* Pelham, 1964.

Chapter 17 - Literary Lions

ABSE, J. *John Ruskin: the Passionate Moralist.* Quartet, 1980.
ANDERSON, N F. *Woman against Women in Victorian England: a Life of Eliza Lynn Linton.* Indiana U P, 1987.

BARTLETT, W and WHALLEY, J I. *Beatrix Potter's Derwentwater.* Warne, 1988.
BURD, V A and DEARDEN, J S. *A Tour to the Lakes in Cumberland: John Ruskin's Diary for 1830.* Scolar Press, 1990.
CASSON, E. *Poems.* Warne, 1938.
COLLINGWOOD, W G. *The Life of John Ruskin.* Methuen, 1893.
DANE, C. *Tradition and Hugh Walpole.* Heinemann, 1930
DAVIES, H. *Beatrix Potter's Lakeland.* Warne, 1988.
DEARDEN, J S. *Iteriad or Three Weeks among the Lakes by John Ruskin.* Graham, 1969.
EVANS, J. *John Ruskin.* O U P, 1954.
HART-DAVIS, R. *Hugh Walpole.* Macmillan, 1952
HILTON, T. *John Ruskin: the early Years.* Yale U P, 1985.
HUNT, J D. *The Wilder Sea: a Life of John Ruskin.* Dent, 1982.
KEMP, W. *The Desire of my Eyes: a Life of John Ruskin.* Harper Collins, 1991.
LANE, M. *The Tale of Beatrix Potter.* Warne, 1946.
LAYARD, G S. *Mrs Lynn Linton: her Life, Letters and Opinions.* Methuen, 1901.
LEON, D. *Ruskin: the Great Victorian.* Routledge, 1949.
LINDER, L. *A History of the Writings of Beatrix Potter.* Warne, 1971.
LINDER, L. *The Journal of Beatrix Potter from 1881 to 1897.* Warne, 1966.
LINTON, E L. *The Autobiography of Christopher Kirkland.* Bentley, 1885.
LINTON, E L. *The Lake Country.* Smith Elder, 1864.
POTTER, B. *The Derwentwater Sketchbook* (Commentary on and edited by J I Whalley and W Bartlett) Warne, 1984.
RICHARDSON, J. *Cummerland Talk.* 1871.
THAL, H V. *Eliza Lynn Linton.* Allen & Unwin, 1979.
RAWNSLEY, H D. *Literary Associations of the English Lakes.* MacLehose, 1894.
RAWNSLEY, H D. *Ruskin and the English Lakes.* MacLehose, 1902.
SESSIONS, F. *Literary Celebrities of the English Lake District.* Elliot Stock, 1907.
STEEN, M. *Hugh Walpole: a Study.* Nicolson & Watson, 1933.
TAYLOR, J. *Beatrix Potter: Artist, Storyteller and Countrywoman.* Warne, 1986.

Chapter 18 - Worthies at Work

ANON. *'The Most Active Volcano in Europe': a Short Life of Canon Hardwicke Drummond Rawnsley, Vicar of Crosthwaite, Keswick 1883-1917.* McKane, nd.
DIXON, J. *The Literary Life of William Brownrigg.* 1801.
LADYMAN, S. *Thoughts and Recollections of Keswick and its Inhabitants during Sixty Years.* 1885.
LIETCH, D. *A Memoir of Jonathan Otley.* 1882.
RAWNSLEY, E F. *Canon Rawnsley.* MacLehose, 1923.
SILWOOD, G. *George Silwood of Keswick: a Brief Memoir and Letters of one who was perfected through sufferings.* McKane, 1894.
WILSON, T. *Jonathan Otley, Clockmaker and Geologist.* McKane, 1956.

Chapter 19 - Walkaround

ARCHER, B H and JONES, D R. *Tourism in Appleby, Keswick and Sedbergh.* Institute of Economic Research, University College of North Wales, 1977.
BINGHAM, H. *Choices for Farmers.* Lake District National Park Visitor Services, 1989.
BINGHAM, H. *A Fragile Environment.* L D N P V S, 1990.
BINGHAM, H. *Learning to Live with Tourism.* L D N P V S, 1988.
BINGHAM, H. *A National Park in the Balance.* L D N P V S, 1988.
BLACKBURN, S. *Keswick for Kids.* Amadorn, 1991.
BOTT, G. *Keswick Town Trail.* L D S P B, 1988.

COUNTRYSIDE COMMISSION. *Pleasure Traffic and Recreation in the Lake District.* (Research Report based on a survey of weekend motorists). Countryside Commission/British Tourist Authority, 1966.
DAVISON, J A. *Traffic in the Watendlath Valley.* Cumberland County Council, 1972.
ENGLISH TOURIST BOARD. *The Marketing and Development of Tourism in the English Lakes Counties.* P A Management Consultants, 1973.
WILSON, H and WOMERSLEY, L. *Traffic Management in the Lake District National Park.* Friends of the Lake District, 1971.

NOTE

The Lake District National Park Authority, Cumbria County Council, and the Cumbria Tourist Board have published numerous reports, many of which contain material relevant to Keswick.

Photographic Acknowledgements

I should like to thank the following individuals and organisations for permission to use photographs.

Calvert Trust - 161
Nancy Chew - 149
Donald Cowen - 8
Cumbria County Library, Carlisle - 5, 6, 11, 23, 29, 34, 37, 44, 48, 49, 53, 57, 58, 64, 70, 76, 80, 95, 101, 129, 132, 136, 146
Cumbria County Library, Kendal and Mrs M Berry - 2, 181, 184
Cumbria County Library, Keswick - 82, 90, 106, 110, 126, 152, 172
Dove Cottage Trustees and Keswick Museum and Art Gallery - 45
Dove Cottage Trustees and John Spedding - 39
Alan Dunn and Open all Hours - 189
George Fisher - 188
George Holt and Gordon Graham - 98, 112, 160
Mrs Hannah Hope - 171
Keswick Museum and Art Gallery - 55, 191
Keswick Museum and Art Gallery and Jim Scott - 94
Keswick Town Council - end maps.
Lancaster City Council - 113
John Marsh - 84, 103, 116, 118, 178
Mike Nixon - 158
Mary Hewetson Hospital and Mrs M Mayhew - 120
Jim Scott - 13, 134, 142, 154
Kenneth Shepherd and Mrs Pauline Tyson - 140
Tullie House, Carlisle and Mrs P H Forrester - 3
Frederick Wilson - 156

Index

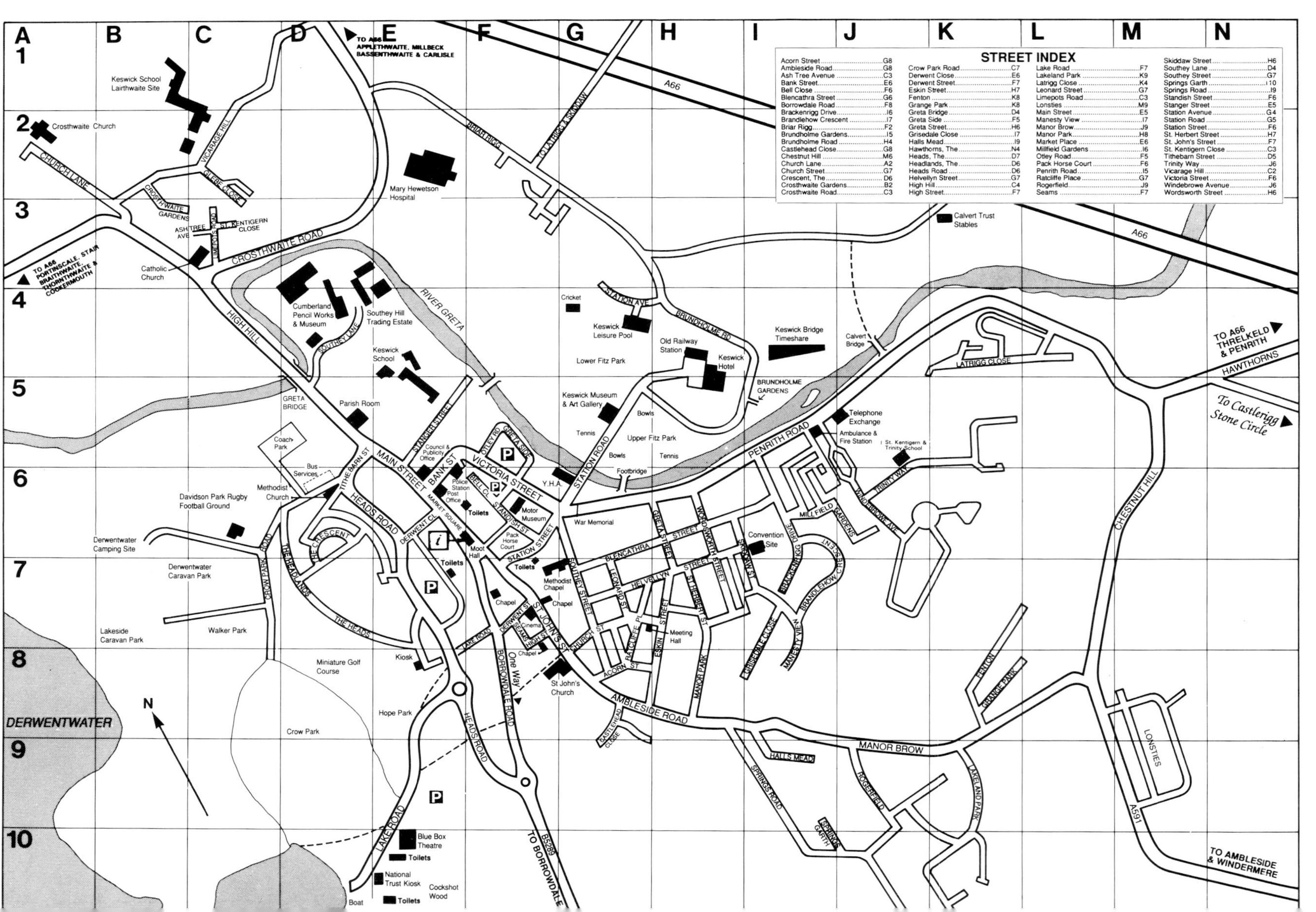
STREET INDEX
Acorn Street G8
Ambleside Road G8
Ash Tree Avenue C3
Bank Street E6
Bell Close F6
Blencathra Street G6
Borrowdale Road F8
Brackenrigg Drive I6
Brandlehow Crescent I7
Briar Rigg F2
Brundholme Gardens I5
Brundholme Road H4
Castlehead Close G8
Chestnut Hill M6
Church Lane A2
Church Street G7
Crescent, The D6
Crosthwaite Gardens B2
Crosthwaite Road C3
Crow Park Road C7
Derwent Close E6
Derwent Street F7
Eskin Street H7
Fenton K8
Grange Park K8
Greta Bridge D4
Greta Side F5
Greta Street H6
Grisedale Close I7
Halls Mead I9
Hawthorns, The N4
Heads, The D7
Headlands, The D6
Heads Road D6
Helvellyn Street G7
High Hill C4
High Street F7
Lake Road F7
Lakeland Park K9
Latrigg Close K4
Leonard Street G7
Limepots Road C3
Lonsties M9
Main Street E5
Manesty View I7
Manor Brow J9
Manor Park H8
Market Place E6
Millfield Gardens I6
Otley Road F5
Pack Horse Court F6
Penrith Road I5
Ratcliffe Place G7
Rogerfield J9
Seams F7
Skiddaw Street H6
Southey Lane D4
Southey Street G7
Springs Garth I10
Springs Road I9
Standish Street F6
Stanger Street E5
Station Avenue G4
Station Road G5
Station Street F6
St. Herbert Street H7
St. John's Street F7
St. Kentigern Close C3
Tithebarn Street D5
Trinity Way J6
Vicarage Hill C2
Victoria Street F6
Windebrowe Avenue J6
Wordsworth Street H6
TO A66 APPLETHWAITE, MILLBECK BASSENTHWAITE & CARLISLE
TO A66 PORTINSCALE, STAIR BRAITHWAITE, THORNTHWAITE & COCKERMOUTH
TO A66 THRELKELD & PENRITH
To Castlerigg Stone Circle
TO AMBLESIDE & WINDERMERE
TO BORROWDALE
Keswick School Lairthwaite Site
Crosthwaite Church
Mary Hewetson Hospital
Catholic Church
Cumberland Pencil Works & Museum
Southey Hill Trading Estate
RIVER GRETA
Keswick School
Parish Room
Cricket
Keswick Leisure Pool
Lower Fitz Park
Old Railway Station
Keswick Hotel
Keswick Bridge Timeshare
Calvert Bridge
Calvert Trust Stables
Keswick Museum & Art Gallery
Upper Fitz Park
Bowls
Tennis
Footbridge
Telephone Exchange
Ambulance & Fire Station
St. Kentigern & Trinity School
Coach Park
Bus Services
Methodist Church
Davidson Park Rugby Football Ground
Derwentwater Camping Site
Derwentwater Caravan Park
Lakeside Caravan Park
Walker Park
Council & Publicity Office
Police Station
Post Office
Toilets
Motor Museum
Y.H.A.
Moot Hall
War Memorial
Convention Site
Methodist Chapel
Chapel
Cinema
Meeting Hall
St John's Church
One Way
Kiosk
Miniature Golf Course
Hope Park
Crow Park
DERWENTWATER
Blue Box Theatre
National Trust Kiosk
Cockshot Wood
Boat
A66
A591
B5289